ROUND TABLE

最有品的英语聊天类节目
来自轻松调频EZFM

圆桌议事

陈沫　刘彦
周赫扬　王玮　编著
牛翊琳　于洋

中国广播影视出版社

图书在版编目（CIP）数据

圆桌议事：汉英对照 / 陈沫等编著. -- 北京：中国广播影视出版社, 2019.1（2024.3重印）
ISBN 978-7-5043-8187-3

Ⅰ.①圆… Ⅱ.①陈… Ⅲ.①英语—汉语—对照读物 ②时事评论—中国—文集 Ⅳ.①H319.4：D

中国版本图书馆CIP数据核字(2018)第215912号

圆桌议事：汉英对照

陈沫 等 编著

责任编辑	杨 凡
封面设计	文人雅士
责任校对	张 哲

出版发行	中国广播影视出版社
电 话	010-86093580 010-86093583
社 址	北京市西城区真武庙二条9号
邮 编	100045
网 址	www.crtp.com.cn
电子信箱	crtp8@sina.com
经 销	全国各地新华书店
印 刷	三河市同力彩印有限公司
开 本	710毫米×1000毫米 1/16
字 数	300（千）字
印 张	21
版 次	2019年1月第1版 2024年3月第2次印刷
书 号	ISBN 978-7-5043-8187-3
定 价	60.00

（版权所有 翻印必究·印装有误 负责调换）

人生中的必然,也是自己的选择

谢谢你来。

我们是中央广播电视总台轻松调频《圆桌议事》(*RoundTable*)栏目。

兴奋与紧张交织在一起,迎接翻阅。

兴奋是因为,出书了。这件事值得纪念,也值得更多的事,比如跟你见个面。

紧张是因为,出书了,竟然是第一本。这么多年以声音靠近你,现在以文字的形式出现,不知道你会不会喜欢。

这本书是我们选择的必然。

最初,当我们在选题、角度、主持、语言等各方面选择去磨炼自己的时候,我们知道,一个午间时段的、英语的广播栏目受到关注,是必然。

渐渐,当我们打开视野和思路,选择去创新、开拓、合作的时候,我们知道,一个以传统媒体为起点的栏目在新媒体上得到热烈的反馈,是必然。

后来,当我们不满足于称赞,选择以匠人的心态稳住心神、杜绝浮躁、精益求精的时候,我们知道,跨界的呼声越来越高,是必然。

当我们选择了在繁忙工作和紧张生活之余，静下心来聆听内容、撰写文字、细致翻译、扩充词汇、解读文化的时候，我们知道，这本书遇见你，是必然。

同样是因为选择，让六位与《圆桌议事》（*RoundTable*）有直接或间接关系的作者陈沫、刘彦、周赫扬、王玮、牛翃琳、于洋必然地走到了一起。

写这本书的过程中，听着熟悉的节目还能又哭又笑，也是一种热爱。我们尽了最大努力，没日没夜听写音频，虽然不是逐字逐句一一对应，但综合考虑了英语学习与分享的习惯，以相对正确或合理的文字呈现了出来。

感谢支持我们的你。

希望你能从书里读懂的不仅是英语，还有情谊。

《圆桌议事》（*RoundTable*）

2018年4月

单身必读

003 ★ 你为什么还还还没对象?

007 ★ 单身? 全怪你宅!

010 ★ 单身贵族都在等待真爱

013 ★ 爸妈的约会建议能听吗?

016 ★ 男友拍照全是坑?!

019 ★ 聊天,意会很重要!

022 ★ 搭讪艺术家

025 ★ 吃不到一起就分手

028 ★ 挑内衣到底为了谁

032 ★ 女强人承受了多少偏见

036 ★ 女人一定要找比自己聪明的男人吗?

039 ★ 男生别抱怨!女生买东西是件大工程!

042 ★ 男人每个月总有那么几天……

婚后感悟

049 ★ 老爸是全能手,老公啥也不会修

053 ★ 把老公存起来,呵呵

056 ★ 爱着同一个男人的两个女人如何相处?

062 ★ "交友神器"还是"婚姻杀手"

065 ★ 剖腹产比割破手痛几倍?

069 ★ 应该这样给中国宝宝起英文名

072 ★ "忽悠"孩子这件事

076 ★ 别让孩子成为"屏奴"

079 ★ 小朋友爱顶撞

082 ★ 都是为你好

个人成长

087 ★ 你的数学

091 ★ 同学们,别叫这些英文名,土爆咯!

094 ★ 大学遗憾排行榜

097 ★ 论文写得怎么样了?

100 ★ 有调性的英文简历这样写!

103 ★ 拒信来了

106 ★ 第一份工作的收入,决定了今后的收入?

108 ★ 自由职业者,想当就能当?

111 ★ 女生为什么爱组团刷催泪片?

114 ★ 一起去厕所是妹子的专利哦!

117 ★ 友情是如何变淡的

生活方式

123 ★ 无Wi-Fi,不生活

126 ★ 廉价航空也不错

129 ★ 飞机点餐法则

132 ★ 西方社交场合着装宝典

135 ★ 有一种寒冷叫"忘穿秋裤"

138 ★ AA制，各付各的

141 ★ 必备砍价技能 get!

144 ★ 真人秀怎么看?

147 ★ 穷游那些事儿

150 ★ 能不能好好过马路?

153 ★ 流浪的喵星人谁来守护

健康呵护

159 ★ 健身去吧!

162 ★ 有氧运动玩起来

165 ★ 无氧运动厉害了

168 ★ 有马甲线才是真女神

171 ★ 你牙好吗?

175 ★ 全科医生

178 ★ 请关注自闭症

181 ★ 整形小知识

娱乐休闲

187 ★ "太长不看"英语怎么说?

190 ★ 去电影院能自带食物吗?

194 ★ 手机使用方式出卖你的年龄

198 ★ 真正的表情帝是谁?

202 ★ 现代人离不开自拍?

207 ★ 朋友圈测试为何这么火?

210 ★ 世界杯

行为心理

217 ★ 哪些事会让人显得很掉价？

221 ★ "鸭梨山大"怎么表达？

225 ★ 洗澡细节暴露真实的你

228 ★ 关闭手机"失联18小时"会怎样？

231 ★ 别让你的少女心恶化成"少女癌"

234 ★ 你是"出门困难症"患者吗？

237 ★ 你比镜子里的自己更丑？

240 ★ 从书架看穿你的性格

243 ★ 完美主义？强迫症？

246 ★ 网络社交达人反而内心孤独

吃很重要

251 ★ 回家吃饭，约吗？

255 ★ 去度假，带什么吃的

258 ★ 吃货普大喜奔：十大垃圾食品名单是假的！

261 ★ 吃方便面哪国强？

265 ★ 中国人为什么爱吃辣？

269 ★ 吃小龙虾的正确姿势

272 ★ 吃货们！中餐再次申遗你知道吗？

275 ★ 如何用英文聊酸甜苦辣

278 ★ 英文菜谱入门教学

282 ★ 吃货+技术宅=美食公式！

285 ★ 土豆拯救世界

289 ★ 独自就餐不再是异类

中外交流

295 ★ 外国人眼中的中国文化符号

298 ★ 外国人看不懂的中式生活习惯

301 ★ 美国学生眼里的中国功夫

305 ★ 中英夹杂太low了？

309 ★ 去洗手间的表达方式

312 ★ 洋明星的中国名

315 ★ 英语花式"打人大法"

318 ★ 到了国外，去银行，说点什么？

321 ★ "OK"是个有故事的词

324 ★ 新年快乐

单身必读
Singlehood

你为什么还还还没对象？

（素材来自《圆桌议事》2016年7月4日节目）

导　语：湖北工业大学一位辅导员给学生布置作业，要求学生写一份300字的自我剖析，要涵盖优点和缺点，思考为什么还没有对象。有男女朋友的要写500字的表白信。发布的平台是微博，还要@辅导员。这样的作业，你接受吗？

What I'm trying to say is by asking the question why you're single, it feels like it's wrong to be single. What's wrong to be single? Maybe I choose to. Maybe I didn't find someone that I like. Maybe the one pursuing me does not come to certain standard. It has a lot of reasons. You can't just say "Why are you still single？" like why you are failing a test. It's not a nice question.

我想说，问出"你为什么单身"这种问题的人，好像把单身看成一种错误。单身有什么错？可能我就是这么选择的，我没有找到我喜欢的人，或者追我的人不够理想。原因可以有很多。凭什么问"你怎么还单身"？好像我没通过某个考试一样。这不是个友好的问题。

Why aren't you in one？ Your life is incomplete. When I was at their age, relationship was the last thing on my mind. I just wanted to have fun with my friends and I was living on my own. I was so excited! I mean, granted of course, relationships are always a nice thing but these kids are young and they need the time to be young.

有一种逻辑是：你为什么没处在一段恋爱关系中呢？你的生活是不完整的。我在他们这个年龄的时候，把恋爱放在最后一位。我只想和朋友们开心相处，自己独立生活，那时的我很快乐！虽然恋爱是美好的，但是孩子们还年轻，他们也需要时间享受年轻。

I think that's something that might be a life-long pursuit for me, but for people who want to have a real and fulfilling relationship, I think you should never stop trying to look for it. You need to look for it. I don't think it's going to fall on your lap if you're just eating potato chips and playing video games at home. But also, I think it's a delicate balance in the mind that if you're too desperate, that just drives good people away. It's about growing yourself stronger inside. Keep looking.

这对我来说是一辈子的追求。对那些希望得到真实的、充实的恋爱关系的人来说，你应该永不停止寻找的脚步。你要去找。只是忙着吃薯片或者打游戏的话，不会等来爱情。把握精妙的平衡也很重要，如果你太绝望，就会把好人赶跑。这需要自我成长、让内心变得更强大。别放弃，一直找下去。

I think for most people, a big part of life is looking for someone to spend it with. But you know what, you need to have patience for that. You also need to be yourself and be okay with being by yourself. I think that person comes when you're independent and when you're happy being by yourself. Because, then it's not like you need them, it's (more like) they complement you. That's how I've always thought of it. But I think it is always so healthy for you to be confident being by yourself. I think this assignment is promoting an ideology of saying that it's not okay and that's not what a young person should be learning in college. They should be learning that it is okay to be yourself and feel good being yourself.

对大多数人来说，生活的很大一部分就是寻找共度一生的人。但是你知道吗，你需要有耐心。你需要成为你自己，与自己相处得愉快。那个人会在你很独立、很快乐地做自己的时候出现。那时，不是你需要他们，而是他们来与你相互成就。这是我一直以来的想法。你自信地做自己，永远是健康的。这个作业的用意是说"单身不好"，这不是一个年轻人在学校该学的东西。他们应该学习的是，遵从自己的内心，做自己很好。

点 评

"你怎么还单身"不是个让人愉快的问题。There's no amenity here. Amenity 是愉快、和悦、礼仪、举止的意思。

拥有一段美好的恋爱关系，不是目的，而是结果。最重要的是做好自己，让自己成为独立、自信的人。处理好与自己的关系，才能处理好与他人的关系。Be yourself. Be independent. Be confident. Your life is going to be amazing.

与你在一起的那个人，不是你求来的，而是你吸引来的；不是你仰望的对象，而是你的伙伴。It's not like you need them, it's (more like) they complement you.

单身的时候应该如何度过？你可以吃薯片、在家打游戏 eating potato chips and playing video games at home，更积极的方式包括与朋友开心相处 have fun with friends，独立生活 live on my own，内心变得更加强大 grow stronger inside。

提到爱情，很多人都会想起经典的《罗密欧与朱丽叶》（*Romeo and Juliet*）。有时也会用 the fighting between the Capulets and Montagues 即"凯普莱特家族与蒙太古家族的战争"来代指"罗密欧与朱丽叶"式的爱情。凯普莱特（Capulet）是朱丽叶的姓氏，蒙太古（Montague）是罗密欧的姓氏。

词汇小百科

single 单身

in a relationship 恋爱中，处在一段关系中

married 已婚的

divorced 离异的

patient 有耐心的

incomplete 不完整的；complete 完整的

fulfilling 令人满意、满足的

delicate 微妙的、纤弱的、易损的

desperate 绝望的、急切渴望的，美剧 Desperate Housewives 即《绝望的主妇》。

（陈 沫）

单身？全怪你宅！

（素材来自《圆桌议事》2015年1月13日节目）

导　语：根据婚恋网站百合网发布的《我们要在一起——2014中国人婚恋状况调查报告》显示，"宅"已经成为导致单身的罪魁祸首。调查结果显示，单身人士往往超长时间"宅"在家里，男性上网，女性追剧。近三分之二的单身人士每天独处6小时以上。你是否同意这个调查结果呢？这个结果又是否证明，连接起全世界的互联网，反而在一定程度上让我们更加不愿意与世界交流了呢？这篇里，我们一起探讨一下"单身"与"宅"的那些事。

I think it seems to have captured the essence of the problem. First of all, this report was released by the matchmaking website Baihe.com and looked at 73,000 net users and it also surveyed 200 single people offline with these detailed interviews. It seems to come to this conclusion that it is because you don't go out enough and you stay in too much and that's why you don't even give yourself a chance to meet people.

我觉得这个报告似乎抓住了问题的本质。首先，百合网的调查综合了7.3万份有效的线上问卷和200位单身男女线下深度访谈的结果。最后报告得出的结论是，随着网络的普及以及生活压力的加大，越来越多的年轻人喜欢"宅"在家里。而总是不出门，也就意味着没有给自己认识潜在"另一半"的机会。

When you look at what people do, if they don't go out, the top three activities are surfing the Internet, hanging out with friends and I don't really understand what that implies here, so maybe hanging out with your friends on WeChat. So still mingling with the people that you know and probably don't really have a prospective relationship with. And thirdly is just do nothing and veg out.

那些宅男宅女不出门都干吗呢？从报告可以看出，排前三位的选项是一、在家上网；二、和朋友聚会，当然，是不出门的那种，可能是通过微信聊天？而且是和原本就熟识的、没什么希望发展成恋人的朋友聚会；第三就是单纯地在家"宅"着，啥也不做。

If you just think of it as a way to make friends as you have done, then perhaps not with the people that you met so far, but maybe in the future you might meet some and then after you meet them through this rather artificial modern way of meeting new people, after that the conventional way of just actually meeting them from time to time would take over. Then maybe a relationship will develop if that's what you are looking for.

如果把网上交友当成普通的认识新朋友的方式，那么虽然现有的朋友好像已经"错过了这个村"，但未来完全有可能通过网络认识更多的新朋友。这些人虽然是通过网络这种好像有些刻意的方法认识的，但是一定会逐渐"奔现"，在现实中加深对彼此的了解。这样一来，你所寻找的恋情也就能水到渠成了。

It would be better to maybe try to go to some events with a group of people. There are loads of interest groups that are online on social media, for people who like a certain kind of musical, or something like that. You can find like-minded people through the social networks.

我觉得更理想的方式是尝试参加一些团体活动。现在社交媒体上有很多这样的线下兴趣爱好小组，方便有共同爱好的人（比如某一类音乐剧的爱好者)一起活动。通过社交网络很容易找到志趣相投的朋友。

点评

宅真的是导致单身的"罪魁祸首"吗?不少人认为百合网的研究报告 captured the essence,抓住了问题的本质!Capture是俘获、夺得、捕捉的意思,essence是本质、实质、精华,capture the essence作为一个固定搭配,可以表达抓住重点、捕捉到精髓的意思。只是capture the essence不够,得有实际行动才行。想"脱单",至少要多出门结交新朋友hang out with new friends,或者参加一些线下兴趣小组 join some interest groups,总之不要继续在家无所事事地宅着,一个人休闲。

词汇小百科

WeChat 微信

nerd 书呆子:智商高,情商低,缺少社交技能,沉迷于学术研究或书本的人

Jock 运动型靓仔:魁梧帅气,热爱交际,很受女孩子的欢迎,尤其擅长American football和basketball等各种体育运动

couch potato 沙发土豆:一有时间就坐在沙发上看电视的人,他们一声不吭,一动不动,就像一个圆滚滚的土豆

weirdo 古怪的人,奇怪的人,也就是网络语言常用的"怪咖"

wallflower 壁花:也就是害羞、不善交际的人,多指女孩

(牛翊琳)

单身贵族都在等待真爱

（素材来自《圆桌议事》2015年10月23日节目）

导　语：某相亲网站对全国用户进行抽样调查发现，月入五万元的单身贵族北京最多，深圳、上海紧随其后。他们都来自什么行业？他们等待的真爱在哪里？

I think a sense of perspective is needed here. We are hearing that Beijing has the highest number of wealthy and single people in China, followed by Shenzhen, and then Shanghai. These are three of China's four first-tier cities. So it very much stands to reason that you have the highest number of wealthy people in the country for a start.

　　我觉得先把判断问题的角度摆正。我们听说北京拥有全国最多数量的富有单身人士，深圳和上海紧随其后。中国的四个一线城市中，这就已经占三个，而这些城市本来就拥有数量最多的富裕人口，所以它们有最多的富有单身人士也就顺理成章了。

Chinese schooling tends to be very rigorous. It's all about "Gaokao" and exam results. Results are king. If you are a Chinese family with disposable income and you only have one child, as a lot of them do, then you'll spend a lot of money on your child to help them achieve these academic goals. So I think the education industry here certainly can be very lucrative.

中国式的教育往往非常严格。"高考"和考试成绩最重要。成绩是王道。一个拥有相当可支配收入的中国家庭如果只有一个孩子，那相当多的金钱可能都投入在这一个孩子身上，以帮助他们达到学业的目标。我认为，这里的教育行业获利颇丰。

What about this very diversified society we live in right now? There are people who don't want to get married, who are in open relationships, or don't have a relationship and is happy to have a connection with his or her cat.

我们所处的这个多样化的社会呢？有的人不想结婚，有的人身处开放式的关系中，或者根本不想拥有两性关系而开心地和他（她）的猫咪建立情感连接。

点 评

在英语讨论中，我们常常要先摆正视角，确认双方语境和理解相同。这句A sense of perspective is needed here大有用场。Perspective是透镜，观点，洞察力的意思。Put it in perspective 是正确看问题的意思。

It stands to reason that 显而易见，理所应当。

Results are king 成绩压倒一切。Cash is king 现金为王。Something is king 就是以什么为王道的意思。欢迎你自己造句哟。

Diversified society 多样化的社会。随着城市的发展，社会能够产生和接纳更多元化的生活方式、价值取向和价值观。

词汇小百科

income 收入，类似词汇有 revenue，earnings，salary 和 wage 等

lucrative 获利多的、赚钱的

diversified 多种的

heterogeneous 异种的，异质的；反义词为 homogeneous，同性质的，同类的

（赫 扬）

爸妈的约会建议能听吗？

（素材来自《圆桌议事》2015年6月10日节目）

导　语：美国新闻聚合网站（www.buzzfeed.com）做了一次调查，让24位女性和24位男性分别给自己未来女儿和儿子写"最重要的一句约会忠告"。这些忠告究竟靠不靠谱？是金玉良言还是实力坑娃？我们一起来看看。

I think for these women to give such tips to their future daughters or daughters that already exist. I think it's a very open kind of attitude, and it sounds like, you know, they are friends. That's something that's a little bit rarer in China, I think, when mothers are usually in a way hiding their mistakes from their kids, and always trying to give the good advice in their eyes, and make their offspring follow.

我认为从这些女人给她们的女儿或未来女儿的建议来看，她们有一种非常开放的态度，就好像朋友一样。我认为这在中国比较少见，妈妈通常都在孩子面前隐藏自己的错误，并总是试图给一些她们眼中好的建议，并让孩子遵从。

On the list for men, because there's some advice that fathers give to sons, there's a very similar one, No.17 on that list of 24 items, which is "Don't spend all your life looking for the right person. Make yourself the right person". I think that's the only one similar for men and women on both lists.

在父亲们给自己儿子的建议中有一条非常相似的，就是这24条里的第17条"不要用你的一生去找那个对的人，让你自己成为那个对的人"。这是男人和女人单子上唯一相似的一条。

I think the best advice when you're on a date, you know, is don't talk so much about yourself, listen to what the woman has to say. I think that's absolutely key to a successful date. That isn't on the list. I don't know why. I think there's one similar to that on the list. Pretend… oh, I'm sorry, be interested in what she's saying. Did I nearly say pretend to be interested?

但我认为最好的建议就是当你在约会时，不要过多地谈论你自己，要听听对面的女士想说什么。我认为这绝对是成功约会的要点。我不知道为什么这一点不在单子上。我认为单子上有一点类似的，是"假装"对她所说的内容感兴趣。我刚才是差点说假装感兴趣吗？

Did you see that episode of Two and a Half Men where Charlie Sheen was saying his key to a successful date is that every few seconds when the girl is talking, pretend to be interested in what she says. You just go "ah ha", "yeah", "keep going". And then in your mind, you can be thinking about other much more important things than what she is saying.

你看美剧《好汉两个半》的一集中，查理·辛说他成功约会的关键是当女生说话时，每隔几秒就要假装对她说的内容感兴趣。你只用说"啊哈""是"或"继续说"就好了，在你脑子里可以想一些比她说的更重要的事情。

I think that's the tricky business, because sometimes waiting is just not enough. Maybe showing your true colors, I don't know, at some point, but don't do that like right up front, if you're an outrageous person, and that works for both men and women.

我认为那挺不好掌握的，因为有时候单纯的等待不足以解决问题。也许在某些时候表现出你真实的一面。但如果你是一个很出格的人,不要立刻表现出来,这一点对男女都有效。

点 评

爸妈给的约会建议中到底哪些是靠谱的?与其 spend all your life looking for the right person 耗费一生找一个对的人,不如 make yourself the right person 让自己成为那个对的人。talk so much about yourself 与其过多谈论自己,不如 listen to what the woman has to say 倾听女方要说什么,并且 be interested in what she's saying 对她说的内容感兴趣,或 pretend to be interested in what she says 假装你对她说的内容感兴趣。是不是很套路?也许有时候适当 show your true colors 表现出你真实的一面会更好,毕竟恋爱还是要多点真诚,少点套路嘛!

词汇小百科

give somebody a date / go on a date with somebody　与某人约会

make an appointment with somebody　和某人定个时间见面

first date　第一次约会

double date　两对男女一起参加的约会

(王　玮)

男友拍照全是坑？！

（素材来自《圆桌议事》2015年5月29日节目）

> **导　语：** 自拍的时候，每个女孩子都有沉鱼落雁、闭月羞花之容。然而当她们交了一个不会拍照的男友后，就再也没有翻身之日了。即便你再美若天仙，也赢不了"男朋友的镜头"。

Well, I certainly think there are times that would give you a big plus if you can become a good photographer, especially when you are traveling with your girlfriend, you want to take a photo for her or she demands you to do so, if you can do a good job, not put your finger blocking it at the lens, or taking a photo when you can't even find where she is. Then I'd say, you'd be doing a good job.

　　我的确认为，如果你是一个好的摄影师，有些时候可以给你加很多分，尤其是当你和女朋友旅行时。当你给她照相或她要求你给她照相时，怎么才叫做得好呢？就是不用你的手指挡镜头，也不会去拍一张连你都找不到她的照片。这已经算好的了。

But sometimes I think it's less of a requirement that girls have on their boyfriends. It's more like that guys, if you have the extra skill, it will boost your chance of ending up with the girl.

　　但是有时候我认为女孩们不会把它当成对男朋友的要求，而更像是如果男孩子们有这项额外技能，就会大大增加你和这个女孩子在一起的概率。

There are a lot of technicalities when it comes to photo taking. One of them is to crouch down a little bit if the boyfriend is taller. Take more photos, take some snapshots. Maybe take a hundred photos, and maybe one of them would be good, right? Be a little bit more diligent.

照相有很多技巧,其中一个就是如果男朋友个子高的话就稍微蹲下来一点拍。多拍几张,或连拍。也许照100张照片,其中一张会很不错,对吗?更勤快一点。

Just show that you care, and you make attempts to impress her. I think it's that heart that really matters, not always the results. Although if the results are good, it would be a plus.

你只需要表现出你在意,试图让她印象深刻。说到底,心意才真的重要,而不是结果。当然,如果结果好的话,会加分。

点评

男朋友的拍照水平到底重不重要呢?会照相这项额外技能的确会给你加很多分 give you a big plus,大大增加你和这个女孩在一起的概率 boost your chance of ending up with the girl。

要怎样才能拍好照片呢?有几个小技巧 technicalities。比如不要用手指挡着镜头 not let your fingers block the lens;不要拍一张你根本找不到她在哪里的照片 take a photo when you can't even find where she is;如果男友比较高的话就蹲下来 crouch down;照得不好就连拍多照几张 take some snapshots,拍100张总会有一张好的,所以要勤快(diligent)一些。

女孩子真正在意的是你试图让她印象深刻 make attempts to impress her,尝试做某事 make attempts to do something。心意最重要,但是如果结果好的话,自然会加分。

词汇小百科

take a picture / photo for somebody　为某人照相
pose for a picture / photo　为照相摆姿势
group picture　团体照
timer　定时器
tripod　三脚架
shutter　快门
lens　镜头

（王　玮）

聊天，意会很重要！

（素材来自《圆桌议事》2016年7月20日节目）

导　语：聊天的时候，你是否真的听懂了对方在说什么？当你听到"有空再约""改天再聊"的时候，或许就是"永远都不要见面""我们别再聊了""到此为止，就这样吧"的意思。

I think it gets more complicated, doesn't it? Because sometimes even if I would say "we'll meet another day", meaning "we'll never gonna meet again. Thanks, goodbye", you might actually think "Oh, no, he really means it. That's great." Because you've interpreted it in a different way. So I think there is still plenty of room for misinterpretation, or hope, maybe the word is.

我觉得这事儿变得挺复杂的。有时候我会说"改天见"，实际想表达的意思是"我们不会再见了，谢谢，拜拜"，但听到的人可能会理解成"他真的要与我再次见面呢，太棒了"——完全是另外一种解读。所以我认为每个人还是有很大的被误解的可能，会让对方失望。

I don't know, maybe different people have different expectations. Personally, even if someone says the sentence to me in a very sincere way, I would still take it as goodbye, 'cause as far as I can see, if you really want to say "let's meet some other time", you will say something more than this. Probably say "okay, I will reach out to you on WeChat later and we'll set a date." If he adds that sentence, then I will believe what he actually means.

我不清楚，或许不同的人有不同的期待。就我个人而言，即便有人用很真诚的态度对我说"改天再见"，我也会认为是"拜拜"。如果对方是真要再见的话，他会说多一点，比如"咱们微信上聊，确定个日期"。有这句话，我才会相信他真要再次见面。

Okay, so I think here is sort of a time for people to comb through their previous social experience and there are so many of these situations that you kind of need to read between the lines.

好吧，我认为是要梳理一下自己以往的社会经验了。现在确实有很多情况需要你听懂"言外之意"。

I'll tell you what's the simple way of telling it, that is to see how long they breathe before they actually give you a reply. Because if they do it quick, that means they're delaying in giving you an answer, which means it's probably not the answer that you want. So just look at how they breathe.

我来分享一个简单的办法——观察他们在回答你之前是否特意吸气。如果他们快速吸气（有吸气的声音，但没说话），说明他们在拖延时间，他们给出的答案很可能是你不想要的。所以，看看他们怎么吸气吧。

点 评

read between the lines 本意是"读出字里行间的内涵"，引申为"读懂言外之意"。无论中国还是外国，东方还是西方，如何理解别人的"言外之意"都是一门学问。很少有人会直接说出自己的想法，那样会显得 cruel，残忍、刻薄、让人难为情。

当有的人 go over the top 表现得有点过的时候，例如用 absolutely fabulous "超赞的" "棒极了" 这样的词汇来形容本来很普通的人和事，他们实际上想表达的很可能是完全相反的意思。这就叫作 disingenuous，不真诚、不坦率，也可以理解成twisted，扭曲、纠结。

虽然"改天见面"在很多时候听上去没有实际意义，但也可以了解一下这句话应该怎么说：We'll meet another day. Let's meet some other time. I'll see you again.

词汇小百科

complicated　复杂的
comb　梳理、仔细查看、彻底搜查
misinterpretation　误解
plenty room for　充足的余地，大量的空间/机会

（陈　沫）

搭讪艺术家

（素材来自《圆桌议事》2014年6月28日节目）

> **导　语：**两性关系是永恒的话题，而男追女则是两性关系里最常见的相处模式。要想"泡妞"成功，还是需要一定技巧的，尤其在搭讪这个环节。

So, a pick-up artist is a man who trains in the skills of finding, attracting, and seducing women. And the use of "pick up" in this context is actually slang for making a casual acquaintance with the stranger in anticipation of sexual relations. It dates from at least World War II.

　　Pick-up artist就是所谓的搭讪大师或者是搭讪艺术家，说白了也就是非常善于和女性搭讪的男性。这里的pick up可不是我们以前在课本里学过的"捡起（某样东西）"，而是一种俚语表达，有几分"泡妞"的意思，至少在第二次世界大战期间就已被广泛使用。

Certainly, picking up a girl may lead to a relationship. But the point of picking her up at a club or a bar is not necessarily thinking in the longer term. And so part of picking up a girl is having a wingman. A wingman is a role that a person may take when a friend needs support with approaching potential partners in order to pick them up.

　　"泡妞"行动虽然可能带来一段恋情，但男性在俱乐部、酒吧等公开场合进行"泡妞"行为时往往不会想得那么长远。他们很多时候会带着一位

"托儿",给他们出主意或者帮他们打气,让"泡妞"行动相对顺利一些。

In general, a woman's wingman will help her avoid attention from undesirable partners whereas a man's wingman will help him attract desirable ones. Right, and so what happens a lot of times with the wingman is, the wingman will befriend or talk up the target's partners while the person who is trying to pick up the girl will talk to the girl herself.

女性也可以有"托儿",不过男性和女性的"托儿"有比较明显的区别。男性的"托儿"主要是帮当事人跟其心仪女性搭讪,而女性的"托儿"则主要负责帮当事人挡开其没有兴趣的对象。所以,男性的"托儿"很多时候选择跟目标周围的人聊天,这样可以制造机会让他的朋友跟心仪对象单独聊天。

And also when you try to pick up a girl, you need to come up with a line. An opener. Those are called, as you might have guessed, pick-up lines. Sometimes they are also called chat-up lines. That's basically just a conversation opener trying to engage an unfamiliar person in an actual conversation for romance or perhaps even dating.

当然,"泡妞"的聊天跟一般的聊天不一样,开场尤其重要。这种打开话匣子的开场白就是所谓的"搭讪语",英文是pick-up lines或chat-up lines。好的搭讪语可以带来进一步发展关系的机会。

Pick-up lines are commonly used by men who pick up women. They can be very straightforward, they can be very subtle, they can be very tasteful, they can be very brash as well. But novice pick up artists are advised to avoid standardized hackneyed lines. For example, are you an interior decorator? Because when I saw you, the entire room became beautiful.

"搭讪语"主要是男性为了"泡妞"而使用的。因为每个人的风格不同,所以"搭讪语"可以很直接,也可以很含蓄。可以很有品,也可以很无礼。有一条建议适用于所有人：尽量避免陈词滥调。比如：你是室内设计师吗？因为你一出现，整个房间都变漂亮了。

点评

虽然绝大多数的人都希望自己成为搭讪大师，但搭讪这种事儿还真没有标准答案，hardly teachable 不好教。一般来说，最保险的原则就是 be your true self 做真实的自己，多几分 sincerity 真诚，少几分 glibness 油嘴滑舌。做到了这两点，该来的自然会来。如果什么也没来，那只能说 it's not meant to be 没有缘分。

词汇小百科

pick-up artist   搭讪大师，特别擅长和心仪对象搭讪的人
in anticipation of...   期待……
wingman   舵手，托儿，帮朋友跟心仪对象搭讪的人
pick-up / chat-up lines   搭讪语
conversation opener   对话的开场白
brash   无礼的，自以为是的，盛气凌人的
novice   初学者，新手
hackneyed   陈腐的，陈词滥调的
interior decorator / designer   室内设计师

（刘 彦）

吃不到一起就分手

（素材来自《圆桌议事》2016年9月23日节目）

> **导　语**：能吃到一起去，对两个人来说到底有多重要？对于"吃货"来说，最感人的表白莫过于"我还是很喜欢你，像吃着糖醋里脊，就着两碗大米饭"。

He likes spices and she likes sweets. He eats noodles all the time, whilst she wants rice as the staple food. Can this couple reconcile their differences and stay happy together? Apparently, different eating habits can be a deal breaker for some couples.

他喜欢吃辣，她喜欢吃甜；他总吃面条，她的主食却是米饭。这样的两个人能弥补分歧、愉快地在一起吗？很明显，不同的饮食习惯会成为一些人分手的原因。

But I painted it in a different way when I look at this. Let's say, something that means a lot to me is my diet, and I try to eat healthy. Yeah I'm dating a girl that doesn't care about eating healthy, and we are living together, and often when we decide to go out to dinner, we have this fight. I wanna go to X, she wants to go to Y. Um, those things could create that friction in a relationship that would be that catalyst for breaking up.

我会从另一个角度看这种事。比如说，我在乎的是饮食是否健康，但我交往的女孩不在乎这个,我们住在一起,商量去哪儿吃饭的时候就会有矛盾。我想去这家,她想去那家,这就产生了摩擦,可能会成为分手的导火索。

We say in the West all the time, it's the small things that make the big difference in a relationship. And I think this is one of those things. You know at first you are looking at eating habits and you are saying: "Oh it's not a big deal. And I'm not saying that you have to eat the same food."

在西方,我们会说,小事对一段关系的影响往往会超出想象。这就是个例子。最开始大家都觉得饮食习惯不是个大问题,毕竟谁也不会要求对方与自己吃同样的食物。

When two individuals who are not family, and they come together, you are kind of molding yourself into ways that fit the other person, and are you willing to do that? And how far willing are you to agree to go down that path? I think that is if you can manage to go down that path together, then it will work.

两个不是亲人的人要走到一起,就要改变自己去适应对方,你确定要这么做吗?你会在这条路上坚持多久?如果你能这么一直走下去,才可以长久。

Love is one thing, support is another, and I think it's okay to have one person that likes an unhealthy diet, and one person that likes a healthy diet. But to find the support for both of you supporting each other with such fundamental differences, I think it's easier to speak those words and say it's easy, but when you are actually in that relationship, it is pretty difficult.

爱是一回事,支持是另一回事。我觉得一个人喜欢健康饮食而另一个不喜欢,也没什么问题。但是让双方在原则性的问题上彼此包容,说起来容易,做起来真难,尤其当你处在一段关系中,就会发现真的不容易实现。

点 评

几种味道的说法：spicy 辣的，peppery 胡椒味的、火辣的，pungent 辛辣刺激的、浓烈浓郁的，sweet 甜的，salty 咸的，sour 酸的，tart 酸涩的，bitter 苦的，tasteless / bland 无味的、淡的。

这是一次由"吃"引发的感情讨论。吃不到一起去，多多少少会产生矛盾（have fights / frictions），这就需要让步妥协（comprise），让自己试着适应对方（mold yourself into ways that fit the other person）。

让关系变好的建议还有：mind your manner 注意举止，fight right 正确地争执，don't call his or her name 不要直呼他 / 她的名字（尤其是全名），sound it out / communicate 说出你的想法 / 沟通。相信在处理亲密关系方面，大家都有自己的心得。

词汇小百科

staple food　主食
reconcile　和好、和解、调停、排解
catalyst　催化剂、导火索、触发因素
fundamental　基础的、基本的、根本的

（陈　沫）

挑内衣到底为了谁

（素材来自《圆桌议事》2016年8月2日节目）

> **导　语**：在挑选内衣这件事上，女性们究竟在想什么呢？一方面，女性似乎更愿意在内衣上花钱；另一方面，购买高端内衣的过程却不是那么愉快。还有，男性在这件事上究竟有多少发言权？

A lingerie is definitely a piece of underwear but it is fancier usually comes with a heftier price tag and underwear is just undergarments. Often it is a lot more economical and what we are talking about today is that apparently high-end lingerie sales are outpacing China's generally downbeat luxury market, and there is a heating-up competition between international centers and local rivals that are looking to go to this up market area. Yeah, for ladies it's a bit of a paradox. On the one hand, we are spending more; On the other hand, we are complaining that the purchasing experience and the whole thing all together kind of sucks.

　　Lingerie 是指那种价格较高的内衣，underwear就是普通内衣，相比之下更经济实惠。今天我们讨论的是领跑中国普遍低迷的奢侈品市场的高端内衣。国际大牌与本土品牌在这个领域竞争非常激烈。面对高端内衣，女性常常陷入矛盾：我们一方面在这上面花了更多的钱，另一方面也抱怨购买过程不太愉快。

There is one notion from the guys that think, you know, it's sort of dressing up to please your lover. But I think there is more to it. I think when you are dressing in nice lingerie or just nice underwear, fancy stuff the girls like, you know with the laces and things. It makes you feel confident. It doesn't always have to do with some guys.

男人们会觉得，这种内衣是用来取悦爱人的。但是我认为内衣的意义大于这点。当你穿上漂亮的内衣的时候，那些精致的部分，比如蕾丝，会让女人感到自信，并不总是与男人有关。

Do you think women are going to Victoria's Secrets to just buy everyday use underwear? Probably not. I know in the US, many guys do go with their girlfriends, because they want their boyfriends' opinion and I see no problem in that.

你以为女人去维多利亚的秘密，是去买普通内衣的吗？不是吧。我知道在美国，有很多男士陪他们的女朋友买内衣，因为女性也需要男性的意见。我觉得没有什么问题。

I can only assume that for those couples that do not want to purchase their lingerie together, it is possible that the girl's trying to surprise her boyfriend. It is possible that she's just buying it for herself, like you said, it makes her happy. Maybe you like it, maybe you don't like it. I don't care. I think I look good in it, it's like everyday clothes. It's the same thing. And maybe it is possible that the guy is shy. He doesn't want to step into such a store. There are so many possibilities.

可有些情侣不愿意一起买内衣，我想肯定有他们的原因。比如有些女性想给男友制造一个惊喜。也有可能她就是为自己而买的，让自己高兴。另一半喜不喜欢，她不在乎，她自己感觉好就好。又或者男士比较害羞，不愿意进入内衣店。总之有很多可能性。

If you are shopping at these stores for your guys, you need to be pulling money out of their pockets too, because this is just as much involving them. Make them have a say.

女士们，如果你们和另一半去高端内衣店购物，记得让他们付钱，这事跟他们也有关，让他们也出出主意。

As a woman, I'm gonna share with the world today. That is, girls, it is so important to get the right piece of underwear or lingerie. Because a lot of Chinese girls, you don't know what fits you well, you might not even know what your correct size is. I know a lot of our listeners are young and you should definitely go into one of the brick and mortar stores that sell lingerie or underwear and have a professional (help you). She can be overly friendly sometimes, in truth, maybe, but you need her help. So figure out your right size and it will help you in life and you feel so confident and your posture is improved, so go for it, ladies.

作为一名女性，我要与世界分享的是：女孩们，选择合适的内衣太重要了。很多中国女孩不懂什么是适合自己的，甚至不知道自己的尺码。我们的受众大多非常年轻，你们真的应该去销售内衣的实体店，与专业导购沟通。她们可能会超出寻常的热情，让你感到不自在，但你也确实需要帮助。找对自己的尺寸，这将有助于你的生活，让你感到自信，体态也更优美。赶紧行动吧，女士们。

点 评

形容昂贵，除了用 expensive，还可以用 with a heftier price tag。Heftier，（体积、数量、重量）巨大的，hefty 的比较级；Price Tag，价签、价格、费用；英国女歌手 Jessie J 有一首非常流行的单曲 Price Tag，是这么唱的：We don't need your money, money, money... Forget about the price tag.

To please your lover 是指"取悦你的爱人"，please 在这里是动词，是"讨好，让某人高兴满意"的意思。在一段关系中，女人做什么事都要与男人有关吗？答案是否定的。It makes you feel confident. It doesn't always have to do with guys.（购买内衣）会让女性自己感到自信，并不总是为了男性。女性也会对男性说：Maybe you like it, maybe you don't like it. I don't care.或许你喜欢，或许你不喜欢，我不在乎。

内衣不是一件小事，因为它涉及一个女人是否了解自己的身材know what your correct size is, 是否知道什么适合自己what fits you well, 最关键的是，它影响一个女人的自信you feel so confident with the right lingerie / underwear. 从内衣开始，知道自己适合什么，你将会拥有更好的人生。

词汇小百科

lingerie　内衣，多指带蕾丝的高级内衣

high-end　高端的

downbeat　低迷、沉闷、黯淡的，可以形容市场，也可以形容情绪氛围

paradox　矛盾

brick and mortar stores　多指零售业的实体店。Brick 是指"砖"，mortar 是指"灰浆、砂浆"

overly　过度地、极度地

posture　姿态、姿势；看法、态度

（陈　沫）

女强人承受了多少偏见

（素材来自《圆桌议事》2016年3月8日节目）

导　语：现在的女性真是越来越出色了。她们有丰富的学识、精彩的经历、美满的家庭，有的还有让人羡慕的高收入和高职位。她们活出了自己最好的样子，不少人都是"女强人"。但是，社会对女性的判断依然有所偏颇。

A lot of the time when women are described in the news reports, you'll hear descriptions of their age, their appearance, you know, their family roles or whatever, far more often than you hear with men, and people are just used to that, used to thinking of women in these sorts of ways.

很多时候，新闻报道中出现女性话题时，大都谈论的是她们的年龄、外表、家庭角色等；而报道里出现男性话题时，就很少涉及这些。人们总是习惯这样评判女性，一谈论女性就谈论这些。

And you hear people talk about women in politics, for example, Angela Merkel. There were some comments said about how she looks, and how she dresses, and really, that's not what we should be focusing on. We should be focusing on the great job they do, or you know, how they think, their skills, their talents, rather than how they look.

当你听到人们谈论政坛女性，比如安吉拉·默克尔，有一些评论是关于她的外表和服装的。我们真的不应该关注这些。我们应该关注她们的工作、思想、技能、才华，而不是她们的样子。

Exactly, and it often appalls me, when these female world leaders, or women in leading positions in big companies, and they've worked that hard to get there, and they are making important decisions, and what the viewer or the audience cares about is—where did she do her hair, what kind of suit is she wearing, and is she getting a little bit fat? And it's like, people, can't you just grow up a little bit, and look at what the real problem is here? That is you, looking at these ladies in that very biased eye.

　　的确如此，这样的判断经常让我觉得震惊。这些女性领导人或者公司高管，她们那么努力地工作，要做重要的决策，但是大家关心的却是她在哪里做的头发、她的衣服是什么样子或者她是不是有点变胖了。我想说，大家能不能成熟点，去关注真正应该关注的问题。像那样看待这些女性是种偏见。

Right, right. And there are so many more important things going on. Like Angela Merkel for example, she is probably the most important leader in all of Europe, and she has way more stuff on her plate, way more important things to do, than you know, what is she wearing or these trivial sorts of things there, I mean, you sometimes see that for men as well, but there is also a far more scrutiny on women.

　　是的，毕竟有很多重要的事情要关注。比如默克尔，她可能是欧洲最重要的领导人，她有那么多事情要处理，她如何工作比她穿什么衣服这些琐事重要得多。这种情况在男性身上就很少见。现在对待女性的偏颇审视太多了。

It's not just about elevating women's right, but it's also meaning that guys can get a wider scope of option. It's like guys, you shouldn't be confined into your gender role either, it's fine to be a little bit metrosexual maybe. Pluck your eyebrows, that's fine too, although that's a little bit too much for my taste. But still, it means more choices, more options for everyone, and that is what we are hailing for.

这不仅是提升女性权益,这也是建议男性有更广泛的选择。男士们,你们不应该局限在自己的性别角色里,做个都市美男也不错。拔掉眉毛也可以啊,虽然这有点超出我的口味。无论如何,我们倡导的是每个人都有更多的选择。

The golden tip is to remember, you can do whatever you want, so remember to be yourself, and remember to strive to achieve what you want to achieve no matter your gender.

给大家一条黄金提示:无论男女,做你自己,做你想做的,去实现你想实现的。

点 评

优秀的女性努力工作 work hard,有很多事要处理 have a lot on her plate,做重要的决策 make important decisions,依然有人只是盯着她们的外表 appearance,发型 hairstyle,服饰 dresses,甚至体重 weight。这是一种偏见 this is bias。

同时,只注重内在,不注重外在,也是一种偏见。还是平衡的好。

总的来说,活得漂亮才是真的漂亮。女性应该怎么生活呢?几点建议 advice:了解自己 know who you really are,做你自己 be yourself,爱你自己 love yourself,建立自信 build confidence。

词汇小百科

family role 家庭角色
talent 才华、才干
trivial 琐碎的、细微的、没价值的
scope 范围、眼界、视角
eyebrow 眉毛
option 选择、选项

（陈 沫）

女人一定要找比自己聪明的男人吗？

（素材来自《圆桌议事》2016年4月25日节目）

导　语：美国布法罗大学日前公布一项针对900人的调查显示，那些希望另一半比自己聪明的女性对科学、技术、数学和工程方面的兴趣很低，她们更愿意扮演传统女性的角色。那么，两个人的理想状态是什么呢？究竟是互补好，还是相似好？

My sister has been published for trying to cure cancer. And she did not marry a guy that's less smart than her. She married another scientist who is also very very intelligent, his name is Chris. And he's a really nice guy. But I don't think that women, if they are very smart, the smart women would settle for dumber guys.

我的姐姐是治疗癌症的专家，她就没找一个比她笨的男人。她的丈夫也是位科学家，非常聪明，人很不错。所以我觉得聪明女人不会找笨男人。

I'd like to share a little story. As you know I was that girl that kind of look for a guy that wasn't as smart as I was. But he was still super cool and a really wonderful guy. That was just in high school. So basically I would ask him like math questions and I totally knew the answer. I just asked him and pretended I didn't know. We had fun together.

我也分享个故事。我可以接受一个不如自己聪明的男人。高中时的那个他非常酷、非常棒。我总会去问他数学题，其实这些题我也会，只是装作不会。我们在一起很开心。

I have heard that opposites attract. I'm not one to buy that. I feel like people that you share stuff in common with you will be able to go do things together, like you will be excited to do the same thing, you will share common interests. We can talk about that for hours. Having things in common I think is actually really important in a relationship and of course you won't have everything in common but having the important stuff in common I think is necessary.

  我听说过"差异产生美",但我不这么认为。与你相似的人可以与你一同做事,这让彼此都开心,有相同的兴趣,两个人可以聊上好几个小时。在两人关系中,相同点真的很重要。当然,两人不可能在所有方面都具备共同点,但在重要的事情上有相似之处还是很有必要的。

Jingdaihuakai says "my major is English and I hate math. I prefer to choose my significant other to be excellent at math". And Jessie says "I want someone that is kind of having that part that I don't have. So I can kind of look up to him". But I would say I would go for, I just can't help but share my own opinion, that is, I think we should work as a team. We should be equals. And he is not dumber than you. And you can work together and move forward together. That's the best thing I think.

  网友静待花开说,我是英语专业的,我讨厌数学,但我希望另一半数学好。网友Jessie说希望另一半具备她不具备的,然后她才可以仰视他。我的观点是,两个人应该像一个团队,旗鼓相当,一起前进,这是我认为最好的状态。

点 评

  两个人的理想关系是什么样的?We should work as a team.我们应该像一

个团队一样，team 团队。We should be equals.我们应该旗鼓相当。Equal，做名词时是指（地位、实力）相同的人，同一个段位的人。两个人在一起可以干什么呢？do things together 一起做事，share common interests 分享共同的兴趣爱好，talk for hours 聊上几个小时，move forward together 一起前行。很有画面感是不是？

词汇小百科

intelligent　聪明的、智商高的

smart　也是聪明、有灵气的意思

cool　形容很赞或者很冷静

wonderful　意思是很棒，非常不错

dumb　蠢笨的。当然，还可以用最常用的stupid

（陈　沫）

男生别抱怨！女生买东西是件大工程！

（素材来自《圆桌议事》2015年4月28日节目）

导语：女人在买东西前犹豫不决是出了名的，研究显示，女性在掏出钱包之前最多要经历10个步骤，据称现代女性至少要花40个小时才能买到自己满意的衣服。在本篇中我们将学习与购物相关的说法。

Look through celebrity magazines, check out online stores to see how much they are, send links to friends to get an opinion, post photos on social networks to get a wider audience, send the links to mom or other close relatives, make a special trip to the store to try it on, take a fitting room selfie and send the selfie to friends, boyfriend or partner, and then the last step, 71 percent, according to the survey, make the purchase there and then, a third head back home again to complete the process by ordering it online.

看明星杂志，上网店看价钱，把链接发给朋友询问意见，把照片放上社交网络获得更多观众意见，把链接发给妈妈或其他近亲，专门去商店试穿，在试衣间自拍并把自拍发给朋友、男友或伴侣，然后是最后一步，根据调查，71%的女性会在店里买，而大约1/3的女性会回家在网上下单来完成整个买衣服的过程。

But I think it is sort of necessary these days. In the old days, you probably find someone to give you their opinion on an outfit, but nowadays you've got so many other ways to do so.

但我认为在这个时代（这些步骤）有必要。在过去，你可能就找个人让他给你关于衣着的建议，但是现在你有很多其他方式做到这些（指询问他人意见）。

I think for these people, they are either too indecisive or they are just obsessed with the shopping experience, some people are just into that. I'm not one of those people.

我认为这些人要不是太不果断了，就是沉迷于买东西的经历。有些人只是太喜欢这些事（指买衣服）了。我并不属于这类人。

Well, you know, the gay best friend is a girl's best gift, I suppose. But I mean these ladies...they seem to really rely on the third person's opinion a lot and that sometimes is a little bit not good.

你知道，gay蜜是一个女孩最好的礼物。但我认为这些女孩子（指通过十个步骤买衣服的女孩子）真的是太依赖第三方的意见了，有时候这并不太好。

But the worst part of it is after all the consultation, half of the women end up making choices that they don't like.

最糟的是在经过所有的咨询之后，一半的女性最后做了她们不喜欢的选择。

点 评

女性买衣服之前可能会经历很多步骤，比如 post photos on social networks 把照片放上社交网络，social networks 社交网络（如 Facebook, Twitter, Weibo, WeChat 等），make a special trip to the store to try it on 专门去商店试穿，try something on 试穿什么衣服，take a fitting room selfie 在试衣间自拍，

fitting room 试衣间，take a selfie 自拍。如果有人真的按照所有的步骤做的话，they are too indecisive, 这些人太不果断了，indecisive 不果断的，从 decide（决定）这个词演变过来，她们也有可能太沉迷于购物（into shopping），be into something 与 be obsessed with something 相似，表示沉迷于某事。最终经历了这些购物步骤后，仍然可能 end up making choices that they don't like 最后做了她们不喜欢的选择，end up doing 最后发展为……，以做……而告终。If he continues like this, he will end up lifting a stone only to have it drop on his own foot, just as the saying goes 如果他继续如此，就会像俗话所说的那样，最终将搬起石头砸自己的脚。

词汇小百科

selfie　自拍、自拍照

go shopping　购物

window shopping　光看不买

discount　折扣

promotion　促销

black Friday　黑色星期五

shopping spree / festival / frenzy　购物节 / 购物狂欢节（如双十一）

online shopping / cyber shopping　网上购物

overseas online shopping　海淘（网上海外代购）

（王　玮）

男人每个月总有那么几天……

（素材来自《圆桌议事》2015年12月3日节目）

导　语：英国一项调查显示，四分之一的男性认为自己每个月都会有特定的"大姨夫"时期，在这段时间内他们会觉得非常容易疲劳、烦躁、嗜吃和烦恼，症状类似于女性的"经前综合征"。男士们真的会有"大姨夫"吗？

This is a bit of a delicate subject to discuss with two gentlemen. And I suppose as the lady here I will take the liberty of explaining the term *dayima* or "periods". So basically in Chinese it's quite funny. Translated into English it literally means "big aunty".

这个话题要和两位男士讨论有点敏感。作为（现场唯一的）女性，由我来担负起解释关键词"大姨妈"或"月经周期"的工作吧。中文里"大姨妈"这个词很有意思，按字面翻译成英文是 big aunty。

I think maybe this is pointing at a hormone fluctuation that maybe men experience more or less similar to what women feel. So we are not talking about the physical side of things but more of the psychological side of things. So guys, do you feel that every month there's a few days you feel cranky, you feel grumpy, you feel unhappy, unsatisfied, you wanna eat a lot and you just hate people around you? Do you feel that?

我想这是指荷尔蒙波动可能给男性造成和女性（月经周期）类似的感

觉。是一种心理上的体验，并非身体上的。那么男士们，每月会不会有那么几天，你们易怒、脾气不好、不快乐、不满足、想大吃一顿，还讨厌身边的人？你们有过这种感觉吗？

I feel that all the time. For a man, that's my default setting.

我天天都这样，这是我的默认设置。

And since I've got married, my wife has offered me this valuable lesson about this other dimension about this world that is emotional dimension. So I began to realize that our emotions fluctuate through time. And I came to pay attention to these small changes in the state of mind especially.

自从我结婚后，妻子给我上了珍贵的一堂课，事关这个世间的另一个维度——也就是情感维度。我因而发现我们的情感会随着时间波动。后来，我开始关注这些情绪上的小变化。

But I wonder if maybe men are sort of cashing in on this a little bit.

不过我怀疑也许男人们有找借口的嫌疑。

Don't you just sympathize with people who don't pay attention to their emotional wellbeing? I remember talking with one of our colleagues who is from Sri Lanka, who pays a lot of attention to her psychological wellbeing. She said a very famous quote I would like to say on this show. She said our mind is kind of like our body. If we don't wash our bodies every two days or every day, your body will stink. It is the same case with your mind. If you don't pay attention to your mind, to your psychological wellbeing, your mind gets dirty.

难道你不同情那些不注意自己情感健康的人吗？我记得和一位来自斯里兰卡的同事聊天。她非常重视自己的心理健康。她引用了相当著名的一句话，在此与大家分享。她说我们的精神就像我们的身体。如果我们不是每天或每两天清洗我们的身体，身体会发臭。其实精神也一样。如果你不注意你的精神健康，心理健康，你的脑子也会变得肮脏。

I'm not sure if I really buy into all this, to be quite honest with you. If you think too much about this, because you don't have enough else going on. I think if you keep yourself busy, you don't occupy yourself with thoughts like this. I think it's very easy to overthink when you are a bit bored or you are at a loose end. I think maybe that's contributing to this sort of phenomenon.

老实说，我不确定我是不是相信这一切。如果你能有这么多的解读，那是因为你的闲暇时间太多了。我觉得，如果你很忙的话，你不会想这些的。我认为常常是你无聊和没事做的时候，你才会想太多。这也许和"大姨夫"这种现象的出现有关系。

点 评

take the liberty of 冒昧地，斗胆地。The meeting had to be postponed, as I couldn't take the liberty of deciding on the action plan without my boss present. 会议必须延迟，因为我无法在老板不在场的情况下冒昧决定行动计划。

That's my default setting. Default setting "默认设置"是电脑语言进入日常用语的例子。生活中很多时候我们都按照习惯做事。比如，一早起床、刷牙、洗脸、上厕所、换衣服、吃早饭、出门上班或上学。你思考过下一步要做什么吗？大部分情况下，好像没有吧。We sometimes live our lives in default setting. 有时候，我们生活得好像进入了默认设置一样，有些枯燥。但如果脱离这种固定制式，也许一方面多了许多可能性，但另一方面会失去一种安全感呢。

offered someone a lesson 给某人上了一课。

cash in on 靠……赚钱，趁机利用，从中获利。原文中这个词组被用来形容男人借"大姨夫"的名义为自己的行为找借口。

I'm not sure if I buy into all of this... 我不相信……的委婉说法。这也是发表

反方意见的开场白。Buy 是一个很有用的小词，除了你一定知道的"买"，还有众多其他含义，比如"相信，接受"，例如 I'm not buying any of that nonsense. 我才不相信那些胡扯呢。另外，buy 有"获得、赢得"的含义：This is a bold move, but may be able to buy us more time. 这是一个大胆的行为，但也许能为我们赢得更多的时间。Buy 做不可数名词的时候还有"性价比高的商品"的意思。This is still a good buy even with the price hike. 即便价格提高了，这还是很合算的。全球知名的家用电器和电子产品零售集团——百思买集团就叫 Best Buy。是不是一个很符合商业定位的公司名称呢？

词汇小百科

period 女性经期

I have my period 大姨妈来了

period cramp / pain 经痛

menstruation / menses / monthlies 都是月经的意思

cranky 脾气暴躁的

irritable 急躁的、易怒的

grumpy 脾气坏的

grouchy 好抱怨的

choleric 易怒的、暴躁的

neurotic 神经质的

（赫　扬）

婚后感悟
Marriage

老爸是全能手，老公啥也不会修

（素材来自《圆桌议事》2014年10月13日节目）

导　语：水龙头坏了、水管堵了、灯泡烧了……小时候，家里的这些事，老爸总能分分钟搞定，但是，现在老公竟然根本就不会。相对爸爸一辈的无所不能，不少家庭主妇认为，自己老公"技能退化"了。对此，老公们也很委屈，现在的东西科技含量那么高，本来就不是非专业人士能随随便便修好的啊。再说我们小时候连手工课都没上过，哪里会修水管呢？那么修修补补到底该不该是老公们的必备素质？"技能退化"这个锅到底该由谁来背？

Anyway, so it seems like sometimes, the newer version of lights we get now isn't all that user-friendly. Sometimes, it is not as simple as sticking a different light-bulb on, but there's like hooking the wire and stuff. So I mean if it is like a more advanced technology that requires more advanced knowledge in fixing it, come on, I don't think even the dads have that kind of knowledge that's required sometimes.

或许，我们现在使用的"新版本"电器，比如灯具，并不那么"用户友好"。比如说，换灯泡不像过去那么简单了，不是拿一个新灯泡装上去就能修好了，你可能还得重新接个线什么的。我想说，现在使用新科技的产品也需要相应的新知识才能驾驭，所以爸爸们或许也不具备把它们修好的高级技能哦。

It is kind of interesting, because they are actually being very honest about where their archetypes of masculinity are coming from... Inevitably, we do end up marrying a version of our parents, whether it is composite of your mother and father, more father or more mother. For either sex, I think it just kind of happens. Because it is what we are familiar with, this is what we are used to. And also, especially with the daughters to fathers, and sons to mothers, that's our archetype of how the other sex is formed or what we are supposed to expect from them and things like that.

对我而言，最有趣的其实是，参加这个调查的这些妻子都很诚实地表达了她们心中"强壮而有魅力"的男性原型来自父亲。或许不可避免地，我们最终都会和另一个版本的父亲或者母亲结婚，无论这个结婚对象是兼具母亲和父亲的特点，还是更像他们中某一个。这个规律对于男女其实都适用，因为父母类型的人是我们所熟悉的、所习惯的。而且，特别是父亲对女儿、母亲对儿子的影响会更大一些，因为他们形成了我们对异性最初的认知和期待。

But at the same time, the gender archetypes with the huge generation gap. And of course, your husband is not going to be able to do the same things as your father. And it is actually quite insulting to be like what... Why can't man fix stuff anymore? Or okay fine, but why can't you cook anymore? Why can't you sew my clothes anymore? Why are you now at work instead of staying at home watching the kids all day? I mean come on, grow up, we are living in a different world.

但同时我想说，这种"性别原型"和你所能接触到的同辈异性之间，其实是有巨大的代沟的。你的丈夫当然做不到你父亲能做的所有事儿。要求老公修这修那，或者对他说"我爸就会修，你为什么不会？"其实很不公平。而且其实老公们也可以说"为什么女性现在不做饭了？""为什么我老婆现在不给我补衣服了？"或者"为什么她要出去工作，而不是天天在家带孩子呢？"我的意思是，让我们成熟一点看这件事，我们现在生活的世界毕竟和长辈那时的不同了。

I think there is a problem with our education system here as well. Because during your primary school days, I think it is hugely useful for both boys and girls to learn how to sew or how to fix things or do some easy manual work. And I think that part is often lacking.

我觉得现在年轻人动手能力差其实也和我们的教育制度有关。在上小学的时候，学习一些类似于如何缝制衣服或者如何修理工具之类的简单技能，无论对男孩还是女孩都很有帮助。很可惜，这部分的培训往往是空缺的。

点 评

孩子眼中的父亲常常是无所不能的，而全能的人、多面手，用英文表达就是 all-rounder。除了表示在很多方面都很有才华之外，这个词也可以指体育运动中的全能型选手。另外，有连字符的 all-round 可以指全能的、综合的，比如 All-round Championship 总冠军、all-round play 技术全面的打法……而不加连字符的 all round 则是指周围、到处，等于 all around。

在讨论完孩子们会以父母为标准寻找另一半之后，主持人们又聊了聊现代人动手能力差的事。当我们要表达"我想再回去说说之前那件事"或者"我对刚刚那个观点还有话要说"的时候，就可以用 just to bounce back on。Bounce 本意是反弹，向后跳，而 bounce back on something 就形象地表达了"让我们跳回刚刚那个话题"。当然，bounce back 也可以表示恢复、弹回、退回，以及恢复元气、重整旗鼓的意思。

词汇小百科

fix　修理、解决

mend　较简单的修复

repair　需要较高的职业技能和较复杂的工具进行的修理

patch　用类似材料修补破洞、裂缝或磨损的地方

straighten　整顿、使……挺直

maintain　维护、维修

trim　修剪、修整

（牛翃琳）

把老公存起来，呵呵

（素材来自《圆桌议事》2016年8月1日节目）

导　语：一个不争的事实就是，女性喜欢逛街，男性对逛街没有太大兴趣。女人拉着一个不情愿的男人逛街，会影响购物的乐趣，也会让男人很不舒服。现在商场推出的"老公寄存处"能解决这个问题吗？男人们，你们愿意被寄存吗？

We men are offended, okay? I am proposing Girlfriends Storage when guys want to play video games with their buddies.

我们男人觉得被冒犯了。我提议成立"女朋友寄存处"，在我们想和兄弟打游戏的时候能用上。

I cannot believe that you think this is girls just ditching their beloved significant other, and so she can enjoy her shopping. It's not about that at all. (What is it about?) It's about thinking for your significant other. Do you honestly wanna be dragged around looking at shoes and dresses?

我不敢相信你认为"寄存老公/男友"的行为就意味着女性把她们的另一半抛弃了。根本不是这样的。这是女性为另一半着想的表现，难道你真的喜欢被拖拽着去看那些鞋子和衣服吗？

I disagree. I would love to go around with my girlfriend and do shopping and tell her what I think looks good and have a say on maybe some of the wardrobe she picks. And at the same time, I'm realizing that at least in a relationship when you work at nine to five Monday through Friday, when you go out on the weekend, that's your time to spend time together, quality time. And even when she's shopping and even when you are shopping, you can be talking and catching up on all the gossip or whatever happening at work, just sharing those moments together that you don't get throughout the week. That's my personal view on it.

我不这么看。我就很乐意跟我女朋友逛街，告诉她我觉得她穿什么好看，对她的着装提一些建议。另外，很多人的工作是周一到周五朝九晚五的那种，那么周末才是你们比较高质量的相处时间，逛街时可以好好交流，分享八卦，说说工作中的事，用周末来弥补工作日不能在一起的时间。这是我个人的看法。

If you're sharing a life together and you're sharing a lifetime together, there's plenty of time to do stuff together.

如果你们要共同生活，要共度一生的话，会有大把的时间一起做事。

And choosing a dress can feel like a lifetime.

选衣服的时间仿佛就有一生那么长了。

点评

争论时的常用句式：I am offended. 我被冒犯了。I cannot believe that you think... 我不敢相信你认为……It's not about that at all. It's about... 根本不是这样的，其实是…… I disagree. 我不同意。That's my personal view on it. 这是我个人的看法。

如果两人 work from nine to five Monday through Friday 周一至周五朝九晚五地工作，到了周末，才可以好好 spend time together 共度时光，talk 说话交谈，catch up on all the gossip or whatever happening at work 聊八卦和工作琐事。

两个人的长远打算是 share a life together 共同生活，更长远的是 share a lifetime together 共度一生。但建议女性朋友逛街不要太久，正如节目所说，太久了就会让男性觉得，挑衣服的时间仿佛就是一生了 choosing a dress can feel like a lifetime.

词汇小百科

significant other　另一半
wardrobe　衣柜，也可以指个人全部衣服
lifetime　一生，有生之年

（陈　沫）

爱着同一个男人的两个女人如何相处？

（素材来自《圆桌议事》2015年11月4日节目）

导 语：婆媳关系是永远的难题，哪里都一样。数之不尽的以婆媳大战为主题的国产电视剧更加说明，这个问题在中国尤其突出。难道婆媳真的就不可能好好相处？

Well, I have a whole speech to make on this topic. Great! We are waiting for that! Although I don't have this issue, I think a lot of people in China are experiencing this issue.

针对这个话题我可以发表一整篇演说呢。太棒了！洗耳恭听！尽管我没有这方面的困扰，但我知道好多中国人都在经历这个问题。

This associate professor Xu Chong said in the explanation that his wife had many conflicts with his parents, including marriage customs, raising the child, and preferred taste of food. This guy thought that must be the key factor causing the breakdown of his marriage. See, how gruesome this issue can be in law relationships.

这位副教授许冲在解释文书里说他的妻子和公公婆婆产生了许多争执。争执的内容包括婚礼的习俗安排，教育孩子，还有饭菜口味等。这位男士认为这成了婚姻破裂的主要原因。看看吧，婆媳问题不解决可能酿成大祸。

There's a saying from Shakespeare—she doth protest too much, which means if you've gone about something too much, people will think you mean the opposite.

莎士比亚说过"她解释得太多",意思是越解释,越让人觉得你口是心非。

From history books, from literature, several thousands of literary works, we have a lot of examples of this. But the most famous one is the famous poet Lu You who had to divorce his beloved wife because his mother didn't like her. So that's the damage this relationship can do to a marriage.

从历史书里,文学作品里,几千部文学著作里,我们可以找到大量的事例。不过最有名的例子来自著名诗人陆游。因为母亲不喜欢自己深爱的妻子,陆游最终还是和妻子分开了。这就是不好的婆媳关系可能对婚姻造成的伤害。

To be serious about it, I think it is awful the fact that there can be this influence on a relationship. For me, a romantic relationship is about two people, not two families. It's about two people. Perhaps because I am from a different culture, there isn't this intertwining of families. There isn't this relationship between the daughter in-law and mother in-law.

严肃地说,我觉得婆媳关系能对一段感情产生这么大的影响实在很糟糕。对我来说,一段感情是两个人的事,并不是两个家庭的事。也许因为我来自不同的文化,在我的文化里并没有这种来自家庭的羁绊,并没有这个媳妇和婆婆关系和睦与否的问题。

I know that in some cases in China, traditionally people have lived under the same roof. It's not uncommon in the past for maybe three or four generations to live under the same roof. Although I know that's changing now. So obviously when you think about marriage, you do have to think in practical terms. Not just about two people being in love, but is everyone else going to get along with each other…It's a shame, because I like the purer thoughts of romance between two people.

我知道在某些中国家庭的案例中，传统上是一家人住在一起。过去一家人三代同堂或是四世同堂并不罕见，尽管我知道这也在发生改变。显然当你在考虑婚姻时，你会想一些现实的问题。这不只是两个人相爱那么简单，还要考虑家庭其他成员能否和睦相处。这真的很遗憾，因为我喜欢更纯粹的两个人的恋爱关系。

In this case, between the mother-in-law and the daughter-in-law. To my way of thinking, a marriage is about those two people, So therefore the mother-in-law should always give way to the daughter-in-law.

在这个例子里，是婆婆和媳妇间的问题。我觉得婚姻是两个人的事，所以婆婆应该永远让步于媳妇。

There is one more issue. Who is going to be the head of the family? Who is going to be the head of two families?

还有一个问题。谁是一家之主？谁在这两个家庭里说了算？

I'm just helping thousands of depressed women airing their views, both on the side of the mothers-in-law and daughters-in-law, right?

我只是在帮助大量情绪低落的女性讲出她们的想法，既包括婆婆，也包括媳妇，不是吗？

There are many old superstitions and misconceptions that the older generations still have. I know from Chinese friends with children that they don't really like the kinds of things that grandparents tell their kids. Old myths, superstitions, nonsense, unscientific rubbish and so forth. But the grandparents think they have that right, simply because they are old.

老一辈依然坚持很多古老迷信思想和错误想法。我从有孩子的中国朋友那里知道，他们并不喜欢祖父母告诉孩子的这些话。诸如古老传说、迷信、谬论、不科学的废话等。但祖父母们往往认为他们有这个权利，仅仅因为他们年纪大。

I understand their frustration. And here I think they have a say too. And they are probably the mothers-in-law. Because don't forget these older ladies work so hard in their life saving up. And what do they use that money for? More often than not, to get an apartment for their sons. When you've put the down payment of your life savings for your son, and now some stranger woman comes in and lives with him. Why can't I have a say when it comes to family matters? For a second I felt like a mother-in-law, and I don't even have a boyfriend.

我了解她们的无奈，我觉得她们也有发表意见的权利。她们大多是婆婆了。不要忘记有些女性工作一辈子就是为了攒钱。这份存款是拿来做什么？往往都是为儿子买房。当你把毕生积蓄都给儿子付了房子的首付，现在有个陌生女人和他一起居住，那为什么我不能就这个家庭内部事务发表看法？有那么一瞬间，我觉得自己好像变成了婆婆，但其实我连个男朋友都没影儿呢。

I disagree with you because I think it's selfish to give a gift but really it's not a gift, it's a tool of coercion and oppression. Therefore if someone gives a gift, it should not come with strings attached which they then pull and expect everyone to dance to their tune.

名义上送出礼物但实际上不是礼物，而把它当成强制和压迫的手段，这是很自私的行为。所以如果有人给了礼物，那就不应该带有附加条款，还指望别人听你的摆布。

Respect has to be earned. It cannot be demanded, because that's true. It does have to be earned. True respect does. You can pretend to be respectful of somebody, but really you resent them, which I think is that we are talking about in this situation. So if the people who buy the apartment, they are the older generation, they want true respect, give as a gift and don't expect anything in return. That's the true essence of giving.

尊重是需要靠争取的，不是张口索要就可以获得的。这是真的。至少真正的尊敬是这么来的。你可以假装对某人很尊敬，但你实际上很讨厌他们。这可能就是我们讨论的情况。如果老一辈想要真心实意地尊重，那么给出礼物就不要计较回报，送出房子也别想着我将来可以如何如何，那才是真正意义上的给予。

点评

The lady doth protest too much, methinks 出自莎士比亚的名作《哈姆雷特》。有越解释越欲盖弥彰的意味。

It's a shame 这实在是个遗憾。It's a shame for us to part. 我们分开是多么可惜的事啊。

give way to 让步；让某人在先。Give way to traffic coming from the left. 给来自左边的车辆让行。

The head of... 是某某头领的意思。在实际应用中至少有三种用法。原文中 the head of the family 是一家之主，the head of state 是国家元首。这个词组还有部门负责人的含义，例如 the head of marketing 营销部门的管理者。

Strings attached 是口语里附加条款的意思。dance to their tune 是和某人周旋的意思。It would be a stupid mistake to dance to their tune. 和他们周旋会是个愚蠢的错误。

True essence 真谛 The true essence of love is mutual trust and respect. 爱情的真谛是相互的信任和尊重。What do you think the true essence of love is? 你认为爱情的真谛是什么呢？

如何能改善婆媳关系？根本上还是要双方达到相互尊重和谅解。关系中的核心男性，即婆婆的儿子、媳妇的丈夫，要发挥润滑剂的作用。两边都顺心了，家庭才能少些摩擦。

词汇小百科

persuasion　说服（名词）
convince　说服（动词）

（赫　扬）

"交友神器"还是"婚姻杀手"

（素材来自《圆桌议事》2015年6月17日节目）

导　语：当手机成为二人世界的"第三者"时，真正的第三者可能就在社交软件的那一头。据中国民政部数据显示，微信、陌陌等"交友神器"引发婚外情而导致离婚的案例增加了20%。这些"交友神器"真是"婚姻杀手"吗？本篇我们来聊聊婚姻中为什么会出现某些问题。

I think it's rather absurd to blame social apps for divorce rate. I think as we've talked about, it seems like it's extramarital affair itself but not the kind of devices you use to enable it to happen that actually causes the rise of divorce rate.

我认为离婚率高怪社交软件很荒谬。就像我们讨论过的，我认为是婚外情本身而不是你使用了这类容易发生婚外情的工具导致了离婚率升高。

There's a thing on WeChat, isn't there, where you can see who's in your vicinity or something. There're apps like Tinder, which is used by people who are looking for someone to have a fling with, and lots of other things like that. So I think if it's made easier, then people are more likely to give in. We're already human, and people can sometimes be quite weak-willed, can't they? So if it's easier for them, maybe they're more likely to engage in this sort of thing.

微信上有一个功能，能让你看到周围都有哪些人。还有类似于"探探"

之类的APP，可以让人们找个人放纵一下。类似这样的东西有很多。所以我认为这些东西让（出轨）变得更容易，而人们更容易屈服。我们是人，有时候人的意志力很薄弱，不是吗？所以如果（出轨）变得更容易，也许人们就更可能发生类似的情况。

If you imagine someone in an unhappy marriage 15 years ago for example, suddenly they're sitting at home one night, and they think I wish I could be with someone else.

你可以想象，比如一个人15年前处于一段不愉快的婚姻中，突然某一天晚上他坐在家里，开始想"我希望能和另一个人在一起"。

So there is no way out. The only thing is that people should be more disciplined and more aware. And just work on your marriage and be aware what you're getting yourself into as you get married. Don't go into it hastily.

那时并没有什么解决办法。唯一的方法就是人们更自律更有（防范）意识。努力维护你的婚姻，并且想清楚：当你结婚时，你会让自己面对什么。不要仓促地进入婚姻。

点 评

如果离婚率升高，可能会是什么原因呢？I wish I could be with someone else 我希望我能和另一个人在一起；it's extramarital affair itself that actually causes the rise of divorce rate 是婚外情本身导致了离婚率升高，extramarital affair 婚外情；people are more likely to give in. 人们更容易屈服，give in 屈服、让步，give in to somebody 屈服于某人，对某人让步；If you always give in to others you will end up feeling like a doormat 如果你总是屈服于人，你最终会觉得自己像一个受气包；出轨还可能因为人们是 weak-willed 意志力薄弱的，反义词是 strong-willed 意志力坚强的。而化解这个问题的方法就是人们要 more disciplined and more aware 更自律，更有（防范）意识，disciplined 遵守纪律的，对应名词 discipline 纪律。

词汇小百科

one-night-stand　一夜情

cheat on somebody　对某人不忠，背叛某人

have an affair with somebody　与某人发生婚外情

be unfaithful to somebody　对某人不忠

have a fling with somebody　和某人放纵一下

love-rat　爱情骗子，指那些经常在恋人背后出轨的人

cuckold　被戴绿帽子的人

two-timer　脚踩两只船的人

（王　玮）

剖腹产比割破手痛几倍？

（素材来自《圆桌议事》2015年8月26日节目）

导　语：十月怀胎，一朝分娩。近年来选择剖腹产手术的产妇越来越多。不少人存在认知误区，觉得顺产很痛，而剖腹产不怎么痛。其实不然。我们就一起来了解一下生小孩儿这件事。

Health authorities in Anhui have issued a provincial guideline for cesarean sections, aiming to bring down the excessively high level of such procedures. It is the first regulation of this kind. How should we choose between natural birth and C-section?

近日，安徽省卫计委推出了全国首个有关剖腹产的省级指导方针，旨在降低过高的剖腹产手术率。那顺产和剖腹产，我们该如何选择呢？

I don't understand why this is all necessary. But I think ultimately it comes to the choice of the woman who is giving birth to the kid. I don't understand why this has to have a requirement or a guideline to restrict it.

我不明白这个指导方针的必要性。我觉得归根结底应该由产妇来决定生孩子的方式，我搞不懂为什么需要出台个指导方针来限制剖腹产。

Traditionally, cesarean section was only used in case of some sort of problem with the natural child birth situation. It was done in emergency. Now it seems to be preferred by almost 50% of women in China. In fact, the figure is 46% of women in China have a C-section. It is one of the highest rates in the world according to the World Health Organization, which recommends a rate no higher than 15%.

传统的做法是，只对那些在顺产过程中遇到问题的产妇实行剖腹产，这属于不得已而为之的无奈之举。但是目前，全中国大概有50%的女性都更加倾向于选择剖腹产。数据显示，中国有46%的女性实行剖腹产，是全球比例最高的地区之一。世界卫生组织建议这个比例不要高过15%。

A lot of times the women want to have a C-section for various reasons. Number one, thinking that it's less painful, which is wrong. Number two, thinking that therefore, I can choose to have my baby on a certain day that is auspicious, quite absurd. And there are some other concerns. Sometimes they are afraid of complications during natural child birth, so they think: why not just have it taken out of me?

很多时候，女性会因为各种各样的原因选择剖腹产。首先，她们可能认为剖腹产没有那么痛，这种想法是错的。其次，她们觉得选个好日子生宝宝比较吉利，这种想法是荒谬的。又或者，她们还有其他顾虑。比如担心在顺产的过程中出现一些并发症，于是心想：为什么不剖腹产把宝宝从肚子里取出来呢？

For the women who sometimes experience pain during their monthly period, it can be quite painful for some people, but try to enlarge that by 10 to 100 times. (But I can't relate to that though) For guys, there is nothing that can be compared to, like a cut, or like a physical pain tearing off your flesh or something. It's a completely different feeling, and also of a different level. And because it's like the whole of your stomach is engrossed in this twisted kind of pain that you think would never stop, and that is going to last for at least two hours.

拿女生痛经来做对照，有人痛经很严重，但是生孩子要比这疼上十到一百倍。这种疼痛男人无法想象，可以说任何生理上的疼痛都比不上它，割破后的伤口啦，身上掉块肉啦，完全不是一个层次的疼痛。那就像你的胃疼得扭曲了，你还感觉这种疼痛似乎永远不会停止，一般会持续至少两个小时，或者更久。

And the worst thing out of the whole thing is, ladies tend to think that C-section is the less painful way to go about it, but actually, after the operation, like right after you give birth, that part is not that painful, apparently. But it's when you recover, like the first time you are trying to pee, or even to pass some gas, the pain is like hell.

最糟糕的是，许多女性认为选择剖腹产相对没有那么疼痛，但其实手术做完以后，除了刚刚分娩完的这个阶段没那么疼外，在恢复阶段，可是相当难受的。当你第一次想要尿尿甚至排气的时候，那种疼痛简直像人间地狱。

People think that your body recovers faster after C-section, but it's not.

人们可能还会认为在剖腹产后，体形恢复更快一些，其实不然。

点 评

生孩子选择顺产（natural birth）还是剖腹产（cesarean section）这件事也需要政府出台个指导方针？归根结底，应该由产妇来决定生孩子的方式 Ultimately, it comes down to the choice of the woman who is giving birth.

Cesarean section 剖腹产这个名字的由来与古罗马的皇帝朱利亚·恺撒 Julius Caesar 有关，据说他是剖腹而生的。但关键词是"据说"，恺撒大帝剖腹而生这一点完全是后人的猜测。

许多女性认为选择剖腹产相对没有那么疼痛，这完全是认知上的误区。当你在恢复阶段，那种疼痛简直是闯关。当然，顺产也是非常疼的。总之，生孩子就是一件苦差事，疼痛是怎么样都避免不了的。所以，要对妈妈们好一点，再好一点哦！

◆词汇小百科◆

cesarean section　简称C-section 剖腹产
natural birth　顺产
monthly period　生理期
restrict　限制
World Health Organization　简称WHO，世界卫生组织
auspicious　吉利的

（于　洋）

剖腹产比剖手痛几倍

应该这样给中国宝宝起英文名

(素材来自《圆桌议事》2016年9月22日节目)

导　语：大家的英文名都是怎么来的？英语老师随机分配的，还是充话费送的？起英文名是门学问，对有些人来说竟然成了生意。英国女孩Beau Jessup建立了起名网站，专门为中国宝宝起英文名。首先家长们要选出孩子的五个性格特征，然后Beau根据这些性格特征给中国孩子取英文名。

I think it's ridiculous. You need not be lazy, people. I mean even like parents in the US, we use baby books. So I mean the thing is, picking a name should be your thing that you share with your child, that special connection that you give to them. But at the same time, some parents in China have picked names like Rolex, oh...

我觉得有点荒谬。家长不能犯懒啊，美国的父母给孩子起名的时候还找专门的书呢。起名应该是家长要做的事，名字是你与孩子之间的一个纽带。但话说回来，一些中国父母给孩子起的英文名竟然叫劳力士，真是……

But she wouldn't know that connotation that's attached to that English name if she's from a different culture.

如果人家来自另一种文化背景，可能就不知道某个英文名的内涵和寓意。

Yeah, all of that can be done in a website and connecting people from two completely different continents. And actually it's filling a demand that is very real for today's Chinese people, because for various reasons, people want that English name.

这个起名网站做的事就是将两个大洲的人联系起来，的确也满足很多中国人的需求。出于多种原因，人们需要英文名。

点评

在中国，给孩子取名是很重要的事，有"女诗经、男楚辞"的讲究。但在取英文名这件事上，同胞们曾闹出不少笑话：有人叫"法拉利""丘比特"，还有人叫"灰姑娘"。

取名为何重要？在西方，有一种说法是，名字会影响一切，包括一个孩子的自信、他在学校的成绩和未来的事业成就。There's the belief that names have been proven to affect everything from a child's self-confidence to his grades in school and his future professional success.

同时还有另一种相反的看法认为，名字影响外界对一个人潜在的吸引力或智力的判断。但当这个人真正的特质显示出来的时候，这种判断就销声匿迹了。Names influence perceptions of a person's potential attractiveness or intelligence, but those perceptions fade away once the real person and his or her real qualities appear.

根据美国 www.babynames.com 网站介绍，2017年最受欢迎的女宝宝名字前五位是 Amelia / Emilia, Charlotte, Aria / Arya, Violet, Nora / Norah；最受欢迎的男宝宝名字前五位是 Oliver, Declan, Henry, Theodore, Liam。

词汇小百科

ridiculous 可笑的、荒谬的、荒唐的
connotation 内涵、含义、深意

（陈　沫）

"忽悠"孩子这件事

(素材来自《圆桌议事》2015年7月13日节目)

导　语："不准撒谎"是绝大多数中国父母对于孩子的要求，然而谎言却是他们自己在教育孩子过程中的常用手段之一。有研究显示，相对于中国父母而言，美国父母在对待说谎的态度上显得更加谨慎。

Do you think it is right in saying that Chinese parents seem to employ lying as a strategy more often?

你们认为中国父母更常用谎言作为教育孩子的手段这种说法正确吗？

Well, if we look at lying in a broader sense, then it seems like American parents verses Chinese parents don't seem all that different. Because 84% of the American parents and 98% of the Chinese parents admit to some sort of lie to their kids when they try to make them obey parents' orders. And, when it comes to the more threatening type of lies, maybe Chinese parents tend to use that tactic a little bit more often.

嗯，如果我们从更广泛的意义上看，84%的美国父母和98%的中国父母承认他们对孩子说过某种谎言，目的是想让他们服从自己的命令。也就是说，美国父母和中国父母似乎没有多大的不同。当然，如果涉及更具威胁性的谎言，也许中国父母使用这种策略的频率要高一些。

Yeah, I noticed that. Let's look at the data. 78% of Chinese parents might say "I will leave you alone here if you don't obey me", only 67% of American parents would say that. There's another thing. Chinese parents like to scare their kids by saying they'll be abducted by a stranger. 67% of Chinese parents said they did that. Only 17 % of American parents （admitted to that）.

是的，我也注意到这一点。让我们来看一组数据。78%的中国父母可能会说"你要是不听话，我就不带你走"，相比之下，67%的美国父母会这样做。还有另一个现象是，中国父母比较喜欢用"如果你不听话，就会被坏人带走"这样的话吓唬自己的孩子。事实上，67%的中国父母承认他们这样吓唬过孩子，但只有17%的美国父母会这样做。

I think what we have here is very interesting. We have the difference between the Chinese society and American society in an understanding of psychology. And, it's extremely damaging to tell a child that they'll be "abducted by somebody" or they'll be "abandoned." This can have long-term repercussions on a child's mental state. And, I think psychology is not as popular, it's not as ingrained in the culture here in China as it has been in the West for over a hundred years. And, I think there's less of an understanding here about the damage you can do to a child by making these kinds of threats.

我觉得今天讨论的话题很有趣。中国社会和美国社会对孩子心理的理解存在差异。跟孩子说他们"会被某人绑架"或者"被遗弃"是极其有害的，可能对孩子的精神状态产生长期的影响。而且，我觉得心理学在中国不那么受重视，是因为它在中国文化中没有那么深厚的根基，而它在西方已有一百多年的历史，可谓根深蒂固。我觉得中国家长还不是很清楚这些威胁可能对孩子造成的伤害。

One of the reasons for saying that is, actually, there are reports of children being abducted, and then, it sort of becomes a sad reality that parents would naturally think that "if the kids don't follow my order then they will be abducted". It's not like they're trying to scare their kids. They're just trying to tell them what the worst could be.

有个重要原因是确实有一些关于孩子被绑架的报道,于是父母们很自然地想到,如果孩子不听我的话,就会被坏人绑架。这是很不幸的现实。所以有时候并不是父母故意吓孩子,他们只是试着告诉孩子最坏的情形。

Well, here's another one. 60% of Chinese parents might threaten their children by saying "you will not grow tall if you don't eat" — 60% of Chinese, only 10% of Americans parents would say that.

这里还有个数据。60%的中国父母会对孩子说"如果你不吃饭就长不高",60%喔,不小的数字。只有10%的美国父母会那么说。

Maybe the parents are just not studying their science well enough when they were in school, so they did not realize that it was not true. But I think it's actually an interesting cultural difference, involved in terms of eating and not eating. Because I think American parents or parents in the West (in general), they wouldn't care that much whether their children eat or whether they eat enough. But, Chinese parents, especially grandparents, seem to care so much about how much they eat. Are they eating enough meat? Are they eating enough vegetables? And will they grow up healthy or not? It's a sign of over-doting.

也许父母只是没有在学校掌握好科学知识,所以他们没有意识到这不是真的。但我认为这实际上是一个有趣的文化差异。我们可以说一下吃和不吃的问题,因为我观察到美国的父母或西方的父母,总体来说不太关心他们的孩子吃不吃,或是吃得饱不饱。但是中国的父母,特别是祖父母,极其关心孩子吃多少,是否吃了足够的肉,是否吃了足够的蔬菜,是否能健康成长——种种迹象表明,部分人对孩子过分溺爱了。

点 评

还记得小时候父母是怎样哄你入睡的吗？还记得每当自己不听话、不吃饭或者不写作业的时候，父母是怎么教育你的吗？让我们从更广泛的意义上来看待父母的谎言 Let us look at lying in a broader sense，看看他们为什么会喜欢用这种策略 strategy / tactic。

父母们爱说"你再不听话就会被坏人绑走了" You'll be abducted by somebody if you don't obey my order. 孩子胆小，或许会乖乖听话，但长此以往可能会对孩子心理产生不良的影响 This can have long-term repercussions on a child's mental state. 所以家长还是要三思而后行。

词汇小百科

threatening　威胁的

abduct　绑架

abandon　抛弃

psychology　心理、心理学

over-dote　过度溺爱

（于　洋）

别让孩子成为"屏奴"

（素材来自《圆桌议事》2016年6月11日节目）

导　语：全球儿童安全组织发布《青少年因电子设备在步行时分散注意力》北京专题调研报告，倡导青少年不要在步行时使用电子设备，以减少交通意外的发生。这项调查涵盖北京1000名中学生，他们平日的行为是怎样的呢？

When a conversation gets boring, we pull out our smartphones and start playing with it. This is been called phubbing.

当交谈变得无聊，我们就会玩手机。这叫作phubbing，即"低头症""低头玩手机"。

It's been revealed that 93.1% of students surveyed in a survey possess smartphones. 60.9% of those surveyed said they got distracted by the use of their electronic devices while walking. And nearly half（45%）of the respondents admitted that they themselves or their friends and family have nearly experienced pedestrian clashes while using smartphones, tablets or gaming devices.

93.1%的受访学生拥有手机，60.9%的受访者表示自己曾因电子设备而在步行时分心，45%的受访者承认他们自己或亲友因为手机、平板电脑或者游戏机在步行时差点发生冲撞事故。

So these are kids. And of course they are ridiculous. Kids do ridiculous stuff. I'm saying that you can't hold them to the standard of adults. These kids need guidance and basically tablets are more available now than ever and kids are getting them. So parents need to join the current situation we're living in right now and be able to tell their kids "Hey, while you're walking, put that phone away."

这些是孩子。他们当然不靠谱，孩子们就是会做不靠谱的事。我想说，你不能拿成人的标准要求他们。孩子们需要指导，现在毕竟是一个很容易拥有平板电脑的时代。家长们需要了解我们现在所处的情况，然后告诉孩子"你走路的时候，把手机放在一边"。

I think you really did hit the nail on the head with saying that it's actually the adults that haven't really been setting the best example or being the role model. They don't really realize themselves or they don't have a stance to say that you should get off your digital device when they themselves are probably doing the same thing. So now it's actually a bigger problem. It's not just teenagers being a bit crazy and immature and those things.

你真的说到点子上了——大人们没有做好示范、成为榜样，他们没有意识到这一点，也没有想着告诉孩子们走路时候别玩电子设备，实际上他们走路时候也玩。这就是个大问题了。这不仅仅是年轻人疯狂、不成熟的问题。

点评

Phubbing is the act of snubbing someone in a social setting by looking at your cell phone instead of paying attention. Phubbing是一个在澳大利亚被创造出来的合成词汇，phubbing=phone手机 + snubbing 冷落，意为低头症、由于玩手机而冷落别人的行为。这不仅会影响沟通，还容易让人分心distracting。很多公益活动以Stop Phubbing为主题，呼吁大家与身边人切实沟通。

青少年沉溺于各种大大小小的屏幕带来的乐趣，很大程度上是因为大人们没有及时给予指导或者以身作则。Parents or adults do not set the best examples. They are not acting as the role models.

词汇小百科

smartphones　智能手机

tablets　平板电脑

gaming devices　游戏设备，这些都是电子（数码）设备digital devices

ridiculous　可笑的、荒唐的、愚蠢的、不靠谱的

hit the nail on the head　切中要害、一针见血、说话中肯

（陈　沫）

小朋友爱顶撞

（素材来自《圆桌议事》2016年4月19日节目）

导　语： 辛辛苦苦生个孩子，发现他/她很爱顶撞你，是个不怕争论、敢于向你说"不"的小家伙。这时候，你还能保持镇定吗？在教育孩子这件事上，不妨听听心理学家的意见。

Well, in this case, the expert is a clinical psychologist called Kelly Flanagan and she says that the behavior is actually healthy for kids'development. And she says that the inability to say no is one of the most common causes of human suffering in later life, which sounds rather sinister when it is put like that. But I think she means that, you know, if you learn to say no to your parents about little unimportant things at an early age, then that in creases your ability to say no to, you know, peer pressure kind of things later in life, like being forced to drink Baijiu, for example.

一位名为 Kelly M. Flanagan 的临床心理学家认为这种行为对孩子来说其实是健康的。"不会说不"是成人苦恼的一大根源，这更加危险。我觉得她想表达的意思是，如果你在小时候敢于就一些不太重要的问题向父母说"不"，那么，你长大了之后会有更强的能力去向同龄人给的压力说"不"，比如当小伙伴劝你喝白酒的时候。

And another psychologist called Joseph Allen at University of Virginia said he tells parents to think of arguments with their kids not as a nuisance but as a training ground for the kids' future development. So they are learning all of these skills like negotiation, how to present your own points of view and you know generally how to interact with other people when you disagree with them and not just have a shouting match.

另一位心理学家Joseph P. Allen来自弗吉尼亚大学。他建议家长不要把孩子的争论当成麻烦事,而是要把这当成儿童未来发展的课堂。孩子们在这个过程中可以学会如何谈判、表达自己的观点、在他人与自己意见不一致的时候与他人互动,而不是比谁会大喊大叫。

When the kid says no to the parents or challenges the parents, I mean the parents take it pretty badly, because they think you are either disagreeing with my way of raising you or my beliefs and views in the world or you are just making a fuss when you shouldn't.

当孩子向父母说"不"或者挑战父母的时候,父母肯定感觉糟透了,他们会认为孩子不认同自己教育的方式、理念和观点,觉得孩子不应该制造麻烦但却制造了麻烦。

I think it very much depends on the individual people on the kind of relationship that they have in their family. I think it's changed quite a bit over the last few generations. Maybe it's not as strict as it used to be, the style of parenting, and of course nowadays we have all of these parenting experts with various strategies and all these TV programs about how to raise your kids better. And some people you know agree with this kind of strategy, the kids should be allowed to argue and other people still think I am the parent, I should be in charge.

我觉得这很大程度上与家庭内部关系有关。几代人下来,教育孩子的方式有所变化,或许不是那么严格了。如今我们有很多教育专家,他们很有办法,还有电视节目教你如何把孩子教育得更好。有些人同意专家的做法,认为应该允许孩子的争论或者顶嘴;可有些人依旧那样,认为我是家长,一切由我说了算。

点评

顶嘴可以是 talk back 或者 mouth off，通常指孩子对家长的顶撞行为。根据一些心理学家的研究，这不一定是件坏事，至少孩子们在理论的过程中可以锻炼如何与人沟通、表达自己的观点、尝试说服他人：they learn all of these skills like negotiation, how to present your own points of view and how to interact with other people when you disagree with them。

顶撞的方式包括：say no to your parents 向父母说"不"，challenge the parents 挑战父母，disagree with the parents' way of raising you or beliefs and views 不认同父母养育你的方式、理念和观点，make a fuss 惹麻烦。

说到育儿电视节目，国外有一档叫《超级保姆》（*Super Nanny*），helping a family where the parents are struggling with their child-rearing，child-rearing 是育儿的意思。国内有一档叫《超级育儿师》，也可一看。

词汇小百科

sinister　危险的、险恶的、不吉祥的
peer pressure　同辈压力、同龄人压力
nuisance　麻烦事，让人讨厌的人或者行为

（陈　沫）

都是为你好

（素材来自《圆桌议事》2016年9月17日节目）

> **导语**："我们这都是为你好"可以算是中国很多父母教育孩子的金句。最近有一个针对这个现象的调查，让我们来听听大家的心声。

Most respondents say that they hate it when parents say this. What's more, most respondents say that their parents' approach in educating them at home has actually cast a negative effect on their psychological being.

大部分受访者说他们受不了父母这么说。大家觉得父母用这种方式在家教育子女会对孩子的心理健康产生负面的影响。

This sounds like the kind of parents a hundred years ago in terms of making all the decisions and the kids have to do whatever the parents think is the best, and don't make the decisions by themselves. It sounds like that kind of approach can't be healthy for any kid to grow up under. I think, you know, telling a little child what to do is one thing，but（doing that to）a grown up child is maybe a bit too much.

这有些像旧时代的父母，喜欢决定一切。孩子就要做父母认为最好的事，而不能自己做决定。这种方式听起来对任何儿童的成长都不是有益的。教一个很小的小孩应该做什么是一回事，但当孩子长大之后还这么做就有点过了。

I think tradition sort of runs deep in our culture, and even till today. Some parents still feel that they have um, that's the part I really don't understand, they have ownership to your ideas or your decisions in life in some way.

我觉得我们的传统文化是根深蒂固的，当下也是一样。一些父母认为他们拥有（嗯，我不太理解）对孩子人生的所有权，包括孩子的思想和决定。

But also I have a different way of looking at this line. I think sometimes today's parents are feeling a little bit desperate in trying to get their point across. Because often, the kids or the grown-up kids have a lot to say, and can argue in a very effective way too. And then, the parents feel what is my last line, what is my last resort that I can try to tell my kid that I'm wholeheartedly thinking in your shoes, and trying to get this point across and I want you to understand me. So I think that is a possibility too.

我会从另一个角度来看这个问题。现在的父母有时候与孩子沟通时会感到绝望。孩子长大了，都有自己的主见，也会争论。家长觉得"都是为你好"是万不得已才说的一句话，是能用的最后一招。他们想表达的是"我在竭尽全力告诉你，我是真的全心全意为你着想，希望你能理解我、明白我的心意。"也有这种可能。

This is the thing. Obviously these parents do have their kids' best interests at heart. They are not trying to, you know, upset them and make them angry. They've made these decisions for probably perfectly valid reasons.

正是如此，很明显家长心里还是最为孩子考虑。他们不是要打击孩子或者让他们生气，他们这么做可能事出有因。

点评

Get one's point across 是指"把自己的想法/观点说明白",这在父母与子女之间沟通时却成了难题。家长觉得"这都是为你好" it's for your own good,孩子觉得"我知道你们是为我好,但我想自己做决定"。

心理学家给父母提出的建议包括:利用非正式场合,多来些非正式的对话,孩子更容易敞开心扉 take advantages of informal moments and have casual chats. Teenagers are more apt to open up. 说话的方式简单点 keep it simple;认真倾听 listen carefully;引导,而不是命令 Guide, do not dictate;不要动怒,保持镇定 stay calm。

词汇小百科

negative 负面的
psychological 心理的
approach 方式、方法

(陈 沫)

个人成长
Growth

你的数学

（素材来自《圆桌议事》2016年4月7日节目）

> **导　语：** 21世纪教育研究院基于"为什么要学数学、要学多难的数学"主题调查发布了《公众对于数学学习评价的网络调查报告》。对于中小学阶段的数学学习，超过半数的受访者认为比较难或很难。

The thing is, it's great that we've got a scope to show how many people find the subject of math difficult and how many people like it. I read a fantastic research paper on the BBC. The British government did a great study that showed the correlation between mathematics and income. And they found that on average in the United Kingdom, if you compare people who have a good grade at math at the age of 10 and someone that doesn't have a good math grades at the age of 10, the person that was good at math on average will make 7% more at the age of 30 than the person bad at math, regardless of their being in the same industry（or not）.

这提供了一个视角，让我们知道有多少人觉得数学难、有多少人喜欢数学。我从BBC找到一篇很棒的研究报告。英国政府做了一项研究，分析数学成绩与未来收入之间的相关性。它们发现，平均来讲，一个数学成绩好的10岁孩子会比一个数学不好的10岁孩子在他们30岁的时候收入高出7%，无论他们是否处在同一行业。

It showed why we learn math. It really does benefit you in life. People often think, well if I do great in math, I have to work in finance, or I have to be an accountant, or I have to do a job that is related to numbers. No!

这解释了我们为什么要学数学。它会让你终生受益。但人们经常觉得，如果我数学好，我就得去从事金融业或者成为会计师，总之是要做与数字有关的工作。其实不是这样的！

Definitely! I think math is the quantitative way to measure everything in the universe, both real, like the nature or the abstract things like money. You know it's not only about the calculus, radius or diameters. It's about nurturing your thought and improving your overall thinking.

的确如此！我认为数学是可以衡量宇宙中一切事物的计量方法，具象的包括大自然，抽象的包括金钱。它不仅是关于微积分、半径或者直径这些内容。它可以训练你的思维，提升你思考的能力。

I think certainly studying math, getting all logical and training your mind to think in a logic way, all the things, that's great. But it's not the kind of quality that you can't get by studying some other stuff. Math is not the only road to Rome in that sense.

没错，数学会让人有逻辑性，有很多好处，这很棒。但是学习其他学科也会让人获得这些素质啊，数学并不是唯一的方式。

I actually do agree. I suck at math. I'm terrible. I really am. If you were hoping for me to solve a math problem to save your life, I'd be busy ordering your grave stone. I'm that bad at the subject. But it is a regret of mine. It's not something I say proudly. It's something I wish I was better at. I know these foundation skills are important, but I also realize math for me is not the best medium to learn it. So I'm also around thinking of an alternative I could study as opposed to studying math extensively, because you've got to work towards your strength.

我同意你的说法,我数学就不好,糟糕透了,真的。如果你指望我通过学好数学来拯救你的人生,那我会给你订好墓碑。我在这科目上差极了,这是我的遗憾,不是一件让我骄傲的事。我希望我能学得好点。技能是很重要的,但是对我而言,数学不是提升技能的最好途径。我也想找一门替代的科目,而不是钻研数学,人毕竟要扬长避短。

点 评

爱数学的人认为它可以 nurture your thought, improve your overall thinking, train your mind in a logic way and solve problems, 训练你的思维、提升你的思考、培养你的逻辑和解决问题的能力。

但很多人并不擅长数学。"不擅长"有几种说法:I suck at it. I'm terrible. I'm that bad at it. I'm not good at it. It's not my strength.

无论你是否喜欢数学、擅长数学,至少要尊重这门学科。关于数学或者数学家的经典电影有《美丽心灵》(*A Beautiful Mind*),a biographical drama film based on the life of John Nash, 以数学家、现代博弈论创始人之一约翰·纳什为原型;还有就是《心灵捕手》(*Good Will Hunting*),讲述的是有数学天分的问题少年如何蜕变的故事。

词汇小百科

scope　眼界、见识、范围
fantastic　极好的
calculus　微积分、运算、演算
radius　半径、半径范围
diameter　直径

（陈　沫）

同学们，别叫这些英文名，土爆咯！

（素材来自《圆桌议事》2014年10月24日节目）

导 语：如今很多中国人与西方人打交道的时候，都喜欢用自己的英文名。然而一些不了解英语文化背景的国人，给自己选择的奇葩英文名往往让人啼笑皆非。除了根本不是名字的 Dragon 龙、Fish 鱼、Chlorophyll 叶绿素，还有引人侧目的 Obama 奥巴马、Einstein 爱因斯坦或者 Madonna 麦当娜。快看看你的英文名有没有"触雷"吧。

I've heard my fair share of weird English names picked by Chinese people and I know a whole bunch of Candies, Lollies or Sugars. It just doesn't seem to occur to these girls that actually these are kind of like stripper names that certainly are not associated with ladies. And that hasn't stopped girls to pick these sweet names. But I'd advise you to stay away from them.

我也知道一些中国人给自己取的奇葩英文名，比如我认识不少叫 Candy（糖果）、Lolly（棒棒糖）或者 Sugar（糖）这类名字的女孩。她们好像并不知道这些"甜美"的名字一般都是专属于"脱衣舞女"的，也没有因为这些词完全不"淑女"而放弃用它们作名字。不过我还是建议大家不要取这些名字哦。

These naming conventions are very, very different. In English, most European languages, you find that they are just a set list of names, pretty much. And these names originally did have meaning. They were in fact created because they had certain types of meaning. But those meanings have been lost in history. Certainly you can go online and do some research to get specific meaning your name has or a name has. But culturally speaking, it really doesn't matter what it means, people usually just give the name because they like the sound of it. Whereas in Chinese, when your name is Xiang, there's somehow some kind of logic in having your English name being elephant, but the problem is that elephant is not an English name.

不同文化背景下的命名规则是非常不一样的。比如在英语以及大量的欧洲国家的语言里，存在这样一个名字的列表。这些名字最初是有含义的。事实上，它们也正是因为具有某种意义而被用作名字的。现在，很多名字的意义已经随着时间的消逝而不复存在了。当然，你也可以去网上做一些关于你的名字或某个名字具体含义的研究。但是从文化角度来说，这些其实已经不重要了，人们起名字的时候大多只是单纯喜欢这个名字的发音而已。然而在中文里，如果你的名字是"象"，你就会觉得自己似乎应该叫 Elephant（大象），但问题是 elephant 在英语文化里根本不是一个名字。

Some of the problem I think is the transliteration. Because a lots of people, when they are coming to China, when they're learning Chinese or they have Chinese friends, rather than trying to find a meaningful Chinese name, they'll just transliterate. So my Chinese name is not my transliteration, but you think about my last name in English is Artman, if you transliterate that into Chinese, it's Ao Te Man!

我觉得一部分的问题来自音译。很多外国人，当他们来到中国，或者当他们学汉语、交中国朋友的时候，他们开始给自己起中文名。但他们并没有努力去找一个有意义的中文名，而是简单地把自己的英文名音译出来。比如我，虽然我的中文名字并不是音译，但是你想一想，我的英文姓氏是 Artman，如果直接音译，那可就是奥特曼了！（这在俚语里又有落伍的意思，我可不想要这样奇葩的名字！）

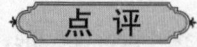

圆桌主持人讨论的奇怪英文名，你有没有遇到过呢？如果遇到过，那

么你就可以说 I've heard my fair share of those names. Fair 是公平的意思，fair share 本身也有公平分配、公平分摊的意思。然而在口语中，使用 fair share 则可以表示得到了应有的、足够的、合理的份额，比如 He has more than his fair share of problems. 他的麻烦已经很多了。

词汇小百科

一些相对安全、常用的英文名及其含义：

Jason　杰森，治愈伤口的人、具备丰富知识的人

Harold　哈罗德，领导者、勇猛的战士

Walter　沃尔特，率领军队的人，或有权势的战士

Dylan　狄伦，海洋、波浪之神

Eli　伊莱，伟大、杰出的人

Felix　菲力克斯，幸福的或幸运的人

Derrick　戴里克，民族的统治者

Ryan　莱安，很有潜力的国王

Maggie　玛姬，珍珠

Charlotte　夏洛特，娇小的，女性化的

Alice　爱丽丝，尊贵的，真诚的（爱做梦的）女孩

Amanda　阿曼达，值得爱的

Bridget　布丽姬特，强壮，力量

Doris　多莉丝，来自大海的海洋女神

Claire　克莱儿，灿烂的、明亮的、聪明的

Vanessa　瓦妮莎，蝴蝶

（牛翃琳）

大学遗憾排行榜

（素材来自《圆桌议事》2015年4月15日节目）

导语：一年又一年的毕业季，回望匆匆而过的四年大学生活，有哪些遗憾事涌上心头？一条关于"大学最遗憾的16件事，你中枪了吗？"的帖子一经发出，迅速得到了众多网友的关注和热议。在本篇中让我们来聊聊怎样用英文表达遗憾。

I think this ranking reflects what the parents and the teachers are really thinking, and has nothing to do with the graduates at all. OK, No.1 on the list: waste time and lost the chance to be a better person. How do you define what's wasting time? I think that is going to be a source of conflicted views between the parents and the students right there already. And it just seems like the whole thing is trying to tell students to focus more on study, having a limited social life, and study is really important.

　　我认为这个排行榜反映了父母和老师的真实想法，和毕业生并没有什么关系。好吧，榜上第一名是"浪费时间并失去让自己变得更好的机会"。你要怎么定义什么是浪费时间呢？我认为父母和学生之间的看法会有冲突。这整个排行榜似乎都在试图告诉学生要多关注学业，社交生活不用太丰富，学业是非常重要的。

What do I gain from regretting? What do I gain by dwelling on the past? Yeah, I played a lot of video games when I was in university. I skipped a lot of classes when I was in university. And maybe that was a mistake. But here I am now, and I get to make the choices, and I can decide now who I want to be.

我能从遗憾中学到什么？总想着过去，我又能得到什么？比如，是的，我在大学时玩了很多电子游戏，逃了很多课。也许那是个错误。但是我现在发展得挺好，我能做选择，我能决定我想成为什么样的人。

But if you enter the workforce, you're allowed fewer mistakes, because your boss may scold you, you may be fired, and you might be poor, and you might end up in the streets, and things like that. But college is the time when you're given the freedom to make mistakes.

但是当你进入职场后，你的犯错空间就小了很多，因为你的老板可能会指责你，你可能被炒鱿鱼，你可能会很穷，可能会流落街头。但是大学是一段你可以自由犯错的时间。

I would still like to sort of give people advice. If you are so lucky so young, and college, I think, really makes that balance, like study is important, but don't forget to go out a little bit as well. Don't just do one thing, because otherwise I'm sure you will regret.

我仍然想给大家意见。如果你还很幸运很年轻，我认为大学可以帮你学着掌握平衡。学习很重要，但是不要忘记也出去玩玩。不要只做一件事，不然的话我肯定你会感到遗憾的。

点 评

这个遗憾排行榜真的准确吗？也不一定呢，因为它可能只是 reflect what the parents and the teachers are really thinking 反映了父母和老师的真实想法，reflect 反映，但是 have nothing to do with the graduates at all 和毕业生并没有关系，have nothing to do with somebody 和某人没有关系，have something to do with somebody 和某人有关系。遗憾并没有用，因为 dwell on the past 总想着过去，dwell on something 总在想着某事，并不能给你带来任何好处。也许你在大学时 play video games 玩电子游戏，skip classes 逃课，但是你有犯错的自由，成本不会太高，不会像等你进入职场后，犯错会让你 be fired 被解雇，甚至 end up in the streets 流落街头。最后，记住 don't just do one thing 不要只做一件事，不然 otherwise 你肯定会后悔的。

词汇小百科

regret　后悔

remorse　悔恨、自责

compunction　内疚

repent　感到懊悔或忏悔

make up for something　弥补某事

remedy　补救、改正

（王　玮）

论文写得怎么样了？

（素材来自《圆桌议事》2014年5月10日节目）

导　语：喜不喜欢都好，我们每个人总有要写论文的时候。论文的英语表达有讲究吗？Thesis 和 dissertation 是一回事吗？

I was under the impression that thesis could apply to high school or undergraduate, but as it turns out, thesis and dissertation are in fact in many cases interchangeable.

有一个比较普遍的误区：thesis 指本科的毕业论文，而 dissertation 是指那种更长的，比如博士生的毕业论文。事实上，这两个词在很多时候是完全可以互换的。

Yeah, So the thing is usually the word thesis is going to be used for part of getting a bachelor's degree or a master's degree, and dissertation is usually applied when you get a doctor's or a PHD, but really, the only difference between the two is going to be length. Thesis is going to be shorter and dissertation is going to be longer.

Thesis 和 dissertation 的区别只有长度，thesis 相对较短、dissertation 较长，仅此而已。只不过本科或硕士的毕业论文确实较短，而博士的毕业论文较长，才有了按学历来区分 thesis 和 dissertation 的常见错误。

Also, let's talk a little bit about quotes. Exactly how much quoting is allowed or accepted when you're writing a thesis or a dissertation? So the most important thing is actually going to be citations. Usually, you want to have as few direct quotes as possible. You're going to use quotes in certain block formations perhaps or fairly small quotes. But in general, for research paper which is a thesis or a dissertation, you want it to be your own actual ideas.

说到论文，当然要说说引用的问题。论文里面虽然可以出现引用，也就是 quotation，但是直接引用最好还是比较少出现为妙。无论是 thesis 还是 dissertation，最重要的还是呈现你自己的想法。

It also depends on what exactly we're talking about. On a technical research paper, like for chemistry, or physics, mathematics, you want no quotes whatsoever. Whereas papers on philosophy, psychology and things like that, a lot of the actual paper and research is going to be based on what other people have done.

引用的多少跟论文的具体内容也有关。如果是比较技术类的话题，比如数理化之类的，最好多用自己能展示的实例，少用别人的原话。但如果是哲学、心理学之类的话题，肯定就需要大量引用别人的观点或发现了。

But usually thesis and dissertations include some form of actual research, whether they're secondary or original research, whereas essays are going to be much shorter, so a thesis may be ten pages whereas an essay is going to be two pages. Also, it usually comes from an author's personal point of view, so really no research involved whatsoever.

无论是 thesis 还是 dissertation，或多或少都包含一些原创的调研。这跟另外一个常见概念 essay 有明显区别。Essay 就是阐述作者自己的观点而已，并不包含调研。而且 essay 一般比较短，可能也就两页而已。

点评

说到论文，我们首先要改变常见的错误，即以学历来区分 thesis 和 dissertation。两者的区别仅仅在于长度（length）而已，前者短，后者长，在大多场合是完全可以互换的。此外，写论文离不开引用，如何引用、引用多少适宜，取决于论文的内容和专业领域。只要引用，就一定要标明出处（citation），这是对他人劳动成果起码的尊重（respect），同时也可以避免抄袭（plagiarism）的争议（controversy）。

词汇小百科

thesis　（较短的）论文

dissertation　（较长的）论文

interchangeable　可以互换的，没有明显区别的

quote / quotation　引用

citation　引用注明出处的做法

block formation　大段文字的架构

essay　随笔，杂文

（刘　彦）

有调性的英文简历这样写！

（素材源自于《圆桌议事》2015年7月11日节目）

导　语：本期节目介绍了写好英文简历的几点建议，比如简历内容中词语的选用，帮助求职者更好地展现自己的优点，赢得面试官的青睐。

So, when you are talking about yourself in your résumé, you might want to talk about your personality, and some good things to put would be, for example, that you have a stable personality, and a high sense of responsibility.

　　所以当你在简历中介绍自己的时候，最好谈谈你的性格，而这时候你可以用以下短语，如性格稳重，富有责任感。

The other thing you should do is to try to use lots of positive words, and avoid words with negative connotations. For example, you use words like bright, ambitious, self-motivated, and the word positive itself is always good on your résumé.

　　另外你应该尽量多用一些积极词汇，避免使用有消极含义的词汇。比如，可以在简历上使用聪明、有进取心、能够自我激励等的描述，或者直接用"积极"这个词也不错。

When it comes to working in a team, which is again, something that employers like to read（is）that you are a team player. That has become a bit of a cliché actually in western résumés and CVs in recent years, but it is very important in an increasingly diverse and multicultural workforce in some countries, too. That's very important to say you can work with just about anybody.

说到团队协作这方面，重申一下，招聘者肯定希望在简历上看到你说自己善于团队合作。这样的用词在近几年西方的简历中已经落入俗套，但是一些国家的多种族、跨文化企业对此却很看重。表明自己能和任何人共事，这非常重要。

But it is not all about team work. You should also emphasize the fact that you can work well independently unsupervised. Putting words like resourceful, self-motivated, you use your initiative and so forth. Again, these are words with very positive connotations.

除了团队合作以外，你也应该强调你能在无人监督的情况下独立完成工作。你可以用上"聪明机智""能够自我激励""做事主动"这一类有着积极含义的词语。

There are some other characteristics which go down well on your résumé: the fact that you are highly organized and efficient, and that you have good presentation skills. Because, remember your employer might be thinking that they want someone that would stay with the company for quite a long time.

简历内容中提及的这些特征也能够成为你的闪光点：比如你做事有条理有效率，你有很强的展示能力等。为什么这招有用呢？你要谨记，招聘者可能想找一个会为公司长期服务的人。

But make it clear that you do have potential to be more than the requirements of the jobs you are applying for. So you could say you have good presentation skills. You have good managerial skills and organizational capability.

但是，你要表明在所申请职位的应聘要求之外，你还有更大的进步空间。你可以说你善于作展示，你具备出众的管理技能和组织能力等。

点评

"性格稳重"可以表达为 have a stable personality,"积极主动地做某事"可以表达为 use someone's initiative to do something,"善于团队合作"可以表达为 someone is a (good) team player,"包含多元文化的公司"英文表达为 multicultural workforce,"做事有条理"英文表达为 someone is highly organized。

词汇小百科

résumé　简历
stable　稳重的
organized　井井有条的
self-motivated　自我激励的
cliché　陈词滥调（来源于法语）
resourceful　机智的、资源丰富的
managerial　管理的

（于　洋）

拒信来了

（素材来自《圆桌议事》2016年9月3日节目）

> **导　语**：港中大（深圳）向未被录取的学生发出拒信，以诚挚、温馨、感人的遣词造句鼓励学生们继续努力，并期待有缘再聚。在中国，发拒信这样的做法还不是很普遍，或许逐渐会被认同。无论如何，希望大家以后收到的都是录取信。

So basically a denial letter is letting you know as soon as it's been decided that "Hey, you don't have to wait any longer for our words. You didn't get in and I'm sorry". And this is very common in the US.

　　基本上，拒信的意思就是告诉你"别再等消息了。你没有被录取，很遗憾"。这在美国很常见。

I think all universities in the US would do this and say "We regret to inform you", so when you see those first words, you know how the rest of the letter's gonna go. But as I understand it, people really appreciated this, because they took the time to apply and this guy took the time to send them a message back, saying some really poetic words like "there are neither hard nor easy paths. Life comes with happiness and sorrows".

　　美国大学的拒信通常会以"我们遗憾地通知你"作为开头，当你看到这几个词的时候，就知道信里接下来会说什么了。但是大家还挺欣赏这种做法的，因为你之前投入了时间去申请学校，现在学校也花时间给你回了消息，还说了些很诗意的话，比如"世事没有难易之分，生活总是伴随快乐和忧伤"。

I think for Chinese students, it's kind of important, cause in the old days when you get rejected from your dream school, what do you get? Nothing. So you, the young person who's waiting to get the acceptance letter, would be waiting at your door for months and you've been waiting for so long. That is…yeah, that's not very humane I think. So now maybe there's a change in things slightly.

我觉得对中国学生来说，这还是很重要的。以前被心仪的学校拒绝时，能得到什么吗？什么都没有。想象一下，等了几个月消息，石沉大海，杳无音信，这实在不太人性化。现在这种情况可能会有所改观。

Right and I think I can't speak for China, but being from the US, this is as I said a common practice. And I think that's something to do with encouragement. In our culture, if you fail, people don't put you down. They try to help you and say "Hey, you can do better next time and this failure was just a small bump on the path of your successful life story".

我不能代表中国的立场，但在美国，拒信很平常，这也算是种鼓励吧。在我们的文化里，如果你失败了，人们不会贬低你。大家会试图帮助你，说："嘿，你下次会做得更好，这次失败只是成功人生路上的一次小小的颠簸。"

◆ 点 评

在很多西方国家，拒信 rejection / refusal / denial letter 非常普遍，大学通常都会给没有被录取的学生发这样的信，公司也会给未被录用的面试者发这样的信，明确地表示拒绝。有时候让人抱有幻想空等是不礼貌的 sometimes it's rude to give false hopes to applicants，另外对那些一直没有申请其他学校或公司的人来说，没有反馈也不公平 it is quite unfair for the applicants who must be waiting to know the result, especially those who have not applied for other universities or companies.

通常拒信的结构是：首先感谢你申请 thank you for applying for a position / sending us your application and we appreciate your time，其次说明学校或公司经过慎重考虑和仔细筛选，你不合适 after careful review and selection, we regret to inform you that you have not been qualified for the position，最后祝你成功 we wish you success in the future，期待"万里江河，有缘再聚"there's a long road ahead of you, and if we were meant to cross paths one day, we will.

但在中国，拒信还是很少出现，可能在我们的文化里，没有消息就是拒绝的意思；用在人际关系里，就是分手的意思。Sometimes in the Chinese culture, silence is rejection.

词汇小百科

sorrow　　悲痛、悔恨、惋惜
humane　　人性化的、慈善的、高尚的
slightly　　轻微地、略为
bump　　颠簸、冲撞、碰撞、撞击

（陈　沫）

第一份工作的收入，决定了今后的收入？

（素材来自《圆桌议事》2016年8月23日节目）

> **导　语**：美国麻省（没有理工）大学一项研究认为，提升收入可能比你想象得要难。你的第一份工作带来的收入将决定未来的收入层级。一开始挣得就少，以后也很难翻身了。呃，不会吧。

I disagree wholeheartedly with this actually, upon really looking and getting into this research. At least from my point of view, this doesn't even apply to me, because into my twenties, into my mid-twenties, I was pursuing higher education. So I wasn't really thinking about a job.

我完全不同意这个研究结果。至少从我的角度看，这就不适用于我。二十多岁的时候，我还接受高等教育呢，根本没想过工作的事。

At the same time, the reason why I think this is happening is because higher education is becoming more and more common. So you need something else to make you stand out. Those middle-class jobs now are harder to get, so if you just had your first job with working at a grocery store, that's not experience, I'm sorry. If you want that, what we call in the US, a big kid job, then you need to have experience relevant to that field as well as the higher education.

高等教育越来越普遍，你需要有过人之处。那些中产的工作越来越难找，如果你的第一份工作是在杂货店，不好意思，那不叫工作经验。如果你想要一份我们在美国所说的"正式工作"，你必须有教育背景和相关领域的经验。

I don't really get that this can determine the end, because we don't see the end yet.

我不明白，难道这就决定了结局？我们还没有看到结局呢。

Twenty to thirty is about establishing yourself. Don't stress it, enjoy your life, try to establish yourself, get those skills, get that experience.

二十几岁是塑造自身的时期。不要有压力，要享受人生，尝试打造自己。去学习技能、获得经验。

点评

提升收入可以说 climb up the earnings ladder 或者 increase / improve your income。

开始第一份正式工作 start your first big kid job，感到既兴奋又紧张 you may feel excited and nervous。

做好第一份工作的建议是：不断学习 keep learning，努力工作 work hard，不要炫耀 don't show off，自己把握成长路径 create your own growth plan，交好朋友 make good friends。

记住：在第一份工作中，你学到的比你赚到的重要得多。In your first job, what you learned is more important than what you earned.

词汇小百科

wholeheartedly 全心全意地、全身心地、完全地

pursue 继续、追求

establish 建立、树立、打造

（陈 沫）

自由职业者，想当就能当？

（素材来自《圆桌议事》2015年1月15日节目）

导　语：不用朝九晚五打卡上班，不用看老板脸色，穿着睡衣拖鞋就能赚钱。在互联网高度发达的今天，自由职业者的收入甚至可能高于白领族。但是自由职业者的工作方式真的如同看上去那般美好吗？他们是否也有自己需要解决的各种困难和问题呢？

I think it's certainly for some people, with the right skills and right way to market and promote themselves, and actually earning quite a lot of money, yeah it's a great idea! But it's not for everyone, I mean, a freelancer by definition is a person who is self-employed and is not necessarily committed to a particular employer long-term. The key here is being self-employed, meaning you are your own boss, you'll have to shoulder all the costs that the job entails. Sometimes, people are not able to bear that. So, not for everyone!

我觉得有一些人是适合自由职业的，他们身怀技能又熟知如何在市场中推销自己，并且的确有能力通过自由职业赚到钱，这样当然很好。但这并不意味着自由职业适合所有人。我们来看看自由职业者的定义：一个自我经营，不长期为某个特定雇主服务的人。这里的关键其实是自我经营，也就是说你是自己的老板，你必须承担所有的工作成本和风险。有的人其实没有这种能力，所以自由职业这条路并不适合所有人。

Yes, as a freelancer, you get to choose your own hours, but you don't always get to choose your own jobs, you'll have to take a job you don't like because it's the only contract available at the moment. So being a freelancer seems very attractive because you can hang out in the coffee shop all day pretty much, and just kind of work from home or whatever. But there's no guarantee that you are gonna be making enough money every month to actually cover your living expenses, your business expenses and things like that.

对，作为一个自由职业者，你可以自由选择工作时间，但并不总能自由选择工作内容。有时候你得做一些自己不喜欢的工作，因为它可能是这段时间里你唯一能接到的活儿。所以归根结底，大部分自由职业者都是"看起来很美"。似乎可以天天泡咖啡馆，或者一直在家办公，但其实自由职业不一定能保证你每个月赚到足够的钱来支撑生活中的所有开销。

So actually what I've seen is that, some of these top employees for some of these major institutions who are well known in the field... when they leave that institution that they used to work for and then become a freelancer, already got the contacts, that makes sense. Because, for someone who's sort of a nobody just starting to get into the field and you are a freelancer? Who knows you? Who wants to employ you?

实际上，就我见到的情况而言，一些大公司的顶级员工辞职转做自由职业者时，因为在业内享有盛誉、有足够优质的人脉，他们自然会做得很好。但是对于初入行的菜鸟而言，你还默默无闻，刚进入这个新领域就要从自由职业者做起吗？谁了解你？谁又想雇用你呢？

点 评

在表达"供职于某大公司"时，主持人没有说 work for a big company 或者 employed in a big company，而是使用了 committed to a big company。Committed to 直译过来就是忠诚于某人、决心做某事的意思。在这个语境下用这种方式表达，显得更生动活泼。commit 原本有承诺、委托的意思，因此许下承诺也就是 make a commitment。而犯下某种罪行可以表达为 commit a certain crime。

讨论自由职业者所面临的挑战与困难时，主持人表示，最基本的一条就是他们并没有公司的经济支持，而需要自己承担一切相应成本，也就是 shoulder the cost themselves. Shoulder 本来是肩膀的意思，作动词就引申出了扛起、承受的意思。除了 shoulder，承担、负担也可以使用 bear，比如 bear the burden，bear the expenses；当然也可以使用 take on / upon，例如 take on / upon the responsibility。

词汇小百科

journalism　新闻业
publishing　出版业
screenwriting　剧本创作
editing　编辑
photography　摄影
copy editing　文案编辑
proofreading　审稿
computer programming　编程
web design　网页设计
graphic design　平面设计
tour guiding　导游业

（牛翃琳）

女生为什么爱组团刷催泪片?

(素材来自《圆桌议事》2015年4月1日节目)

> **导　语**：女生似乎天生喜欢看催泪电影，尤其是和闺密一起边看边哭成一团。而最新研究显示，和朋友分享这些悲情片，有助于减少这些影片对她们情绪上的负面影响。

It seems like when you're with someone, the happy images seem happier to you and then the negative ones don't seem so sad either, so it's good experience overall. So it's about sharing and bonding.

似乎当你和其他人在一起的时候，快乐的画面会看起来让你更快乐，而消极的画面则看起来不那么糟了，所以总体来说是好的体验。核心是分享和联系。

So this idea that being with someone makes the happier moments happier and the bad moments not as bad just makes complete sense. But I think that in general when we look at gender or sex differences between men and women and how they bond, men usually bond over activity and women usually bond over emotion or communication.

所以和别人在一起会让快乐的时光更快乐，悲伤的时光不那么悲伤，这个理论非常说得通。但是我认为通常我们看到男女性别不同，他们之间的联系方式也不同。男人经常通过活动联系在一起，而女人则通常通过情绪和沟通联系在一起。

And I think with ladies, it's not just watching a weepy movie, also like shopping and talking about girls' stuff. I think men and women have different ways to relax.

我觉得对于女性来说，这不只是看一个催泪片，这很像一起购物或谈论一些女孩子的事。我认为男人和女人有不同的放松和沟通的方式。

This is why I see some of the advertisements targeting women, oh, this is why I see so many restaurants and coupon things targeting women because this is how women bond. They go out together, they walk around in a mall together, they window shop together, they have lunch together, and they're just talking and sharing the entire time.

这就是为什么我看到一些广告会针对女性，这就是为什么很多餐厅和打折券针对女性，因为女性就是这样联系在一起的。她们一起出去，一起逛购物中心，一起浏览商店的橱窗，一起吃午饭，全程都一起聊天和分享。

And Draco says maybe that explains why the situation comedies insert the canned laughter background because they let you feel you're laughing with someone.

听友Draco说也许这解释了为什么情景喜剧中要插入笑声的背景音，因为那让你感觉你是在和别人一起笑。

点评

为什么女生总喜欢组团一起看催泪电影？在这个问题上，男女大不同。Men usually bond over activity and women usually bond over emotion or communication，男人经常通过活动联系在一起，而女人则通常通过情绪和沟通联系在一起。

Bond over something 通过什么事情联系在一起，I love and appreciate every single one of my friends, sometimes I wish they share some of my passions, so we could bond over them 我喜欢或欣赏我的每一个朋友，有时我希望他们也喜欢

我热衷的东西，这样我们可以紧密联系在一起。

Watching a weepy movie is also like shopping and talking about girls' stuff，看一个催泪片很像一起购物或谈论一些女孩子的事，girls' stuff 女生的那些事、女生的小秘密，a weepy movie 催泪片，weepy 让人哭的。

词汇小百科

situation comedy　情景喜剧

tear jerker movie　催泪电影

newsreel　新闻短片

documentary　纪录片

commercial film　商业片

musical　音乐片

thriller　惊悚片

romance film　爱情片

war film　战争片

disaster film　灾难片

action film　动作片

science fiction film　科幻片

feature film　剧情片

detective film　侦探片

ethical film　伦理片

epic　史诗片

dubbed film　译制（配音）片

（王　玮）

一起去厕所是妹子的专利哦!

（素材来自《圆桌议事》2015年9月25日节目）

> **导　语**：男生心中是不是常有一个疑问——女生为什么要成群结队、呼朋引伴、手牵手地上厕所呢？

I think it's not just a Chinese phenomenon that girls tend to go to the bathroom in groups.

我觉得女生喜欢一起去厕所的这种现象不是中国特有的。

Right. I think it's basically a practice everywhere in the world. You can see those kind of groups in western movies too. I think it's a chance for girls to socialize and gossip about all the things. Like if you don't want to discuss something in public, then you will invite a friend, say "Hey, do you need to go to the restroom? Let's go to the restroom together." And then it's not the restroom that you really want to go. It's somewhere outside the restroom where you will have your talk.

是的，这种行为很普遍，哪里都有。在西方的电影里我们也常看到女生一起去厕所。我觉得这是女生们交际和八卦的好机会。你如果不想在公众场合讨论什么东西的话，你可以喊一个小伙伴，说"你要去厕所吗？我们一起去厕所吧"。其实你想去的地方并不是厕所，而是厕所外的某个可以聊天八卦的地方。

I think for ladies certainly, the bathroom is a place to bond. When you grab a girlfriend with you and it's sort of the ultimate signal saying we are besties. And you share that waiting time together. And also after the bathroom experience, you talk about things. I think it's quite a happy time for ladies.

我觉得对女生来说一起去厕所是增进感情的方式。你呼喊女性朋友和你一起去厕所是一种信号,表明你们是好朋友。你们分享共同等待的时间。在一起去厕所之后,你们会讨论一些事。我觉得这对女生来说是很开心的时光。

It's really this kind of mystery. Men are from Mars, and women are from Venus. Is that right? Something like that. But it's this sort of behavior that you don't see in males. It's very weird. For the most part, men and women are roughly the same. This is just exceptional stuff. I remember as a kid, you make jokes about you have never been to the girls' bathroom and it must be this mysterious place. Who knows what sort of stuff is going on there because girls just disappear in packs, in groups.

我们男生一直觉得这事很神秘,女生真是奇怪的物种。人们不是这样说嘛,男人来自火星,女人来自金星。对吧?你是不会看到男生一起去厕所的,那太怪异了。其实男人和女人大部分情况下是差不多的,但上厕所绝对是例外。我还记得小时候开玩笑说,从来没去过女厕所,女厕所一定是最神秘的地方。谁知道那里发生了什么。女生总是成群结队地在那儿消失。她们真的是在上厕所吗?

I think it has to be reciprocal. Because as a woman, I always wonder what the boy's bathroom looks like.

我觉得这是相互的。作为一个女生,我也总是好奇男厕所是什么样子。

点评

妹子们喜欢成群结队地上厕所 Girls tend to go to the bathroom in groups，这种现象不是中国独有 It's not just a Chinese phenomenon。其实一起上厕所是女生亲密无间的表现，她们也许只是想在一起去厕所的路上 gossip 八卦八卦、讲一些小秘密。

当然，男生也喜欢聚在一起八卦，只不过不会选择一起上厕所这种方式而已。他们一起喝啤酒，借着酒兴多说几句倒是司空见惯的，这就是两性的差异吧。毕竟 men are from Mars, women are from Venus，男人来自火星，女人来自金星。

词汇小百科

baffle　困惑、难倒
bond　纽带、联系
socialize　社交、交往
mystery　秘密、迷
reciprocal　相互的

（于　洋）

友情是如何变淡的

（素材来自《圆桌议事》2015年2月11日节目）

导　语：每个人都会有这样的时候，翻开通讯录或者登录很久没上的QQ，看到好多曾经的至交好友，已经很久都没有联系了。回忆起一起玩闹的岁月，似乎觉得那份亲密感仍然触手可及，但想点开那个头像打个招呼，又好像比什么都困难……少年时的友谊真的只能被拿来缅怀吗？友情真的都有保质期吗？又是什么让曾经亲密的朋友渐行渐远呢？

I think it's very natural. It's a natural process for a lot of people, a lot of friends to drift apart. I think one major reason is that we have different growth patterns, right? We tend to have different social status, we have different jobs. It's very easy for friends, even very close and good friends to drift apart. The second reason I think is because of the distances.

我觉得友谊逐渐变淡甚至消逝是很正常的事情。对许多人来说，和曾经的朋友渐行渐远其实是个自然的过程。其中一个主要原因是我们的成长模式不尽相同。我们开始有了不同的社会地位，从事不同的工作，对生活有了不同的渴望。这些因素都有可能让朋友，甚至是非常要好的密友逐渐远离对方。当然还有一个原因，就是空间上的距离，这也会让友谊变淡。

I think of course, what goes on with your life, whether you're married or not, changed your job or lived in a different friend circle or not, has an impact and possibility on the friendship, but I still believe in BFFs, best friends forever. I think they do exist, just very rarely.

当然，你的生活状态——结婚与否、是不是换了新工作或者开始拥有了新的朋友圈……这些都会对你的友情产生影响，带来各种可能。但是我仍然相信BFF，就是"永远的最好的朋友"的英文缩写。我相信这种朋友是存在的，只不过数量非常稀少。

But for me, at least, a lot of it has to do with context. My best friends were friends that I made in university. And I've been not in university for 8 years now, soon to be longer than 8 years. And so, without that context, without that shared experience when we lived together, we went to class together, we ate together, we partied together... Also we shared so many experiences because of that context. And after that context is over, we graduate, we move on, we find jobs, we get married, we have kids and so on and so on, now we live in totally different parts of the world where it's difficult to maintain communication.

对于我来说，友谊很多时候要有一个适用的情境。我最好的朋友是大学时代认识的。现在，我已经毕业8年了，而离开大学的时间很快就会超过8年。离开了那个环境，我们就没有了之前那些共同的经历，就不再一起生活、一起上课、一起吃饭、一起聚会……而我们之所以能有这么多共同的经历，也正是因为一起上大学那个背景。随着那个情境的结束，随着我们一起从大学里毕业，我们的生活就各自继续了。我们找工作、结婚、有自己的孩子……现在，我们生活在世界上的各个角落，要继续保持联系就很困难了。

I think we've seen each other in the most pathetic, ugly state and also the most beautiful ones. I think it's the ups and downs, thin and thick you've gone through in life together. That doesn't mean that you have to speak every day or even all that often. But you are just like a packaged deal and you understand each other. And I think just as you grow older and you realize how precious that is, you want to stick with it a bit longer.

我想，这么多年过去了，我们看过彼此最可悲、最糟糕的状态，也见证过彼此最美丽的时刻。我觉得友谊的真谛是彼此共同经历过的起起落落。这并不意味着你们必须每天都聊天，甚至不意味着你们要经常通电话。但你们就像是成套出售的产品，缺一不可，而且彼此理解对方。我想，随着你慢慢长大，你会越来越意识到这种友谊的珍贵，也就会努力让它久一点、再久一点。

点评

好朋友之间的友情慢慢变淡是很伤感的事，英文中形容这样的感情疏远主要使用 grow apart 和 drift apart 两个说法，grow，成长、长大，grow apart 就像是说共同成长，但渐渐长成了不同的样子，于是慢慢疏离；drift，漂流、漂泊，而 drift apart 则更像曾经并行的两条小船因为选择了不同的方向而渐行渐远。

曾经共同拥有的经历—— shared experience、和那些经历发生的情景——context，才是友谊的本质和核心。就像有一种说法：我们与朋友其实并不一定是一类人，只是缘之所至，在某个时间，我们恰巧共同出现在了某个地点，然后怀着相同的需求彼此陪伴。

这种因为 right place，right time 而形成的连接关系，自然也会随着时间、空间的改变而改变。因此，与其硬拽着朋友走自己的路，倒不如在分岔口温柔道别，再从同路者中寻找新的朋友。

词汇小百科

ASAP，as soon as possible　越早越好

B2W，back to work　回去上班

BBQ，barbeque　烧烤

BM，bite me　去死，不服咬我啊

BTW，by the way　顺便说一句

FYI，for your information　仅供参考

F2F，face to face　面对面

FBFR，Facebook friend　脸书上的朋友

TGIF，thank God it's Friday　感谢上帝，终于星期五了！

（牛翎琳）

生活方式
Lifestyle

无Wi-Fi，不生活

（素材来自《圆桌议事》2014年4月19日节目）

导　语： 随着移动端上网越来越普及，Wi-Fi已经成了我们日常生活中不可或缺的东西。在本篇中，我们就来看看Wi-Fi到底是什么意思，以及相关的英语表达。

The term "Wi-Fi" was commercially used at least as early as August, 2000 and was actually coined by brand consulting firm called Interbrand Corporation. Interbrand Corporation was hired by the Wi-Fi Alliance because they needed a name that sounded better than the "IEEE 802.11b direct sequence." And so what they did was they made a play on words. They said that "Wi-Fi" is the standard for wireless fidelity. The term right now, Wi-Fi, has nothing whatsoever to do with fidelity.

Wi-Fi最早在2000年8月就已经进入商业市场，是一家叫Interbrand Corporation的品牌顾问公司取的名。它们需要取一个比较吸引眼球、能让人立刻记住的名字，于是就玩了一把文字游戏，说Wi-Fi代表了Wireless Fidelity（fidelity有"精准度、确切度"的意思）。时至今日，Wi-Fi和fidelity已经没有任何关系了。

But why is it called "Wi-Fi" and not "weefee？" Again, it's a play on the word "Hi-Fi" and then you have "Wi-Fi."

为什么Wi-Fi的发音是why-fi（ght）而不是wee-fee呢？因为Wi-Fi也可以看成是基于Hi-Fi的基础上产生的新词。Hi-Fi的发音是high-fi（ght），所以Wi-Fi也就依样画葫芦了。

Hotspot is just a wireless access point that usually you use a router to connect to. And a router is just a piece of equipment where you plug it in to the Internet and a wireless router will broadcast a Wi-Fi signal that you can use to connect to your other devices, too.

在使用Wi-Fi的时候，我们经常会提到"热点"这个词，也就是所谓的hotspot。它是指在公共场所提供无线局域网（Wi-Fi）接入Internet服务的地点。这类地点多数是咖啡馆、机场、商务酒店、高等院校、大型展览会馆等。此外，"路由器"的英文名称是router。它是连接互联网中各局域网、广域网的设备，它会根据信道的情况自动选择和设定路由，以最佳路径，按前后顺序发送信号。

The idea is that you have a 3G or 4G-enabled device (that can be a smart phone or a tablet with a 3G connection), and you can turn on something called "tethering". That basically just turns your mobile device into a wireless hotspot.

如果你有3G或4G功能的移动设备，你可以通过该设备来共享互联网连接，这种行为叫tethering。它实际上就是把你的移动设备变成了无线热点。

点 评

虽然Wi-Fi跟我们的日常生活密切相关，但太过技术性的内容我们没有必要深究。只需要记住Wi-Fi是读why-fi（ght）就成。它的读音也充分说明，Wi-Fi的真实意思不是wireless fidelity，不然就该读why-fi（t）了。此外，美剧《生活大爆炸》里曾经开过玩笑，说Wi-Fi应该读成wee-fee。那纯属娱乐，请千万不要当真。

词汇小百科

Wi-Fi　无线局域网
hotspot　无线热点
router　路由器
tethering　使用移动设备共享互联网连接的行为

（刘　彦）

廉价航空也不错

（素材来自《圆桌议事》2014年7月5日节目）

导　语：人人都要坐飞机，但不是人人都能有钱任性，动不动就买头等舱的票。对大多数老百姓来说，廉价航空依然是首选。

Usually it's (a budget airline) is more formally known as a low cost carrier or a low cost airline. It can also be called a no-frills, discount or budget airline.

Low cost carrier（缩写为LCC），是廉价航空正式的称呼。此外，也可以用 no-frills、discount 或 budget airline 等叫法。No-frills 这个词可能需要解释一下。Frill 原本指的是衣服上的褶边，多跟女性服饰挂钩。

Yeah, it's a little frilly, right? It's got lots of extra stuff on the edges. And so if you think about that, something that is frilly has got lots of extra stuff. (The meaning of) No-frills should be quite obvious then. Basically it's just a service or product in which the nonessential features have been removed to keep the price low.

因为frill原来指的是女士衣服上的褶边儿或者装饰，所以 no frills 自然就是指没有装饰。在这个基础上，它引申出卖方不提供那些花里胡哨的、不必要的服务或商品的意思。这样做的目的是保持廉价。

So these days when we are talking about these no-frills or cheaper airlines, a lot of times we call them budget airlines. And so budget basically just means cheap.

Because the word budget itself usually refers to when a person, a company, or a family is coming up with a list of incomes and expenses, and if something is budget, it means it won't affect your budget.

时至今日，当我们说 no-frills 的时候，其实指的也就是 budget airlines。budget 作名词一般是预算的意思，但是它当作形容词的时候也可以表示 cheap，价格低廉的意思。所以 budget airlines 也就是 cheap airlines，即使你不是土豪，乘坐这样的航班一般也不会影响预算。

And interestingly enough, the English word budget is actually derived from the French word bougette which means purse. That's a weird way of putting it, but you know, English is a very weird language.

有趣的是，budget 这个词是从法语单词 bougette 演变过来的，而 bougette 的本义是"钱包"，所以 budget airlines（廉价航空）似乎应该理解成"钱包航空"。这样说似乎有点奇怪，但英语原本就是一门很怪的语言。

What else can you use with budget that means cheap? Really, it's just about whether the industry has a segment identifying themselves as cheaper. A budget TV, I mean pretty much anything, just when you're calling it cheap, when someone's trying to sell it to you, maybe you don't have very much money to spend, they'll call it a budget something or other.

除了航空，还有什么是可以用 budget 来形容的呢？其实，似乎什么都可以，比如 budget TV。只要你觉得可以用"廉价"来形容的东西，都可以叫它 budget something。

点评

我们每个人都有坐飞机的时候。如果经济条件很理想，当然可以选择价格贵的航班，无论配餐 food 和服务 service 都能有优质的保证。但如果经济条件很一般，只是个普通打工仔，那还是选廉价航空 budget airlines 比较实际 practical。除了 budget airlines，廉价航空也可以叫 LCC（low cost carrier）或 no-frills。

◆ 词汇小百科 ◆

budget / discount airlines　廉价航空

low cost carriers / airlines　廉价航空

No-frills　不提供不必要服务的（航空）

frill　（女性服饰的）褶边

budget　名词：预算；形容词：便宜的

（刘　彦）

飞机点餐法则

（素材来自《圆桌议事》2015年8月31日节目）

> **导　语**：能遇到好吃的飞机大餐大概是三生有幸了。我们不能改变飞机餐的味道，但是我们可以学学飞机上点餐的黄金法则。至少呢，一顿不太差的飞机餐是妥妥的。

There are a few tips that we can give out. The one that comes from me that I recommend to everyone is being active to ask for alcohol. You can even make your own cocktail on a flight if you want to. There's juice and there's alcohol. Mix them together and you get a cocktail. I think when you get a beer or a glass of wine and you get a little bit tipsy, everything just looks better.

我们可以给一些小建议。有个窍门我想推荐给大家，就是积极地要酒喝。你甚至可以自己整鸡尾酒。这其实很简单，航班上又有果汁又有酒，把它们混在一起，你就做出一杯鸡尾酒啦。我觉得吧，当你有杯啤酒或葡萄酒，喝得有点微醺的时候，所有事情看起来都会更美好一些。

The other thing about airline food is that it is supposed to be really strongly flavored. Because apparently when you are put thirty thousand feet, which is about ten thousand meters, your taste buds become less sensitive. Although I doubt whether any of us have ever tried it, I have heard that if you ate an airline meal on the ground, it would taste really strong. You know, because they have to enhance the flavors.

另一点是，飞机餐都比较重口味。这是因为据说当人们处于三万英尺，也就是万米的高空时，味蕾会变得没那么敏感。虽然我很怀疑到底有没有人试过，但我听说如果在地面上吃飞机餐，会觉得非常重口味，因为飞机餐是加重了口味的。

Because noodles will be stuck together like a brick and you don't want to eat that. So go for rice.

因为面条会黏成一坨，你不会想吃的。所以，要点米饭。

During the flight if you are feeling a bit hungry between meals, if you go to the galley, they will have instant noodles there and they will give you instant noodles for free. They are prepared for you. And you could also get extra drinks there like orange juice or water. It's all there in little plastic glasses ready. On the flights that I used to take, which is the big ones back to the UK, I always go up to the back. And on British Airways, if you go to the back, they don't give you instant noodles, they'll give you an ice-cream.

飞行途中，如果你在两餐间觉得有些饿，你可以去厨房那儿，他们会免费给你方便面。你也可以拿到额外地倒在小塑料杯里的饮料，比如橙汁和水。我以前回英国常常乘坐那架比较大的英国航空班机，我总是会走去机舱尾部，因为厨房在那里。跟中航不同的是，英航的厨房不给方便面，而是给冰激凌。

By the way, I was reading this report earlier in the paper actually online. You should never put your peanuts on the tray. Do you know, most of those trays on planes have been used by passengers to change babies' nappies apparently. You should wipe your tray before you even think of putting your hands on it.

顺便提一句，我之前在网上读过一份报告，它说千万不要把花生放在托盘上。不知道你们有没有听说，飞机上的大部分托盘都很悲催——乘客们经常直接在上面给婴儿换尿布。你哪怕把手放上去之前都要好好擦一下，更别说放食物了。

Useful advice here, chicken is the better choice apparently. Chicken is usually tastier than pork and beef.

还有个很有用的建议,就是记得选鸡肉。飞机上的鸡肉总是比猪肉或牛肉好吃。

点评

飞行途中,尤其是长途飞行途中,人们容易觉得压抑和无聊,而本来可以调节情绪的美食却又不那么美好,真的很心塞!不要紧,一些小建议多少能让飞机餐变得美好一些。你可以尝试喝点酒,变得微醺 get a little bit tipsy,因为在那种状态下 everything looks better。当然,这个方法不一定适合所有人。Tipsy 是指 slightly drunk,点到即可,喝得酩酊大醉可不好。此外,在米饭和面条、鸡肉和其他肉类之间做选择的时候,总是选前者。因为实践证明,飞机餐里的米饭和鸡肉相对好吃一些。

词汇小百科

galley　飞机上的厨房
instant noodle　方便面
cocktail　鸡尾酒
tray　托盘
nappy　尿布(英式英语,同diaper)

(于　洋)

西方社交场合着装宝典

（素材来自《圆桌议事》2014年11月15日节目）

导　语： 大家的印象中，美国人平时穿着很随意，T恤牛仔裤人字拖，没那么时尚和讲究。但这并不代表他们在所有场合都没有着装要求。事实上，西方国家在不同的场合有各种不同的着装礼仪。如果你受邀参加一个活动或者party，可别指望一条连衣裙或者一件西装外套就蒙混过关哦。这篇里我们就来了解一下请柬上常见的着装要求吧。

So we are talking about dress code and the thing is, in western culture, dress code in some cases in the formal category is very tightly defined, but as we get into casual areas, it's very loosely defined. So when we look at dress code, usually what we are talking about is formal wear, semi-formal wear and informal wear. Now once we want to get into casual areas, that's no longer considered as dress code, just more of a style.

西方文化中的着装礼仪其实是很有趣的。你会发现通常情况下，正式场合穿正装这个大类下的各种小类规定都非常严格，而非正式场合穿便装大类下的各种小类又都较为随意。首先，在"有着装要求"的大前提下，一般有正式、半正式和非正式等分类。而剩下的归在便装（即"无着装要求"）范围内的，其实不能算着装礼仪，而应该算是一种着装风格。

So formal wear or formal dress code, in the US and Australia for example, is not usually followed any more. It used to be, for a formal occasion, like a state dinner, perhaps a wedding or a very, very serious event, it would be a white tie event. For men, what white tie means is basically a tuxedo but then with three pieces on top, a white shirt, a white vest and a white tie and a black jacket and black pants. These days, again in the US and Australia, most formal dress codes don't include the white tie, instead the black tie perhaps or even just a regular suit.

对于正式场合而言，白领结其实是最正式的。过去，在美国、澳大利亚等国家，如果遇上婚礼之类的极正式场合，可能会遵循这个着装要求。现在，基本上除了在国宴这样的场合外，白领结已经不再用了。之所以叫白领结，就是说男士不仅要穿礼服，还要穿白色的衬衫、背心以及白色的领结。但是现在的正式场合一般戴黑领结，或者穿正规西服就可以了。

For women, it used to be, like ball gowns, like very, very fancy things with long gloves and things like that. Usually these days, in the US and Australia, women just wear like cocktail dresses, you know, just like a nice dress or a nice skirt.

过去，女性在非常高级隆重的正式场合，会被要求穿宫廷长礼服，戴长款手套等。现在，着装礼仪对女士来说，要求也不像以前那么严了。以前是一定要穿长裙，那么现在穿这种鸡尾酒裙或者及膝小礼服也是可以的。

And so then we get into the casual category where anything kind of goes and it's actually very difficult to define. So there's smart casual, business casual and then just casual. Smart casual is basically just when you mix and match casual and formal clothing pieces.

像之前说的，便装这个大类基本上没什么明确的要求，所以也很难严格定义。便装包括 smart casual 日常休闲装（可以在较轻松的办公场合穿）、

business casual 商务休闲装（不需要开会或会见客户时的办公室标准穿着）和 casual 彻底休闲装。Smart casual 日常休闲的种类是介于正式和随意之间的穿着。

点评

　　Dress Code 着装礼仪，dress 是衣着、穿着，code 是编号、代码，如果把 Dress Code 直译成"着装代码"其实也能让人理解。有一点要注意的就是千万别觉得越正式越好，其实穿的过于休闲或过于正式都会怪怪的，所谓"过犹不及"嘛。所以一定看清楚请柬上的 dress code，万一你被邀请参加化装舞会 masquerade，还要早一些去找合适的戏服呢。

词汇小百科

evening gown　晚宴装、正式场合穿着

ball gown　舞会装、女性社交场合最正式服装

one-piece garments　一件套的衣服，多指外衣

sheath　女式紧身裙装

jumper dress　无袖女罩衫

sundress　吊带裙

nightshirt　男式晚礼服

three-piece suit　三件套

dinner jacket / tuxedo　无尾礼服

tailcoat / morning coat　大礼服

overalls　工装裤

dust coat　风衣

plus fours　高尔夫球裤、半长裤

（牛翃琳）

有一种寒冷叫"忘穿秋裤"

(素材来自《圆桌议事》2015年11月13日节目)

导 语:每年一到冷空气降临的时节,穿不穿秋裤,就成了广大青年男女纠结的问题。秋裤这东西,到底穿,还是不穿?

Qiuku in English is called long johns or thermal underwear. It is a style of pants you wear underneath your outdoor pants that keeps you warm.

秋裤在英语里还有连身内衣和保暖内衣的意思。秋裤是一种穿在外裤里面的起到保暖作用的裤子。

Qiuku has been considered as the least fashionable thing. Anybody who's remotely into fashion should stay away from it…That's because in the old days, when Qiuku or long johns were really loose and thick. So when you wear it inside, your legs look really fat…But now how times have changed! As there's a major demand from the Chinese population, men and women. We want our legs to look thinner and we want to look good even in cold weather.

秋裤被认为是最不时尚的物品。任何稍微对时尚有点兴趣的人士都应该尽量远离它。那是因为以前,秋裤往往很松垮和厚重。当外裤里面穿着秋裤,你的腿看上去就非常粗壮。但现在时代不同啦!中国人民对秋裤有着很大的需求,包括男人和女人。我们都希望自己的腿看起来比较纤细。即使天气寒冷,我们也追求视觉上的美感。

It just reminds me of those good old days in middle school in China when you would often hear a lot of static cling kind of zapping sound. Because everybody's wearing Qiuku and there's this friction with the outdoor pants.

这让我想起那些中学时代的好时光。有时会听见静电作响的声音。那是因为秋裤和外裤由于摩擦而产生的静电。

We were talking about the fashion aspect of Qiuku just then. As I mentioned earlier, in the UK, we don't really wear thermal underwear on a regular basis. What is really popular is leggings among the female population in the UK and other countries. It's simply like just wearing a thick pair of tights or something.

刚才我们聊到秋裤的时尚地位。就像我提到的,在英国,我们不怎么穿保暖内衣或秋裤。但在英国和其他国家,女性人群特别流行穿打底裤。这种裤子就像是穿了一条厚的连裤袜似的。

Actually there's a variation on this that I've noticed in the last few years which I believe is called jeggings. It's a portmanteau of jeans and leggings. They are these leggings but are made to look like jeans, like they are made out of denim.

其实我还发现这几年有个(打底裤)的变体叫牛仔打底裤。这是牛仔裤和打底裤的混合词。它们是打底裤,但被做成牛仔裤的样子,看起来好像是由牛仔布制作而成的。

The reason why Qiuku is so prevalent in China is because it's cold and often indoors is cold too. Some places in China don't have heating.

秋裤在中国流行的原因在于外面天气寒冷,而且也可能室内温度很低。中国的有些地方并没有暖气。

I thought medical journals say that arthritis is not created because you are cold outside, but it can be exacerbated if it's cold when you are outside. So maybe it's a bit of a myth that not wearing Qiuku will cause arthritis.

医学期刊好像说过关节炎并不是因为室外寒冷而产生的，而是因为室外温度低而加重的已有的病痛。也许不穿秋裤而患上关节炎只是一个传说。

点评

Into something 对某事很感兴趣。He's into video games. 他喜欢打游戏。

It reminds me of the good old days 这让我想起过去那些好时光。It reminds me of... 让我想起……

Portmanteau 是混合词（或者叫合成词）。英语里有很多这样的词，例如 smog is a blend of smoke and fog 雾霾是英文里烟和雾的组合；其他例子还有前文提到的 jeggings 和下文要提到的 athleisure。

Myth 是神话的意思。例如 Greek myth 是希腊神话；另一个意思是错误的看法、认知或谎言。例句：Contrary to the popular myth, women are more than shopaholics. 翻译：和人们的普遍观念相反，女性并不是只爱买东西。

词汇小百科

althleisure　运动休闲风，athletic 加 leisure
leggings　打底裤
yoga pants　瑜伽裤

（赫　扬）

AA制，各付各的

（素材来自《圆桌议事》2014年6月21日节目）

导　语：谈恋爱约会也好，跟朋友聚餐也罢，埋单付钱是避不开的环节。我们中国人常说AA，也就是各付各的，可是它真的是地道的英语表达吗？在本篇中，我们就来研究一下这个问题。

Sometimes it's just called going Dutch, but it can also be called a Dutch date, a Dutch treat, and doing Dutch. There are two possible ways this could be used: each person pays their own expenses or the entire bill is divided evenly among all participants. In strict terms, going Dutch refers to the former everyone pays their own expenses, and the latter is usually referred to as just splitting the bill.

中文里常说的AA，用英语表达是 going / doing Dutch，或者叫 Dutch date/ treat。如果要深究，going Dutch 其实又分两种：一种是每个人只付自己消费的那部分；另一种是每个人付总额平摊到人头上的数字。严格说来，前者才是真正的 going Dutch，谁都不吃亏；后者的精确叫法是 splitting the bill，自己消费份额少于平均值的人相对比较吃亏。

Looking at the history of this phrase, one person has suggested that going Dutch might originate from the concept of a Dutch door. This is usually farm houses. The door would consist of two equal parts.

为什么AA跟 Dutch 有关呢？有一种解释是说，荷兰人家里的门经常是双开门，也就是对开的那种门，所以 going Dutch 就引申出"费用对开"的意思。

Whereas The Oxford English Dictionary says go Dutch, Dutch treat and other phrases actually come from the 17th century when there was a bit of tension between the English and the Dutch. Another example is Dutch courage, so in that sense, it's used to basically be derisive, a bit of a negative term.

《牛津英语词典》则说，这些短语之所以包含Dutch字眼，是因为17世纪时，英国人和荷兰人之间存在不小的矛盾。当时英国人对荷兰人带有偏见，所以很多短语都有歧视或嘲笑荷兰人的成分，比较负面。Going Dutch 是嫌荷兰人小气，而 Dutch courage（酒后之勇）则是嘲笑荷兰人缺乏勇气。

Another term that's used primarily in China is AA. Interestingly enough, this term does not originate in the English speaking countries. In fact, it originates in Hong Kong.

至于我们非常熟悉的AA，它并非源自英语国家。最初是在中国香港叫开的，如今在中国都很流行。但在中国以外的地方，很少有人这么说。

There are actually a few different theories there, as to what exactly that means. Some people suggest that it's the algebraic average. And there are other theories suggesting that it means all apart.

AA究竟是什么的缩写，目前没有定论。有人说是"代数均值"（algebraic average），也有人说是"全部分开"（all apart），似乎都说得通。

If I say AA to a friend from an English speaking country, they most probably wouldn't know what you are talking about. They'll think you are talking about Alcoholic Anonymous, which is very, very different.

如果跟来自英语国家的人说AA制，他们十有八九不懂你的意思。他们听到AA，第一反应都是嗜酒者互诫协会（Alcoholic Anonymous）。

点评

从语言的角度来看，AA真的是神奇的存在。虽然是英语缩写，但它基本只在大中华地区适用。如果跟英语为母语的人提AA，他们并不会想到"各付各的"，而是会以为你有酗酒的问题。所以，为了交流顺畅、避免无谓的误会，跟外国人还是说 going Dutch 或者 splitting the bill 比较好。

词汇小百科

going Dutch / Dutch date / Dutch treat / doing Dutch　各付各的，AA制
splitting the bill　平摊费用
former　前者
latter　后者
Dutch courage　酒后之勇
derisive　嘲笑的，嘲弄的
algebraic　代数的

（刘　彦）

必备砍价技能get!

（素材来自《圆桌议事》2016年2月18日节目）

> **导　语**：在中国的小摊贩上买东西，卖家报价，买家砍价，别具乐趣。有什么是必备的砍价技能呢？

Bargaining in Chinese markets can be similar to fighting a war, if you are vigilant and calm enough, you can have the upper hand! Let's discuss strategies and compare notes. So we can leave the show with ample ammunition to claim victory in this mental war!

在中国的市场里讨价还价就像打仗。如果你够机警和沉着，你还是可能占上风的！咱们聊聊战略战术，互相切磋吧。这样听了节目后，我们就可以带着足够的弹药打赢这场心理战！

I mean this as a compliment, so please don't take it negatively. When it comes to doing business, Chinese people are relentless. They don't stop attacking until they win.

我这么说是赞美，所以千万别负面地看问题。要说做生意，中国人绝对不依不饶。他们不赢是不会罢手的。

When it comes to these personal vendors or individual stalls in places like the Silk Market or just a general market, bargaining skill is very useful there. There isn't really a tag price, but there's an ask price. It's often something you need to maybe have it or even ask for a lower price than that. That seems to be a piece of useful knowledge for shoppers.

当和秀水市场或其他市场里的小商小贩做生意的时候，讨价还价是一项非常有用的技能。那里的商品并不存在标明的价格，但有一个起始价。你可以按照这个价格付款或者砍价。这是顾客应该知道的信息。

Be calm and don't act like you really want the product. It's like with any business, the more weakness that you show, the more it's going to give them leeway to think they can make you pay a higher price.

保持镇定，别表现出来你真心想要买这个产品。就像任何一项生意，你越表现出你的软弱，他们（卖方）就越觉得可以抬高价格。

Be relentless. Because they will be coming at you with the same mentality. They are not going to quit. So if you want that item that much, you've got to have the same pit bull mentality as the person that's trying to sell it to you.

别放弃，不懈努力！因为他们就是以这样的心态对你的，他们不会罢手。如果你真的很想拥有这个产品，你一定也得用斗牛犬般的心态面对卖家。

If you are spending a lot of money in general, asking for a big bargain is pretty important. But if you are only spending a few Yuan at the fresh market, then maybe not be that aggressive about it? Because every time I go to that market with my dad, my dad always says "let the poor guy have that 5 extra Yuan, he got up at 3 a.m. this morning to get the vegetables into Beijing."

如果你打算大买一通，讨价还价挺重要。但如果你只是花几块钱到菜市场买个菜，要不就别太强势地砍价了？每次和我爸爸去逛菜场的时候，他总是说"就让他多赚5块钱吧，那哥们儿早上3点就得起床把蔬菜运进北京啦。"

To have the upper hand 是占优势，占上风的意思。众所周知，upper 是

上面的；hand 是手的意思。To have the upper hand 除了可以形容人的行为以外，还可以用来指情绪。He let his feelings get the upper hand. 他没有处理好他的情绪，失控了。

Compare notes 交换意见；切磋。想象两个积极好学的学生交换笔记的样子。Mother and Mrs. Smith like to compare notes about baking. 母亲和史密斯夫人喜欢就烘焙切磋技艺。

Ammunition 弹药、军火，也有战斗手段的喻义。在辩论或讨论中，还有可攻击对方的信息，事实，炮弹的意思。He seems confident that his company has ample ammunition to fend off competition from the other company. 他对他的公司有足够战斗手段来阻击来自其他公司的竞争这一点，似乎胸有成竹；He improved trade figures have given the government fresh ammunition to fight the opposition. 有所改观的贸易数据给政府提供了新的弹药，助它和反对派继续斗争下去。

Pit bull mentality 斗牛犬般的心态。Pit bull 是斗牛犬这种犬类的名称。它被认为是有好斗性格的狗。Mentality 是心态的意思，前面可以加上某种具体的呈现形式。例如 victim mentality 受害者心态。

Leeway（航行由于强风所致的）偏航、余地、时间损失。give leeway 留余地。How much leeway should parents give kids? 家长们应该给孩子们多少自由度呢？

词汇小百科

bargain 讨价还价，达成协议。当名词用的时候，还有便宜货的意思。

（赫 扬）

真人秀怎么看？

（素材来自《圆桌议事》2014年7月12日节目）

导　语：真人秀是深受大众欢迎的电视节目类别。从歌唱比赛到相亲配对，似乎每个小类别都有不少铁杆粉丝。在本篇中，我们就来学习一下相关的英语表达。

Reality TV began in the 1990s with MTV's The Real World, basically putting a bunch of college students together and creating situations that led to conflict and other interesting outcomes.

真人秀最早的起源应该是MTV电视台20世纪90年代播出的一档节目：《真实世界》。这个节目基本上就是把一群大学生放到一起生活，制造出一些会产生冲突或矛盾的情形，然后看发生什么样的后果。

So by definition, reality television is a genre of television programming that basically just records unscripted situations and actual occurrences and in many cases features an unknown cast, usually highlighting personal drama and conflict between the different characters. But as we can see with many reality TV shows, especially as they have become more and more popular, these supposedly unscripted events do seem to be highly scripted.

之所以叫"真人秀"，是因为这种类型的节目号称百分百反映真实世界发生的事情，没有预先写好的剧本，演员也相对来说没什么知名度。当然，为了保证吸引眼球，真人秀会在所谓的真实情景里面加强戏剧冲突。而随着某档节目越来越受欢迎，它的真实程度也会越来越低，往往大部分内容都按事先写好的剧本走。

So what happens a lot is that sometimes we are looking at what originally was a spontaneous event or interaction. But producers or directors will stop the cast members and say "OK, that was really good but do it again." And in some cases, they actually coach the actors or the non-actors (as we're supposed to believe) in acting a certain way.

虽然说真人秀旨在反映真实的情况，但制作人或导演有时也会让演员从原本即兴的表演中停下来，给他们一些指点：怎样表演观众会更爱看一些。其实真人秀之所以会走红，大多是因为这类节目迎合了我们普通人的一些偷窥他人隐私的心理。

Also, talent shows, singing shows, and dating shows as well, usually can be considered as reality TV.

还有一种节目也可以叫真人秀，就是 talent shows，选秀节目。这其中又以唱歌选秀最为常见。此外，相亲节目也是真人秀的一种。

Anything that will give us an opportunity to look at what we think actually happens in other people's lives. However, you have to remember that reality TV unfortunately is anything but.

说穿了，任何给我们机会去看别人生活里发生什么事的节目，都可以叫"真人秀"。当然，你得记住，"真人秀"并不一定"真"，大多都是按事先安排好的剧本来拍摄的。

点评

很多人对"真人秀"嗤之以鼻，认为这种类型的节目纯粹就是用来 kill time（打发时间）的，没有营养，没有价值。这种观点不够 objective（客观）。首先，真人秀很大程度上满足了我们普通人偷窥他人隐私的心理需求；其次，唱歌选秀类的真人秀往往很励志，是那句流行语"梦想总是要有的，万一实现了呢"的 best interpretation（最佳诠释）；最后，即使某些冲突和矛盾是事先安排好的，这毕竟是电视节目，主要的目的是 entertainment（娱乐），所以也不必太较真。

词汇小百科

genre 种类

scripted / unscripted 事先（没）写好剧本的

supposedly 据说应该，按推测应该……

spontaneous 自发的，随性的

talent / singing show 才艺 / 歌唱选秀节目

dating show 相亲节目

anything but... 根本不是……

（刘 彦）

穷游那些事儿

（素材来自《圆桌议事》2016年2月29日节目）

导　语：世界那么大，你也想去看看？穷游曾风行一时，但是风险也是很大的！至少，别丢东西，别丢人。

So what we mean is solo backpackers who are staying in hostels that are very cheap, maybe 20 to 30 kuai a night. They hitchhike. They maybe eat instant noodles instead of eating in a restaurant wherever they travel, or they impulse on the kindness of strangers they might meet along the way, those are the kinds of things that can be shoestring backpacker travel.

我们所指的穷游是独自旅行的背包客的旅行方式，他们住非常便宜的旅社，二三十块钱一晚；出行经常搭便车，吃饭常吃方便面，不去餐馆。他们会在路上向陌生人求助。

I wanted to see the world. I wanted to experience life in different places and eat different food and greet people in different ways and（find out）how you say "cheers" in Gaelic.

我想去看看世界，在不同的地方体验不同的生活、品尝不同的食物、结识不同的人。我也想知道用盖尔语怎么说"干杯"。

We are probably be standing in the middle of nowhere, you want to hitch a ride, but you couldn't see any cars, or you've seen millions of cars passing by. Still, there was not even a driver who would like to give you a free trip. A lot of assaults or attacks might be happening.

有时候我们所处的地方很偏远，想搭车的时候没有车，或者有车驶过但没车停下。有时还有可能被攻击。

I think that is definitely something to keep in mind, especially for a solo female traveler. You should be a bit smarter about how you travel, who you take a ride from. You definitely need to be cautious, but being cautious doesn't mean you need to lock yourself in a room and never see anything, you know. I think that there's a healthy balance. There are always risks attached to anything. You could ride the subway.

是的，尤其是单独旅行的女背包客要注意安全。怎么旅行、搭什么人的车都要想清楚。谨慎不等于封闭自己或者什么都不看。我觉得收获和风险是可以平衡的。你可以坐地铁嘛。

I think that the more you do this kind of travel, the more you are gonna find other people with similar values and interests who will help you along the way.

这样的旅行你经历得越多，就越能找到与自己价值观和兴趣相似的人，他们会在路上帮助你。

点评

穷游的说法是 shoestring travel，shoe 是鞋子的意思，string 是带子绳子的意思，放在一起就是以极少的钱、极小的成本来实现一个目标的做法。experience 体验，life 生活，food 食物，people 人，有了这些，旅行才有乐趣。找到拥有相似价值观和兴趣的人 find people with similar values and interests，或许是旅行中的最大幸事了吧。

词汇小百科

backpacker 背包客

hitchhike 搭便车

instant noodle 方便面（必然是旅行常备！）

ride the subway / take the subway 坐地铁

（陈　沫）

能不能好好过马路？

（素材来自《圆桌议事》2014年4月12日节目）

导　语：只要在中国生活过，一定对"中国式过马路"有深刻的体会。这么有中国特色的名词，恐怕没有相对应的英文表达吧？还真有。在本篇中，我们就来说说jaywalking的种种。

In English, "jaywalking" is the illegal or reckless pedestrian crossing of a roadway. So, for example, people crossing between intersections without yielding to drivers or starting to cross at a crosswalk at a signal intersection without waiting for a permissive indication to be displayed.

在英语里，jaywalking这个单词专指行人非法或莽撞过马路的行为。它跟"中国式过马路"非常吻合，因为我们几乎每天都会看到不看红绿灯直接过马路的行为，这正是"非法或莽撞过马路"的体现。"中国式过马路"的另外一大特点就是一大帮人一起闯红灯。

And interestingly enough, the earliest use of the word "jaywalker" in print was in the Chicago Tribune in 1909, whereas the earliest citation was in the Oxford English Dictionary in 1917. Actually, the word "jaywalk" is a compound word derived from the word "jay", which in this case means an inexperienced person.

Jaywalker这个词于1909年第一次出现在《芝加哥论坛报》里，1917年被正式收入牛津英语词典。事实上，jaywalk 是个合成词，也就是 jay + walker。Jay 有"缺乏经验的人"这一层含义，所以 jaywalker 自然就是指缺乏经验、胡乱走路的人。

So "Jay" is actually a very old word that's not used in at least American English. So in the United States usually state laws require that drivers yield to pedestrians at crosswalks and at many other locations. However, sometimes pedestrians are supposed to yield to cars.

  Jay 表示"缺乏经验的人"这种用法已经相当古老，如今的美式英语里不复存在。当然，jaywalking 还是极其常用的。就美国而言，各个州会各自立法，要求司机在许多有人行横道的地方给行人让路。但某些时候，行人也要反过来给车让路。

点评

  "中国式过马路"屡见不鲜，一方面的原因是中国人遵守交通法规（traffic laws and regulations）的意识比较淡薄，另一方面也跟红绿灯（traffic lights）设计不够合理有很大关系。相信大家都见过这样的例子：很短的一段马路，明明几步就可以走完，红灯却要长达两分钟。这确实非常不合理，也难怪大家耐不住性子（impatient），不理红灯就直接过马路了。司机不让行人也很让人沮丧和生气（frustrated and angry），因为有时绿灯的时间特别短，车一直不停，行人就一直过不了马路。等到车终于过完了，绿灯又变红灯了。如果不闯红灯，又得等很久。总之，中国式过马路是个复杂的问题（complicated issue），需要多方共同努力，否则永远无法解决。

词汇小百科

  jaywalking 不遵守交通规则的走路行为，在中国被称为"中国式过马路"

yield to...　给……让路
crosswalk　人行横道
Chicago Tribune　《芝加哥论坛报》
Oxford English Dictionary　牛津英语词典
Jay　缺乏经验的人
pedestrian　行人

（刘　彦）

流浪的喵星人谁来守护

（素材来自《圆桌议事》2014年8月9日节目）

导　语：杭州市政府计划投资30万元为流浪猫绝育的新闻引起了不少人的关注。流浪猫和野猫是一个概念吗？

There is a difference between feral and stray. So let's start by talking a little bit about feral. A feral animal is an animal living in the wild but descended from domesticated animals. And the word "feral" comes from the Latin, fera, which means a wild beast.

　　Feral是指野生的、没有经过驯化的动物，但是它们是由家养的动物生下来的。Feral这个词源自拉丁语fera（野兽）。

Other definitions of a feral animal define them as one that has changed from being domesticated to being wild, natural, or untamed. Common examples include horses, dogs, goats and cats.

　　Feral 也可以指曾经是家养，但后来又逐渐回到野生的动物。常见的例子包括马、狗、羊和猫。

And now we come to the important difference between a feral cat and a stray cat. A stray cat is a pet cat that has been lost or abandoned, whereas feral cats have never been socialized.

　　由此可见，feral 和 stray 的区别还是很明显的。就拿猫来说，stray cat 是流浪猫，一般是指从家里逃出来的或者被遗弃的家猫。而 feral cat 则是在野外长大的猫。

Usually a feral cat is descended from a stray cat. For cats, it's really important, the socialization process when they are very young. If they are not exposed to humans in the wild, then they'll not learn to trust them, and they'll never learn to actually form an attachment with them.

野猫通常是由流浪猫所生。因为它们没有被社会化的过程，所以很难相信人类，也不会与人类亲近。

So usually feral cats are born and live outdoors, without any human contact or care. However, they have been shown to be adoptable and can be tamed by humans, provided they are removed from their wild environment before the feral behaviors are established.

野猫通常在户外出生并长大，而且整个过程中没有与人类接触或者被照料。尽管如此，它们也还是有可能被人类驯化的，前提是在它们的行为还没有定型之前就离开野外的环境。

For example, Hangzhou is doing is a Trap-Neuter-Return（TNR）program which involves volunteers trapping feral cats, sterilizing them by spaying or neutering, and then returning them to the place where there were originally captured.

比如，杭州市政府实施的TNR项目就是这样的努力。TNR的意思是 Trap（诱捕）、Neuter（绝育）、Return（放归），志愿者先诱捕野猫，为它们做绝育，然后再把它们放回被捕捉的原地。

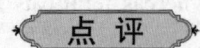

给流浪猫做绝育手术，这消息乍一听可能会引起不少 animal lovers（动

物爱好者），尤其是 cat lovers（喵星人爱好者）的反感。问题是，杭州市政府推出这个项目时，当地已有约30万只流浪猫。猫的繁殖能力极强，如果不控制，要不了几年，这个数字就将以百万计。TNR在全球范围内被证明有效，不失为 smart choice（明智的选择）。但TNR毕竟是一个 long-term project（长期工程），效果不会立竿见影。要让流浪猫真正少下去，还是要靠大家加强 responsibility（负责任）的意识。比如养猫当宠物，不要因为没兴趣了就抛弃它；或是家里的猫怀孕了，生下的猫宝宝大多没法处理，也随便抛弃。

词汇小百科

feral　野生的，没有经过驯化的
stray　流浪的，走失的
descend from　起源于
domesticated　驯服的，驯养的
untamed　未驯服的，难驾驭的
attachment　依恋，喜爱，忠诚
adoptable　可收养的
trap　诱捕
sterilize　使失去生育能力
spay　切除卵巢
neuter　阉割，绝育
capture　捕捉

（刘　彦）

健康呵护
Health

健身去吧！

（素材来自《圆桌议事》2016年3月17日节目）

导　语：不知从何时起，仿佛所有人都在健身，每人至少有一套健身装备。朋友圈里晒步数、发健身照片已经成为时尚，跑马拉松也不仅仅是梦想。健身房的服务你满意吗？健身的人都有哪些期待？

You see the growing number of facilities, the gyms, gym attendees. At the same time it's another very interesting phenomenon that people tend to be more interactive than before: they use wearable devices, they keep track of their data, they share them with other people on social media platforms, discussing and competing with each other. So generally it's a very good sign.

　　现在可以看到越来越多的健身房和健身的人。同时，很有意思的一个现象是人们更加喜欢互动——用着可穿戴设备，记录自己的数据，在社交媒体上分享数字，还与他人讨论、比赛。这总体上是好兆头。

But it does have its problems and the key one being profitability. Now just around 20% of gyms in China earned a profit; about 50% of gyms which offer just a few value-added services are facing tough conditions due to a limited number of customers. And this is according to facts from industry insiders.

　　这也有个问题，就是盈利的能力。现在中国只有20%的健身房盈利；还有50%的健身房，也能提供一些增值服务，但面临着艰难的境遇，因为顾客少。这些信息是业内人士提供的事实。

And there is an abundance of suggestions now being put forward. I think the main school of thinking here is that these gyms need to offer more than just exercise classes, they should be looking at personal trainers, health lessons, diet guidance, outdoor activities and other highly value-added services.

大家提出了很多建议。我觉得主流的想法是希望这些健身房多提供操课以外的高增值服务，比如个人私教、健康课、饮食指导、户外活动等。

I think the problem is that you've really got to ask why Chinese people are going to the gym. If it is because they are trying to lose weight, and I think to a certain level, that is the case. I was reading a story this morning of how Chinese netizens ave now got this popular thing, holding a piece of A4 paper in front of their ust, and if they're thinner than the paper, that means they are "in shape". And t 's actually, that's just aesthetically, though. I think you really got to ask what the consumers want: do they want to look in shape or do they actually want to be in shape?

我觉得问题还是在于：中国人为什么去健身房。如果说是为了减肥，那还有些道理，是那么回事。今天早上我看到一篇报道，说中国网民在比试A4腰：拿一张A4纸在腰前，如果腰比纸瘦，就说明他们身材保持得好。但这实际上是审美上的挑战。我们觉得真需要问一问消费者究竟想要什么，是想看 来身材不错，还是想真正健身？

◆ 点 评 ◆

如今，健身除了其本身意义之外，还有社交的功能：用可穿戴设备 use wearable devices，记录数据 keep track of data，在社交平台上与他人分享 share them with other people on social media platforms，讨论、比赛 discuss and compete with each other。

健身房能提供的增值服务 value-added services 除了提到的个人私教 personal training，健康课程 health lessons，饮食指导 diet guidance，户外活动 outdoor activities，还可以有体重管理 weight management，营养咨询 nutrition counseling，儿童托管 childcare，全套更衣室服务 full locker room services，果汁吧 Juice bar，物理治疗 physical therapy。

几种健身器械 fitness equipment 的说法：跑步机 treadmill，for running and walking while staying in the same place，椭圆机 elliptical or elliptical trainer or cross-trainer，踏步机 stepper。

几种健身服装 fitness clothing / workout clothes 的说法：连帽衫 hoodie，紧身压缩裤 compression tights，运动内衣 sports bra，紧身背心 tank top。

词汇小百科

industry insider　业内人士

lose weight　减肥、减重

in shape　保持健美、健康

aesthetically　审美地、美学观赏上地

school　除了有"学校"的意思，还有"流派"的意思

waist　腰，中国古代就有"楚王好细腰""嬛嬛一袅楚宫腰"的描述

slim / thin / skinny / small waist　细腰

（陈　沫）

有氧运动玩起来

(素材来自《圆桌议事》2014年8月16日节目)

> **导 语**：运动健身是很多人生活中必不可少的一部分。运动主要分有氧运动和无氧运动，而有氧运动当中又分高强度的和低强度的，锻炼者应根据身体情况来做最适合自己的选择。在本篇中，我们主要来看看与有氧运动的相关知识和英语表达。

First, we are going to talk about aerobic exercise, sometimes known as cardio, and basically this is a type of physical exercise of relatively low intensity that depends primarily on the aerobic energy generating process. So aerobic literally means relating to, involving or requiring free oxygen.

有氧运动 aerobic exercise 一般是指在人体氧气充分供应的情况下进行的体育锻炼。强度相对比较低，持续的时间也比较长一些。

Usually when we talk about aerobic or cardiovascular exercises, we are talking about medium to long distance running or jogging, swimming, cycling and walking.

举例来说，常见的有氧运动包括慢跑、游泳、骑自行车以及走路。

And you can actually break it down into two different types of aerobic exercises. High-impact which means both your feet leave the ground simultaneously during the workout, so running, jumping rope, skipping, and things like that. And low-impact means that at least one foot stays in contact with the ground at all times, so things like walking or even technically, although there are really no feet involved, swimming and cycling are also considered low-impact.

有氧运动可以细分为两类。第一类high-impact是高强度的，一般是指在运动中双脚都会离地的运动，比如跳绳、跑步等。第二类 low-impact 是低强度的，一般在任何时候都至少有一只脚是和地面有接触的，比如走路。另外游泳和骑自行车也可以算低强度有氧运动。

And looking at good running technique for everyone interested, actually, leaning forward places a runner's center of mass on the front part of the foot, which avoids landing on the heel. Also you want to make sure you have upright posture with a relaxed frame and keep your core upright and stable.

跑步也有很多技巧。首先是身体前倾，然后重心要放在前脚掌部分。另外就是保持上身正直，且人处在放松的状态。

Now let's take a look at some equipment. A treadmill is a device for walking or running while staying in the same place. You'll see that almost every single gym that you go to is going to have some people on treadmill.

现在来看看运动时用到的仪器设备。最常见的就是 treadmill（跑步机），它可以让人在快走或奔跑时停留在同一个地方。随便去哪家健身房，一定可以看到有人在跑步机上挥汗如雨。

And now we come to my favorite piece of equipment in terms of aerobic exercises elliptical trainer, sometimes even called the cross-trainer or X-trainer. It's a stationary machine that is used to simulate stair climbing, walking, or running without causing excessive pressure to the joints.

除了跑步机外，elliptical trainer，即椭圆机或叫太空漫步机，也是经常看到的一种健身器械。它是一台静止的设备，可用来模拟爬楼梯、走路或跑步，同时最大限度地减少对关节的伤害。

点评

发现我们大多数人所谓的"健身"主要进行的是有氧运动。而且区分有氧运动强度高低的依据是运动过程中是否出现双脚同时离地的情形，而不是身体感觉有多累。此外，涉及运动的许多概念都是 set phrases（固定说法），不能按字面翻译。比如跑步机是 treadmill 而非 running machine，太空漫步机是 elliptical trainer 而非 space walker，等等。这说明无论学什么都不能 take things for granted（想当然）。

词汇小百科

aerobic exercise　有氧运动

intensity　强度

oxygen　氧气

cardiovascular　心血管的

high-impact　高强度的

low-impact　低强度的

center of mass　质心

upright　笔直的，直挺挺的

posture　姿势

elliptical trainer / cross-trainer / X-trainer　椭圆机，太空漫步机

stationary　静止的

simulate　模拟

joint　关节

（刘　彦）

无氧运动厉害了

（素材来自《圆桌议事》2014年8月23日节目）

> **导　语**：运动健身是很多人生活中必不可少的一部分。运动主要分有氧运动和无氧运动。上一篇讲了有氧运动，所以在本篇中，我们主要来看看无氧运动的相关知识和英语表达。

Anaerobic exercise is exercise intense enough to trigger lactic acid formation. It is used in non-endurance sports to promote strength, speed and power. So bottom line, an anaerobic exercise is a high-intensity activity which lasts from mere seconds to up to two minutes.

无氧运动跟有氧运动相对，指的是高速剧烈的运动。运动时会在体内产生乳酸。因为强度很高，所以不能持久，时间一般在两秒钟到两分钟之间。

Yeah, anaerobic exercise increases your capacity to withstand the buildup of waste substances, such as lactic acid, and removes them from the body. This actually means your endurance and ability to fight fatigue will improve.

无氧运动可以加强身体抵抗诸如乳酸之类废弃物的能力，并将其从身体中清除出去。这可以改善你的耐力和抗疲劳能力。

And so weight training is a common type of anaerobic exercise. Sets of one to five repetitions primarily develop strength. Sets of six to twelve repetitions develop a balance of strength, muscle size and anaerobic endurance. And sets of thirteen to twenty develop anaerobic endurance.

负重训练是一种常见的无氧运动，既可以通过负重器械，也可以通过像哑铃、杠铃这样的工具来完成。如果是做一到五次的话，主要是为了增强力量；做六到十二次，是在力量均衡的同时增肌；做十三到二十次，则是在增加无氧情况下肌肉的承受力。

So looking at free weights, there are a few different pieces of equipment you can use. One is the dumbbell. And I'm sure if you have been to a gym, you have seen many of these. The dumbbell is actually a part of a pair. Usually, you take one in both hands and use it in different exercises.

哑铃应该是最主要的力量训练的器械。如果你去过健身房，肯定见过不少哑铃。使用者一般是一手拿一个，用来均衡地训练力量。

Then there is the barbell which is basically just a bar that you can put different weights on and use in your exercise.

然后就是杠铃，你可以根据自己的锻炼需求来调节重量。

Of course, there are the body weight exercises which many people are already familiar with. There is the push-up or press-up. That's used by lying in a prone position and raising and lowering the body, only using the arms. Then there is the pull-up.

还有一些体重训练，其实指的就是用自身的重量，而不是用哑铃、杠铃这些器械来训练力量。最常见的是俯卧撑和引体向上。

And there are also the sit-up and the crunch. The only real difference between the two is that the sit-up has a fuller range of motion and it targets the hips, not just the stomach. The crunch targets mostly only the stomach.

还有两种很常见的体重运动就是仰卧起坐和卷腹了。它们之间的区别是：仰卧起坐的动作幅度更大，而且不只是训练腹部肌肉，还能训练到臀部肌肉。而卷腹基本上只是训练腹部肌肉。

点评

无氧运动对 technique（技巧）的要求相对更高。几乎所有的人都会走路、跑步等有氧运动，但很多人做不了俯卧撑或引体向上之类的无氧运动。如果你想通过锻炼 comprehensively（全面）提高身体各方面的机能，最好有氧和无氧运动兼顾。但是每个人的具体情况都不一样，没有必要过分纠结。如果 time（时间）、energy（精力）或 physical strength（肢体力量）有限，完全可以只选择走路、跑步这些相对较为简单的有氧运动。切记，stick to what's best for you（坚持最适合自己的方式）。

词汇小百科

anaerobic exercise　无氧运动

lactic acid　乳酸

endurance　耐力

fatigue　疲劳

weight training　负重训练

dumbbell　哑铃

barbell　杠铃

push-up / press-up　俯卧撑

prone position　卧姿

sit-up　仰卧起坐

crunch　卷腹

（刘　彦）

有马甲线才是真女神

（素材来自《圆桌议事》2015年5月7日节目）

导　语：对于很多有健身习惯的都市女性来说，长期在健身房锻炼身体，是为了瘦身和健康。但是目前最流行的可并非是瘦身，而是在瘦身的同时不忘锻炼肌肉，直至练出紧实的肌肉、长出马甲线或人鱼线。

I think this is a new trend apparently. And more and more girls are adopting a more healthy way to shape their bodies. And I think it's good, because in the old days, it was just being skinny, you don't eat, you don't exercise, you just try to get as skinny as possible. That is not right. And that is not good for your body.

我认为这明显是一个新趋势。越来越多的女孩在用一种更健康的方式塑形。我认为这很好，因为在过去，大家只想着要瘦，不吃不运动，就是要试着尽可能的瘦。那不对，会伤害你的身体。

If you look at business people, inside China and even internationally, they are looking at the personal fitness market and salivating, because it's huge, it's absolutely huge. You know, because there is more and more demand. More and more people, especially in urban areas, are realizing that they need to be healthy, that they need to be fit. And those two things really do go hand in hand.

如果你看那些生意人，在中国甚至国际范围内，他们都在关注个人健身市场并对它垂涎欲滴，因为这个市场无比巨大，需求也越来越多。越来越多的人，尤其是城里人，正逐渐意识到他们需要健康和健身。这两件事真的是密切相关。

And Vivian is one of them, saying "I've been taking dancing classes for fun and entertainment starting this year. And I have been having a small six-pack already. I didn't expect it to grow bigger after taking these classes. But for me, it's about having fun, and maybe being healthy. Getting the muscle is just a bonus, not a must."

听友Vivian就是其中之一。她说："我从今年开始为了兴趣和娱乐开始上舞蹈课。我现在六块腹肌已经初具雏形了。我并不期待上课后它们会变大。但是对于我来说，这是为了乐趣，或可能为了健康。长肌肉是一个额外福利，而不是必需。"

The thing is, women are never going to become big, unless you're in the gym, and your diet is protein rich, calorie heavy, you're not going to get that big. What is going to happen? It's that if you exercise and eat healthily, women are going to develop the muscle. And it's going to become quite obvious that you have muscle. So you won't get big, but just be like "she has muscles, she has a six-pack, she has really great legs", or something like that.

女性永远不会变得肌肉太强壮，除非你总去健身房，而且你的食谱中有丰富的蛋白质和高热量，否则你不会有太强壮的肌肉。那会发生什么呢？如果你锻炼并吃得健康，你会长肌肉，而且会很明显看出你有肌肉。所以你不会过于强壮，而只是有人会说"她有肌肉，她有六块腹肌，她的腿很漂亮"或类似这样的话。

点评

马甲线已经逐渐成为现代女性锻炼的目标了，这是一个好趋势，因为越来越多的女孩 adopt a more healthy way to shape their bodies 用更健康的方式塑形，adopt 采用，shape one's body 塑形。越来越多的人 realize that they need to be healthy, that they need to be fit 意识到他们需要健康，他们需要健身，而健康和健身这两件事 go hand in hand 密切相关。而且女性不用太担心自己肌肉变得太强壮，除非你 take steroids 吃类固醇之类的药物，或在锻炼之余坚持 protein rich, calorie heavy 富有蛋白质和高卡路里的食谱。

词汇小百科

a six-pack 或 six-pack abs   六块腹肌

Apollo's belt   人鱼线

beer gut   啤酒肚

rock-hard pecs   厚实的胸肌，胸肌在英文里是 pectorals，简称为 pecs

firm abs   马甲线

abdominal muscles   腹肌缩写为 abs

（王　玮）

你牙好吗？

（素材来自《圆桌议事》2016年2月23日节目）

> **导　语**：中国人的牙齿保健一直是个问题。虽然刷牙习惯已然普及，但国人还是缺乏保护牙齿的意识和知识。随着中国经济日益强大，国民生活质量日渐改善，这种状况会改变吗？

Yeah, it's a terrible, terrible experience. It was only when I noticed that guy standing next to me had really bad odor…I think he had Chinese chives the night before, amongst seafood and stuff and it was terrible. So I looked at him at the corner of my eye, and I realized he had bad teeth as well. Okay, why are we talking about this? Sorry if I've disgusted you.

　　是的，这真是非常糟糕的经验。我注意到站在我身边的男士身上散发出难闻的气味……我估摸着他昨晚应该是吃了韭菜和海鲜之类的食物，真的很糟糕。我用眼角的余光瞧了他一眼，接着发现他的牙很不好。是的，咱们怎么聊到这儿了。抱歉啊，如果恶心着你们了。

That's an indication that generally speaking, Chinese people don't pay enough attention to their dental care. I also have two surveys to back up my argument. The very first survey is this oral health epidemiology survey. This latest survey shows that about 80% to 97% of Chinese people have periodontal diseases.

　　那表明了总体来说，中国人并没有注意牙科护理。我有两份调查结果可以佐证我的论点。第一份是一个口腔健康流行病问卷调查。这份最新的调查发现百分之八十到百分之九十七的中国人有牙周疾病。看来绝大多数中国人都有这个问题。

China is by no means the only place with this issue, but obviously you know regular health, if you get sick, you know you need to do something about it because it is bothering you. But say with dental health, mental health, it's not as obvious and there's not this idea or this consciousness about it. So people are less likely to do as many preventative measures as well as going to get care when you need it.

中国绝不是唯一面对这个问题的国家。你也知道如果是一般的健康问题，如果生病了，你需要去治病吃药，因为身体向你发出警告。但遇到牙齿健康、精神健康问题，症状往往不突出。人们没有这个概念和意识。所以人们也不太可能采取防范措施或者及时寻求治疗。

Sometimes I think the Chinese people lack the basic knowledge of how to protect their teeth. For example, when we pick up the brushes, we don't know which brush is the best one for you, when it comes to the stiffness of the bristle.

有时，我觉得中国人缺乏保护牙齿的基本知识。例如，当我们去买牙刷的时候，我们并不知道哪一款牙刷最适合自己。我说的是牙刷毛的硬度。

You have to have money or more often insurance. If you don't have health insurance that covers this, then you are not as likely to do that and afford it.

你需要有一定的财力或（牙医）保险（来负担费用）。如果你的健康保险没有涵盖牙医费用，那你很可能负担不起牙科医疗费用。

Yes, and also I think here is the place that parents have a big role to play as I know sometimes bad teeth or crooked teeth have been passed on from generation to generation. But that is not a general case, I think. Parents need to tell their kids that especially when your teeth change, that's when you need to pay more attention to the kid's teeth and make sure that they are growing in a really straight fashion.

是的，我想家长在这里也应该发挥重要作用。有的时候不好的牙齿或是七扭八歪的牙齿常常是从家长传到下一代那里的。当然，这个不可一概而论。家长在孩子换牙的时候尤其需要叮嘱孩子照看好牙齿，让牙齿能整齐生长。

点评

Chinese chives 为韭菜。Chives 是细洋葱和韭黄的意思。韭菜是中国人民喜爱的蔬菜，把 Chinese 加在 chives 前就成了约定俗成的用英语说韭菜的方式了。

From the corner of my eye 用眼睛的余光看到。

From the corner of my eye, I saw her strut by. From that moment on, I could never take my eyes off her. 余光一瞥，我看到她高视阔步而来。从那个时刻后，我的眼神再也离不开她了。

在美国看牙是非常昂贵的。大多数美国人的雇主或本人会购买健康保险以负担高昂的牙医费用。

这一点和中国国情有所不同。在中国看牙医相对而言并不算贵。这样看来，国人是不是更应该照顾好自己的牙齿呢？

一句笑话这么说：Now thanks to our first-world diet and third-world dental care, we have 19th century teeth. 由于我们享受着第一世界的饮食和第三世界的牙齿护理，我们拥有了 19 世纪一样的牙齿状况。

为了避免这类情况出现，牙齿健康要从宝宝抓起，成人后也不能放松。

词汇小百科

periodontal disease　牙周疾病

tooth ache　牙疼

cavity　牙洞

mechanic / electronic tooth brush　电动牙刷

dental floss　牙线

dental correction　牙齿矫正

wear braces　戴牙套

（赫　扬）

全科医生

（素材来自《圆桌议事》2014年4月26日节目）

导　语：我们每个人都会生病，掌握一些跟医疗体系相关的词汇很有必要，比如"全科医生"这个词和这个群体从事的工作。

Let's start with the term community hospital. A community hospital can be purely a nominal designation or have a more specific meaning. When specific, it refers to a hospital that is accessible to the general public, and provides a general or specific medical care which is usually short-term, in a cost-effective setting, and also focuses on preventing illnesses as (much as) on treating them.

Community hospital 实际上就是社区医院的意思，它通常提供短期的医疗服务，价格比较便宜，对老百姓来说是个省钱的选择。而且社区医院不但治病，也注重预防疾病。在中国，社区医疗真的不太发达，所以社区医院往往只能提供一些打疫苗之类的简单服务，并不能治病。

It seems like there is a difference in the role played by the general practitioner, a doctor based in the community who treats patients with minor or chronic illnesses and refers those with serious conditions to a hospital. Their duties are not confined to specific organs of the body, and they have particular skills in treating people with multiple health issues. They are trained to treat patients of any age and sex.

General practitioner 这个词按字面意思理解是全科医生，但它大多指在社区医疗卫生机构工作的全科医生。这种医生接受了比较全面的培训，可以治疗身体各个部位的疾病，而且不限病人的年龄和性别。

但是，general practitioner 一般只治日常小病，如果你的病是骨折，或者需要住院的大病，他们就会把你推荐到有一定规模的医院去接受更系统的治疗。

A family doctor is a synonymous term used in many countries as a general practitioner. But in the US, after the 1970s, the two terms mean differently. A practitioner who specializes in "family medicine" must now complete a residency in family medicine, and must be eligible for a board recognition.

在美国，家庭医生是自成一体的一个单独体系，跟全科医生有一些区别。

虽然在很多其他国家，family doctor 和 general practitioner 被当成同义词使用。

美国的家庭医生需要专门通过家庭医学的相关培训和考核，才有资质上门给人治病。

点评

中国的社区医院的功能过于简单，缺乏真正意义上的全科医生和家庭医生，去医院看病往往会遇到各种困难。

我们仍需要不断摸索（keep exploring）和改进。

词汇小百科

community hospital 社区医院

general practitioner 全科医生

chronic illness 慢性病

family doctor 家庭医生

register 挂号

medical system / health care system 医疗系统，医疗保健体系

（刘　彦）

请关注自闭症

（素材来自《圆桌议事》2014年4月5日节目）

导　语：每年4月2日是世界自闭症关注日。自闭症在医学上也称孤独症，是一个尚未被全社会知道、了解的病症。

Generally speaking, autism is a developmental disorder that usually shows itself around the age of 3 years old. It's characterized by low social interaction and poor communication.

自闭症在中文里面又叫"孤独症"，是一种由于神经系统失调导致的发育障碍。这种病症的特征包括不正常的社交及沟通能力，通常在三岁的时候就能发现。

The Latin word autismus（the English translation is autism）was actually coined by the Swiss psychiatrist Eugen Blueler in 1910, as he was defining symptoms of schizophrenia.

说到 autism 这个词，它实际上是来自拉丁语的 autismus，而 autismus 最早是在1910年由一位瑞士的精神科医生在定义精神分裂症的时候提出的。在希腊语里，auto 是"自己""自我"的意思，这位医生把 auto 定义为病态的自恋，也就是说病人沉浸在自己的幻想世界中。

In terms of autism itself, it seems for a lot of Chinese people, all the impression they got is from this film *Hai Yang Tian Tang*. And in that film, this autistic adult already has really repetitive behavior and sometimes he's intolerant to any little change in the outside environment.

很多中国人对自闭症的印象都来自电影《海洋天堂》。片中，文章扮演的角色是一名自闭症患者，他有大量的重复动作，受不了外界环境的一丁点变化。

Autistic people in general are very difficult to get along with, mostly because they are prone to explosions, where something is not exactly how it should be or not exactly how they are used to and also you couple that with an inability for their brains to filter sensory input. So, for autistic people, especially more severe cases, you do see a lot of unwillingness to communicate in some ways, but also a tendency towards blow-ups or just losing control emotionally.

由于自闭症患者在分析外界信息方面具有一定的困难，所以经常会表现为重复某一种刻板的行为。而且当外部的环境突然改变时，他们可能会无法理解，由此发生情绪失控的情况。对自闭症比较严重的人来说，不愿意与人交流、情绪突然爆发的趋势尤为明显。

Right. It's important also to mention that autism exists on a spectrum. Actually the way it's referred to now is "autism spectrum disorder". You have very extreme cases on the one end and then very light cases on the other end. Just because someone is diagnosed with Asperger's or autism, doesn't necessarily mean that they're going to be impossible to help or impossible to get along with. Really, you have to look at it case by case.

自闭症是一种谱系障碍，也就是说它是一大类很多种发育障碍的统称。有程度非常严重的，也有程度相对比较轻的。有些患者经过治疗是可以比较好地融入社会的，所以千万不要一听到"自闭症"就认定对方很难相处。还是要具体情况具体分析。

点评

自闭症虽然不算罕见,但确实有很多人对其一无所知。这就是为什么有必要设立世界自闭症关注日(World Autism Awareness Day)的原因。很多中国观众通过《海洋天堂》这部电影对自闭症有了初步的认识,也说明流行文化(pop culture)在寓教于乐、普及知识这方面可以起到非常重要的作用。俗话说,知识就是力量(knowledge is power)。我们只有不断补充自己的知识体系,才能持续跟歧视(discrimination)和偏见(prejudice)做斗争。

词汇小百科

autism 自闭症

schizophrenia 精神分裂症

be prone to... 容易……的,有……趋势的

spectrum 波谱、光谱、范围、系列

Asperger's 阿斯伯格综合征,在分类上与自闭症同属于孤独症谱系障碍或广泛性发育障碍,区别在于此病没有明显的语言和智能障碍。

(刘 彦)

整形小知识

（素材来自《圆桌议事》2014年8月2日节目）

导　语：整形手术已经变得越来越常见，很多经济条件不错的中国人甚至会专门飞到国外去动刀。当然，整形手术是个非常宽泛的概念，有很多不同种类，不能一言以蔽之。

Plastic surgery is a medical specialty concerned with the correction or restoration of form and function of the human bodies. This can be cosmetic or aesthetic surgery, but it could also include non-elective medical surgery that is required, for example, severe burns or broken bones or things like that.

　　Plastic surgery是用来修复人体的外观和功能的手术，也就是整形手术。它可不光是美容类的手术，还包括从医疗角度出发必须要做的手术，如修复烧伤后的肌肤、修复断骨等。

In the term plastic surgery, plastic actually refers to sculpting or reshaping, which is derived from the Greek plastikē, which means the art of modeling of malleable flesh. So the actual surgical definition of "plastic" first appeared in 1839, which predates the modern use of plastic, which is substance made from petroleum. So in this sense, plastic surgery isn't talking about the material plastic. It's talking about how the human body is malleable and you can change how it looks.

我们一般都觉得 plastic 是塑料的意思，但其实它还有塑型、雕塑的意思。这种用法来源于希腊单词 plastikē，1839年第一次出现在英语里，比"塑料"还要早。所以，plastic surgery 里的 plastic 不是在说塑料这种物质，而是在说人类可以被塑型。

Treatments for the plastic repair of a broken nose are first mentioned in the Edwin Smith Papyrus, which is a transcription from an Ancient Egyptian medical text, dating to the Old Kingdom of ancient Egypt 3,000 to 2,500 BC. Reconstructive surgery techniques were also being carried out in India by around 800 BC. So we can see these types of techniques are actually very, very old.

据历史资料记载，早在公元前 3000 年到 2500 年期间，古埃及就已经有了重塑鼻子这样的整形手术。在公元前 800 年前后，整形手术在印度也已经非常普及。由此可见，整形手术历史悠久、源远流长。

And now we come to probably the most well-known aspect of plastic surgery and that is cosmetic surgery, sometimes called aesthetic surgery or perhaps even elective plastic surgery. So abdominoplasty or just "tummy tuck" which might be heard of is basically just reshaping and firming of the stomach area.

一种最广为人知的整形手术叫 cosmetic surgery，有时也叫 aesthetic surgery 或 elective plastic surgery，主要目的是美容。比如 abdominoplasty，也叫 tummy tuck，指的就是腹部整形术。

This is different from liposuction. Liposuction is literally just taking fat out of certain areas and sucking it out.

这跟我们通常所说的吸脂术还是不太一样的。吸脂术可以从字面上理解，就是把过多的脂肪从身体里吸出来的手术。

I think one of the types of surgery that many of our female listeners will probably be familiar with is the blepharoplasty or "eyelid surgery". And then there is the mammoplasty (or mammaplasty), which can include breast implants and breast reductions.

Blepharoplasty 也叫 eyelid surgery，就是割双眼皮的手术，很受女性朋友欢迎。Mammoplasty（或mammaplasty）包括隆胸和缩胸，显然也是在女性中更受欢迎。

点评

整形手术分不同的种类，没法一概而论。如果是因为 disabilities（先天残疾）或遭遇 accidents（事故）而毁容，为了更好地生活下去，当然要整容，无可厚非。

如果只是为了追求 appearance（外观）的某个标准而去整容，那就值得商榷了。

有一句话叫 beauty is only skin deep（外在的美貌是肤浅的），因为说到底，最重要的还是 inner beauty（内心美）。

当然，追求外在美也是每个人的权利，即使我们自己不做这样的手术，也不要对别人judgmental（妄加评判）。

词汇小百科

plastic surgery　整形手术
restoration　恢复
aesthetic　审美的，有美感的
malleable　可塑的，易改变的
transcription　抄本、誊写

abdominoplasty / tummy tuck　腹部整形术
liposuction　吸脂手术
blepharoplasty / eyelid surgery　割双眼皮手术
mammoplasty / mammaplasty　乳房成形术
breast implant　隆胸手术
breast reduction　缩胸手术

（刘　彦）

娱乐休闲
Leisure

"太长不看"英语怎么说？

（素材来自《圆桌议事》2015年4月18日节目）

导　语： 网络世界风起云涌，变幻莫测。几天不看就有一堆新词冒出来，让人摸不着头脑。在英语国家也是如此。尤其是当很多新词变成缩写后，就更让人蒙圈了。

The problem is, this specific abbreviation has become part of our lexicon and part of the words we use. Sometimes to everyone's frustration and annoyance, some people will just say LOL rather than actually laughing.

问题是这个特定的缩写已经成为我们语言和日常词汇中的一部分了。令人抓狂或生气的是，有时候一些人不用laughing大笑这个词或真的大笑出来，而是只说LOL，laugh out loud 的首字母缩写，就是"大声笑出来"的意思。

And there is JFGI. A little bit difficult to say. But it could be kind of fun to write it down when someone's really annoying you. A lot of this is coming from the idea of a website let me google that for you or LMGTFY.com. Let me Google that for you. So the idea being that someone comes to you and asks a question, it's a question they can answer themselves if they only go and search for the answer. So JFGI is just google it.

还有一个是JFGI，有点难说出口。当有人让你真生气的时候，把它写下来还挺好玩的。这个词来源于一个叫 LMGTFY.com 的网站，意思是"让我为你谷歌一下这个"。当有人过来问你一个问题，但这个问题明明是他们上网就能查到答案的，纯粹因为懒得搜索，想从你这里找快捷答案。是不是很讨厌？这个时候就可以用JFGI，表示"就（自己动手）谷歌一下吧"。

It's really interesting too that blog culture on the American Internet at least that re-appropriated this. What they've done is instead of saying this is the summary of an article, they say TL;DR and they give you the summary of the article.

美国互联网的博客文化还赋予 summary 新的用法。它们不直接说我给你看这篇文章的摘要，而是说"TL；DR"（too long; didn't read，意思是太长不看），然后再给你这篇文章的摘要。

Sometimes you may come across a link or an article or maybe some pictures that you think is quite interesting. And then you send it to your friend. And your friend opens the email or they open the link at work. Their boss walks by, they see what they're looking at. And maybe they get into trouble. Maybe they get fired. So next time, instead of just sending it to them, you can put in the subject line NSFW. Not safe for work.

有时候你可能看到一个你认为很有趣的链接、文章或图片，然后你会发给你的朋友。你的朋友在上班时间打开邮件或链接，正好被走过的老板看到（跟工作无关的不合适的内容）。也许这会给他们带来麻烦，或导致他们被炒鱿鱼。所以下次不要只是发给他们邮件或链接，你可以在主题那里写上 NSFW，Not safe for work，意思是"上班时候看不安全"。

点 评

在谈话或发信息时运用缩写让人感觉很潮，很时髦，因为有些缩写（abbreviations）已经 become part of our lexicon and part of the words we use 成为我们语言和日常词汇中的一部分了。但是凡事都不能过度，有时候缩写在不同的语境下会有不同的解读。不过，如果你是上班族，掌握NSFW还是很有必要的。虽然NSFW可以包括无伤大雅的、只是跟工作无关的东西，但一般说来还是指包含裸露、色情、暴力等元素的内容。

词汇小百科

abbreviation　缩写

LOL　表示 laugh out loud，大声地笑出来，多用在网络聊天中

YOLO　表示 You only live once，你只能活一次，该出手时就出手。但是很多西方人不喜欢这个词，认为这是孩子做坏事前的宣言。

TBH　意思是 to be honest，老实说。

IMHO　表示 in my humble opinion，依我愚见，恕我直言。这个词大有"区区在下不才，对这个问题是如此看的，阁下若有高见，尽请说来"的意思。

JFGI　意思是 Just freaking google it，就不能自己查一下吗？当别人问你一个很愚蠢的问题，你很不耐烦，不想回答时请用此句。要是用中文说的话应该就是"自己百度一下会shi吗？"

TL；DR　意思是 too long；didn't read，太长不看，注意这个缩写中的分号不能省略。NSFW表示 Not safe for work，意思是"上班时候看不安全"，就是不适合在工作场合看或读的影像和文字。这也是给收到这个信息的人一个提醒。是非常体贴的举动哦！

FOMO　意思是 fear of missing out，错过恐惧症，可以用来形容天天挂在网上刷新微博和朋友圈动态的社交控。

（王　玮）

去电影院能自带食物吗？

（素材来自《圆桌议事》2015年7月21日节目）

导　语：爆米花和可乐几乎是每家电影院必备的标配，有一些影院贴出告示：谢绝外带食品进入电影院，影院自售的才能带进去。这种条款是否合理？

Why did you pay a handsome price to go see a movie in this black room? That is to watch the movie. It is not for you to wine and dine there, okay? So I think there is a perfect reason why people should not be allowed to eat anything. That is my idea. I don't understand that when you go into the cinema, and get your coke and food there at a super expensive price. But I don't want to violate the rules. I am a very civilized audience. So in order to avoid that feeling of guiltiness that I actually brought food with me from the outside, I simply get prepared. I drink and eat beforehand and go in just feeling prepared to watch that movie.

　　为什么你要花很多钱去一个黑暗的房间里看电影呢？那肯定是为了看电影，而不是为了在那里吃吃喝喝，对吧？所以我觉得这是人们不应该在电影院吃任何东西的充分理由。这是我的观点。同时，我不能理解当你去电影院的时候，花那么多钱买吃的喝的，毕竟电影院里面卖的食物和饮料都比较贵。（也许你会说：那就自带食物和饮料啊？）但是我又不想违反规章制度。我是一个文明的观众。为了不让自己有愧疚感，我不会外带食物去电影院。我会提前吃完喝完，进影院就准备好好看电影了。

Interesting. For me it's all about choice. When I go to the cinema, I do want to have something to eat and drink during the film. But I don't want what they are selling and I don't want to pay the price that they are selling it for. I don't want to have a soft drink that has the equivalent of 20 spoonfuls of sugar in it. And I don't want to have the popcorn because that is too noisy as food. So I must confess that I do take my own food and drink to the cinema. I think it is a question of choice that they are not selling something I want to buy for a reasonable price. If they did sell something I wanted for a reasonable price, then I would be very happy to pay.

很有趣。对我来说这是个选择权的问题。我去电影院看电影时，确实想要一些食物和饮料。但是我不想要电影院里卖的那些东西，而且我觉得他们的定价也太高。我不想买一杯有20勺糖热量过剩的软饮，我也不想买吃起来会制造噪声的爆米花。所以我必须承认，我确实带着自己的食物和饮料进电影院。这说到底就是个选择权的问题，电影院一来没有我想要的东西，二来没有我能接受的价格。如果他们出售我想要的食品或饮料，价钱又合情合理，我会乐意购买的。

I think this is a question of violating the rules or not. Did you not see there was a sign saying "Food and drink from outside are forbidden as you enter our cinema"?

我认为这就是一个是否违反规定的问题。难道你没有看到标语说"禁止外带食物和饮料"吗？

And if it is a UK one, there was a court case about this actually, because the cinema tried to take someone to the court for taking the food in, and they were found there was no case. People could take their own food and drink into the cinema there. The cinema had no right to stop them. That was the ruling of the court.

在英国，以前倒是有过这么一个案例，电影院禁止观众自带食物和饮料，还将违反者告上法庭。结果呢，法庭是这么判的：观众可以自带食物和饮料，电影院无权阻止。

By the way, I think cinemas do have to make money from selling food and drinks. There is research showing that their major revenue is from food and drinks and these other products, not from box office sales.

顺便提一句，我觉得影院确实需要通过卖食物和饮料来赚钱。有调查显示，影院的主要收入来源正是食品、饮料和其他一些衍生产品，而不是电影的票房。

点评

做某事花了你一笔不小的钱，可以说 you pay a handsome price to do something。如果你被敲竹杠了，那就是 you are ripped off。

进影院自带食物算不算违反规定 violate the rule 呢？如果不自带，而是购买影院出售的爆米花和可乐 popcorn and coke，表面上不违规，但在影片播放过程中吃吃喝喝也会影响周围观众的观影体验 movie-going experience。所以，我们还是要努力做文明的观影者 Let's try to be civilized audiences.

词汇小百科

box   包厢
exit   出口
entrance   入口
gallery   顶层楼座
audience / viewers / spectators   观众
aisle   走道座位

full house   客满，满座

open-air theatre，amphitheatre   露天剧场

usher   男引座员

usherette   女引座员

row   排

ticket office   售票处

refreshments room   小吃部

lobby / foyer   休息室

evening show   夜场

sound effect   音响效果

（于　洋）

手机使用方式出卖你的年龄

（素材来自《圆桌议事》2015年6月30日节目）

导　语：除了电话短信这些基本功能，你的手机最常用来做什么？如果是上网浏览、导航、炒股——那么，大叔，你好！如果是听音乐、看电影以及玩游戏——嘿！小伙伴，一起玩儿咩？一项调查表明，尽管现在人们都难以离开手机，不同年龄段的使用者仍然表现出了不同的消费特征。今天让我们了解一下手机使用和年龄之间的联系。

Those born in the 1960s, they want to use it for navigating, so the GPS functions, taking photos and then browsing the online stock market. No wonder they are using the smartphone, because I cannot think of any other way the post-1960s are going to use them. And then for the younger generation, it's more about entertainment, including using them to play games.

那些60后用智能手机导航，即手机的GPS功能，他们还拍照片以及上网炒股。怪不得他们用智能手机，我想不到60后用智能手机做其他事情。至于年青的一代，他们主要使用娱乐功能，包括玩手机游戏。

You can't expect young people to be practical about things. Of course, it's the older people who's gonna be more practical. Oh, I'm going to take a picture of things, I'm going to look up important information online, I'm going to figure out where I'm going. While young people who practically live on their phones all the time, it's like OK, I'm checking this message, I'm watching this little thing, I'm playing a game, or trying to do all three of these, if not more, at the same time. That's not a surprising sort of thing.

你不能指望年轻人做事太实际,当然,年纪大一些的人会更实际。比如我要照张照片,我要在网上查重要信息,我要弄明白自己去哪里,等等。但是事实上年轻人一直生活在手机的世界里,就像我查个信息,我看个小视频,我玩个游戏,或者试着同时做这三件事。这并不稀奇。

But when you see the popularity and prevalence of the usage of WeChat and Weibo these days, maybe particular the WeChat, I suppose, social media APPs in general, I think the smartphone becomes the perfect gadget you use to get on those platforms. That's the only part that we see across-the-board similarity, I think.

但是当你看到现在微信和微博的流行和普及时,尤其是微信,总的来说就是社交媒体应用,智能手机成为你登上这些平台的最好装置。我认为这是唯一一个我们能看到不同受访者相同的地方。

It shows that it's the younger generation, those born after 1995, they tend to listen to music a lot more than other people age groups in the survey. And another interesting thing is across (the) board. Nobody really cares about the quality of music they hear as the sound quality. Maybe you're not listening a lot from a licensed source, you're not gonna get top-quality music anyway.

年轻的一代,即出生在1995年之后的那些人,他们比调查中的其他年龄组倾向于听音乐。另一件有趣的事是不分界限的。没人真的在乎他们听的音乐的质量。也许你从一个没有得到许可的来源听了很多音乐,你是不会在那里听到高质量音乐的。

It seems like younger people are not only doing that, they are more willing to purchase new phones too. I suppose they are not as practical as older people. I'm not older, but I tend to agree with the older ones in this sense. I think it's most important to be rational about these things and not spend too much money on this for show.

似乎年轻人不止做这个,他们还更乐于买新手机。我觉得他们不像年纪大的人一样实际。我年纪不大,但是我在这件事上更倾向于赞同年长的人。我认为最重要的是在这些事情上要有理智,不要为了炫耀而花太多钱。

点 评

年轻人和年长的人在手机使用方面有什么区别呢?

年长的人更实际(practical),他们主要是用手机的 GPS 功能导航(navigate)、拍照片(take a picture)、看股市(browse the stock market online)、上网查重要信息(look up important information online),look up 查找,I looked up your address in the personnel file 我在人事档案里找到了你的地址。

而年轻人的使用更娱乐化(entertainment),如看视频(watch a video)、听音乐(listen to the music)或玩游戏(play a game),有时候甚至同时干这三件事,年轻人可是一直生活在手机上的一群人(live on their phones all the time)哦!

但不同年龄段的人也有相似之处,就是他们都喜欢用微博微信这样的社交媒体应用(social media APPs)。

词汇小百科

smartphone　智能手机

tablet　平板电脑

earphone　耳机

gadget　小玩意儿、小配件、小装置

mobile device　移动设备

smart device　智能设备

electronic device　电子设备

wearable device　可穿戴设备

（王　玮）

手机使用方式出卖你的年龄

真正的表情帝是谁？

（素材来自《圆桌议事》2016年1月4日节目）

导　语：根据公开的数据，2015年，超过八成的微信用户通过使用表情来表达自己的态度。既有的表情符号已经影响了当代人的表达方式。中国人的表情符号和表情包有什么区别？最受欢迎的微信表情到底是什么类型的？

But I think the problem now is not the extent that they are being used, in terms of the number of people, it's more about the style of how they are being used, which I think is causing the problem. When you use emojis, it's meant to be used to highlight a mood…The problem is you have a lot of people which are now using emojis to replace text completely. So they'll just send pictures as responses and not actually use any cognitive thought and actually write a sentence. A lot of people find it quite frustrating. I think it shows a large scale of laziness. What's with that face? Is it something you do?

但我觉得问题并不在于表情符号的使用程度，或者说使用人数，问题在于使用方式。当你使用表情符号的时候，原本可以强调某种感情，但现在有很多人用表情符号彻底地代替了文字表述。他们会发一些图作为回应，不使用任何认知思维，不写一句话。很多人对此感到沮丧。我认为这体现了一种大规模的懒惰行为。为什么你是这个表情？你是不是也这么做？

If you look at the conversations, especially the ones that are reported in China, I think the extent of emojis, it's not just emojis, some of them are clarified as a meme which is basically a picture with some text. They are being used now instead of writing in general.

如果你看一下这些人的对话，尤其是在中国被报道的这些，你会发现，表情符号的使用范围——其实不只是表情符号，有一些看着是一幅图片上面写着字，那应该被称为表情包——它们被广泛应用，很多时候代替了书写文字。

See, there are so many things that are being read out of it. These days if you don't know what an emoji means or the interpretation of it could be, how can you even sustain your relationships? So much is going on online.

看看吧，有那么多层的含义都被解读出来了。现在，如果你看不懂表情符号或是它所代表的引申含义，那你怎么维持你的各种人际关系？毕竟那么多交流都发生在网上。

When emojis are too frequently used, sometimes people tend to be a little bit vain and pretentious.

当表情符号被用得太频繁时，人们难免显得有点苍白和虚伪。

I'm actually genuinely quite speechless. I think that's the problem and I'm going to persist on my point of view here. If we are getting to a point that we feel we can't express a certain emotion with words, then this may sound a bit firm and harsh, maybe we need to improve our abilities to articulate ourselves. We should always be able to express ourselves in our mother tongue. That's why people take pride in being, for lack of a better word, well spoken.

我真的有些无话可说。我认为这是问题，我也会继续坚持我的观点。如果我们到了这个时候，感觉有些情感竟然无法用语言表达——我要说的可能听起来有些刺耳和严厉——那我们也许应该提高我们的表达能力了。无论何时我们都应该有能力用母语表达自己的想法。这同样是人们对谈吐文雅感到骄傲的原因。

But it's not just about you expressing yourself, because when it's communication, it's a two-way street. And sometimes the other end is not expecting a big paragraph.

但这并不只是你想表达自己真实感受的问题。因为这是交流，需要双方的沟通。有时，你的交流对象并不想看到长篇大论。

This is not a Chinese phenomenon at all. When you look at Dictionary's Word of the Year of 2015, it's not any word, it's the smiley face with the tears.

这并不是一个只发生在中国的现象。看一下 2015 年 Dictionary.com 评选的年度词汇，你会发现它竟然不是一个真正的单词，而是一个"笑中带泪"的表情符号（也就是我们常说的"笑 cry"表情）。

I think you have got the best of the two worlds. On the one hand, you are old-fashioned in the sense that you still appreciate being able to articulate every single shred of your emotion, and that's not something that everyone can do these days. On the other hand, you've sent me emojis occasionaly so you are not completely left behind.

我觉得你找到了两全其美的方法。一方面，可以说你有点守旧，你看你这么在意要把每一丝感情都用语言表达出来，而在如今这个年代，这并不是每个人都能做得到的；另一方面，你给我发过表情符号，说明你并没有被时代甩在后面。

点 评

People take pride in... 人们以……为傲。I take pride in being a working professional. 我为自己的专业工作人员身份感到骄傲。

For lack of a better word 找不到更好的词形容某状况。一般会有两种情况，一是词汇有限并没有更合适的表达，二是将说的话有些不妥。Greed, for lack of a better word, is good. 贪婪，其实，是有益的。

Get the best of both worlds 两全其美。I tried to get the best of both worlds, but somehow I just can't fool myself. 我试图找到两全其美的做法，但到头来还是发现没法自欺欺人。

词汇小百科

emoji　表情符号

kaomoji　颜文字

meme　表情包、文化基因

sticker　原来是贴纸的意思，也指特定的聊天工具里带有的贴画

GIF　动图，可交换的图像文件格式

（赫　扬）

现代人离不开自拍？

（素材来自《圆桌议事》2015年12月16日节目）

导　语：随着带有拍照功能的智能手机的普及，自拍也让很多人欲罢不能。有精神科专家研究称，爱自拍是一种病。更有重度"患者"称自拍"根本停不下来，已经放弃治疗"。你的"自拍病"到哪个阶段了？

US Photographer website published a report on web users' photo searching behaviors in 2015, which shows that the word selfie was searched more than 20 times than last year. So this is not a reason to be all that surprised since the word selfie was included in the Oxford Internet Dictionary in 2013, but my query is, how self-obsessed are we that we are still doing this and it is a trend that is growing and wouldn't stop?

美国"摄影家"网站公布了一项 2015 年度针对网民照片搜索行为的调查报告。报告发现"自拍"一词的搜索量比前一年高出 20 多倍。人们爱自拍并不是让人惊讶的事，毕竟 2013 年"自拍"就已经被收入牛津网络词典了。但我的问题是：我们一直沉迷于自拍，而且热潮愈演愈烈，并没有丝毫停止的迹象。我们究竟有多自恋？

It's kind of catchy and this recurrence of, *ZiPai*, *ZiPai* of everything, and yeah, she says like wherever she is, the first thing she does whenever she is in the crowd or just everywhere it has to be selfie, selfie, selfie time, so what do you think is going on? What does it tell about today's modern China?

（这首歌）朗朗上口，还有"自拍"不断被重复。是的。她在唱，不管到任何地方她都先自拍一下。你觉得这是怎么回事儿？这反映了现代中国的什么问题？

I have to admit something that's a little bit embarrassing, but I am part of a WeChat group with some of my friends, and the whole WeChat group is devoted to taking selfies.

我得承认一件有点让人不好意思的事。我和一些朋友加入了一个微信群。这个群就是一个自拍群。

So all of us are living in different parts of the world, some of them are in San Francisco, some of them are in the UK, some of them are here in China, but the thing that connects us, some of them I have not even met, but we all sent selfies of wherever we are, so we're kind of like checking in via selfies, I've got to say it's super fun.

我们处在全球的不同地方，有的人在旧金山，有的人在英国，有的人在中国。但连接我们的是自拍。不夸张地说，有的人我甚至没有见过面，但不管我们去了什么地方，都会分享自拍照片。我们就像用自拍来打卡，真的很好玩儿。

Right, it's actually a global network of sharing selfies.

是的，这就像一个全球范围的自拍分享网络。

Yeah, it's super fun with people I've never even met with. We just like sharing selfies with each other, but we do also share information, any new stories that are about selfies.（Laugh）But somebody recently shared an article in this group, where they are talking about using selfies as a security method. I don't remember what it was for, maybe for ordering something or for paying tickets or something like that, but basically you register for whatever it is, and then you take a selfie to show that it is you, and then submit that, and that they give you the thing that you ordered, so it is sort of like, now it's a security measure.

是啊，和这些甚至我没有见过面的人分享，真的特别好玩。我只是喜欢分享自拍照片，以及分享与自拍相关的种种故事。（笑）最近有人在群里分享了一篇关于用自拍照片作为一种安全措施的文章。我不记得具体目的是什么了，好像是为了订购什么东西，还是买票之类的用途。基本上就是你为了某种目的进行注册，拍一张自拍照以证明注册者是你本人，然后上传照片，对方就会给你预订的物品。你看这不就是一种安保措施吗？

What is really interesting is that because of the popularity, new derivatives are coming from that, such as the selfie stick. Now it is everywhere.

我认为真正有趣的一点在于，由于自拍的流行，新的衍生品由此产生，例如自拍杆。它现在已经无处不在。

It's not about the wider shot, I mean, wherever you go, if you are single on your own, on a business trip, or whatever. For example, when I visited Macau, standing in front of the St. Paul's Cathedral there and I was alone, the only thing I can do is to take a selfie with my selfie stick, otherwise I have to ask someone else for help.

这不是为了拍广角的照片。不论你去哪里，有时难免会碰到一个人的情形，比如你一个人出差。就拿我去澳门出差的例子来说，在大三巴牌坊前我只能拿出自拍杆来自拍，要不然我必须向别人寻求帮助（而因为我当时正在工作，没那个时间）。

You are missing out on a romantic opportunity by taking all these selfies.

因为自拍，你失去了一个结识他人的浪漫机会。

I think so, and because by doing that, you are cutting down the chances of being able to communicate with other people, meeting new people and all that kind of thing.

我同意。因为自拍，你削减了和他人交流和认识的机会。

So I think selfies can only happen in this day and age with the level of technology we have, and the level of narcissism we have here.

所以我认为自拍的盛行只有可能出现在如今这个技术高度发达、自恋程度也令人惊讶的年代。

It's a good challenge because it is like you have this criteria and you try to make different kinds of selfies, maybe a mirror selfie, or like a reflection selfie, or like a behind selfie, you know, you try to find the most creative way to do it.

这是个巨大的挑战，因为我们都有一个（自拍的）标准，我们还想拍出不一样的自拍照片。比如镜像自拍，反射自拍，后方自拍，或者你就是想找到最有创意的自拍方式。

So it's not just about conforming yourself into the kind of beauty that everybody else agrees with.

这么说（自拍）不是为了把自己拍成符合别人认可的审美标准。

That's not pure narcissism.

不是赤裸裸的自恋。

点 评

人类作为群体性社会动物，都有分享和交流的欲望。过去生活节奏慢，物理距离远，人们的交流方式也相对缓慢。而现代快节奏的生活改变了我们沟通的方式。随着网络和智能手机的普及，自拍和社交媒体也应运而生。

每个人都可以把自己的照片贴到网上，通过受到关注和肯定，满足"被看"的心理需求。每个默默无闻的"我"都能展示自己，成为虚拟世界里具有一定名气的"腕儿"，或多或少产生满足感。或者看到别人晒自拍照，也想主动尝试自拍。每个人本能的"窥视欲"也会使这种具有私密性质的自拍照更能受到关注。这多重的心理需求，让自拍成为一种习惯，或者说"一种病"。

自拍发得太多也有可能造成朋友的困扰，于是就有了下面这句话：A selfie a day keeps the friends away. 一天一张自拍照，朋友们不再搭理你啦。（这句话改编自养生名言：An apple a day keeps the doctor away. 一天一个苹果，不用看医生啦。）

Selfie自拍是一种 self-portrait photograph 字面翻译为自我肖像式的照片，其实就是自己拍摄自己的人像照片。

I have to admit something... 我必须得承认…… 这个表达方式往往预示着你对下面要说的事情带着一点点的罪恶感。例如原文中Amy表达的是自己有点不好意思参加了一个自拍微信群。例句：I have to admit that I thought you were pretty annoying when I first met you. 翻译：我必须承认咱们刚认识的时候我觉得你挺烦人的。言下之意是现在觉得你挺好相处的。相似的用法还有I have to say / confess，都是我必须承认的意思。

Devote 是把……奉献给，把……专用于的意思。The group is devoted to taking selfies. 这个群就是发自拍用的；Considerable resources have been devoted to bringing him to court. 为了让他接受审判，已投入了相当多的资源。

词汇小百科

selfie   自拍
belfie   即 a butt selfie，臀部的自拍
welfie   即 workout selfie，运动中拍的自拍

（赫　扬）

朋友圈测试为何这么火?

（素材来自《圆桌议事》2016年7月22日节目）

导　语：微信朋友圈里各种主题测试很容易刷屏，尤其是那些关于个人性格分析、个人运势预言的测试都很火。大家参加这样的测试是为了乐趣，但有没有注意到其中的风险呢？

The latest fad on WeChat Moments or friend circle is this: once you've entered your name and birthday, various tags of your personality traits such as "optimist" "sensitive", and "self-healer" will be put into one picture summary. Of course, in order to see this summary, you'll have to forward it to your friend circle.

微信朋友圈流行的最新玩法是：输入你的名字和生日，然后各式各样的性格标签，比如"乐观主义者""敏感的""自愈者"等就会出现在一张图上。当然，为了看到这张图，你首先要在朋友圈里分享测试结果。

Oh, let me hear some good things, I have this great trait here, my personality is like this, all these kinds of things. Whenever you take these tests, they are not gonna say, oh, you are actually really obnoxious. But they are gonna say almost only good things. So you wanna hear that sort of thing, and there is a desire to be categorized, I suppose like "Oh, I am a this or my spirit animal is that"…These things that people are interested in even though there is no real basis of it.

让我听到些好的描述吧，比如我有这个优点，我的个性像什么什么。你做这些测试的时候，系统不会告诉你你是个让人讨厌的人，系统只会说好听的话。你就是喜欢听这种话，希望被分类，就好比"原来我是什么什么"或者"我的精神动物是什么什么"，人们总是喜欢这些没有真实依据的事。

I think for most people, especially in our generation, if it doesn't happen online, if it doesn't come out online, it's like it didn't happen. What's the point of taking this personality test if you cannot show it to anyone? Obviously, sharing it, publicizing it to the whole world or their friends circle or whatever, is a major part of the point.

对我们这一代的大多数人来说，如果事情不是发生在网络上的，我们就当它没有发生。如果不能分享性格测试结果，那做这个测试干吗用呢？很明显，大家都想分享结果，公开在朋友圈里，这是很重要的一点。

And that's how these online businesses... I think they captured minds in that way, they know it so well. And that's how a gimmick, like this or a campaign like this has been designed. And I don't think this is gonna be the last time that we see this kind of fad. These days, every other week, I think, there is gonna be something, a new design of such nature that people will sort of participate in and it is the popular thing at the moment. In just in a couple of days' time, people forget about it.

那些线上的生意就是这样获取信息的，他们深谙于此。把戏也是这么设计的，这不会是我们最后一次看到这种风尚。游戏总有新的，人们还是会参与，几天之内还是会流行，之后就被忘了。

点评

有一代人是看书长大的，有一代人是看电视长大的，还有一代人是上网长大的。I think for most people in our generation, if it doesn't happen online, if it doesn't come out online, it's like it didn't happen. 这一代的年轻人，相当一部分认为：不在线的事情，都不叫事情。

移动端的、朋友圈的游戏自然也受到了欢迎。做性格测试时，一些常出现的、形容人的性格的词包括： optimistic 乐观的，sensitive 敏感的，confident 自信的，easygoing 随和的、好相处的，determined 坚定的，cowardly 怯懦胆小的，kind-hearted 好心肠的，reliable 可靠的，hardworking 勤劳的、努力的。

微信朋友圈的那些说法：微信 WeChat，朋友圈 moments（官方名称）或者 friends circle（意译），发送至朋友圈 forward it to moments 或者 share it in moments。

词汇小百科

fad　一时的流行、风尚

gimmick　诡计、花招

obnoxious　讨厌的，引人厌恶的

（陈　沫）

世界杯

(素材来自《圆桌议事》2014年6月14日节目)

导　语：足球是全球第一大运动，每四年一次的世界杯自然是万众瞩目的焦点。我们来学习一下跟足球相关的常见概念，以确保自己在世界杯期间跟别人有话聊，不至于太落伍。

The first word we are gonna look at today is hat-trick. So a hat-trick is used quite often in football to describe one player who scored a goal three times.

先来看看帽子戏法。帽子戏法在足球比赛中较为常见，指的是在一场球赛中，一名队员三次将球踢进对方球门的壮举。

What is so interesting is that according to the Extended Oxford English Dictionary from 1999, the term actually came into use after a cricket player took three wickets in three balls. So what happened was—a collection was held for him, and that money was used to buy him a hat.

原来帽子戏法源自板球比赛，当时有一名选手连续三次得到了wicket（三次击中门柱而得分），后来得到了一顶帽子作为奖励。所以"帽子戏法"就引申出了"连中三元"的意思。

The next word we are looking at is round-robin, sometimes called an all–play–all tournament, in which competition each contestant meets all other contestants in turn. So this is obviously very different from an elimination tournament, where if you lose, you are out. In round-robin, it doesn't matter if you win, lose or tie, you are going to face each and every opponent.

  Round-robin 是循环赛的意思，在这种赛制中，每支队都能和其他的队至少比赛一次，这个跟淘汰赛是有明显区别的。循环赛也称 all-play-all tournament，也就是说不管成绩是输是赢还是平局，都要跟所有对手至少踢一场。

While you are watching the game, you are probably going to come across different types of kicks. First, let's take a look at place kick. A place kick is a corner kick, a free kick, a goal kick, a kickoff or perhaps even a penalty kick.

  Place kick 是定位球，既可以指角球，也可以指任意球、球门球、开球，甚至是罚球。

And so a direct free kick is a method of restarting play following a foul. Unlike indirect free kick which we will talk about in a minute, a goal may be scored directly against the opposing side without the ball having first touched another player.

  任意球也分两种，一种是直接任意球，另一种是间接任意球。如果是前者，队员可以将球直接射入犯规球队的球门；如果是后者，球在进门之前必须被其他的队员触及才可以。

Right. So a corner kick happens when the attacking team leaves the field of play by crossing the goal line without the goal having been scored, and also it was last touched by the defending player.

  角球的判罚则是在防守队员将球踢出底线后做出的。

The last word that I want to look at is offside, the way it usually works out is that an attacking player is behind the last defending player and then he receives the ball that is usually considered to be offside.

当进攻队员在对方半场并且站的位置处于所有对方防守队员的前面，同时他接到了队友的传球，这种情况就会被称为越位。

点评

足球虽然受欢迎，但要真正看懂足球，尤其是掌握那些常见的概念，还是颇有难度的。

如果记不住定位球、任意球、越位等技术含量较高的术语（jargon），至少要记住帽子戏法（hat-trick）、循环赛制（round-robin）和淘汰赛制（elimination），因为这些概念都跳出了足球乃至运动的范围，在日常对话中大有用武之地。

词汇小百科

hat-trick   帽子戏法

goal   射门得分

cricket   板球

wicket   板球比赛中的三柱门

round-robin   循环赛

all-play-all tournament   循环赛

elimination tournament   淘汰赛

place kick   定位球

corner kick　角球
free kick　任意球
goal kick　球门球
kickoff　开球
penalty kick　罚球，点球
direct / indirect free kick　直接 / 间接任意球
offside　越位

（刘　彦）

行为心理
Temperament

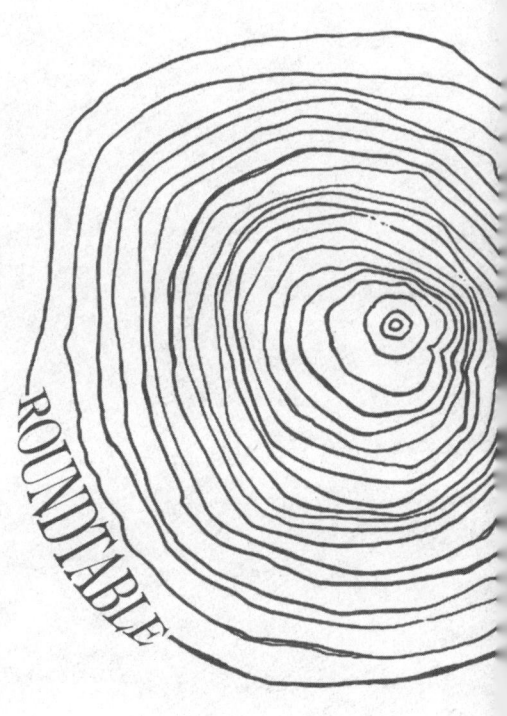

哪些事会让人显得很掉价？

（素材来自《圆桌议事》2015年7月22日节目）

> **导　语**：知名微博博主"同道大叔"发布了两篇文章，历数那些让人显得很掉价的行为，引起网友的热烈讨论。他都列举了哪些行为？你同意他的观点吗？

Number one is beating up your girlfriend. That is not acceptable whatsoever. I think that's definitely the bottom line there. And I think also speaking ill of this girl who's refused to go out with the guy or speaking ill of a girl that has gone out with you, these are pretty bad things from these guys.

一种让男生掉价的行为就是动手打女朋友，无论在什么情况下这都是不能接受的。我认为这绝对是底线。还有就是，某些男生追求女生遭到拒绝后，转身就说人家坏话；或是女生和你出去了，相处得不那么愉快，于是你在背后说人家坏话。这些都是很低俗的行为。

Talking about details of your romantic life to your friends… That's going to upset your girlfriend if you start doing that kind of thing. Being stingy is on the list as well. I mean there's a difference between being careful with your money and being stingy. Eventually, there comes a time when yes, you do have to pay for things, but it's no good expecting to sponge off other people all your life. But being careful with your money is another issue.

把你和女朋友相处的具体细节告诉你的朋友……这会让你的女朋友不安。此外，吝啬小气也被列在单子上。我认为"小心看好自己的钱"跟"为人吝啬"是有区别的。生活中不能总是期盼揩别人的油，有时终归还是得自己埋单。小气和谨慎处理自己的钱是两码事。

Do you know there's one thing on the list that I strongly disagree with, which is number six. It says, "Posting selfie photos, showing your body even though you don't have a good figure. This makes others feel disgusted. If you have nothing good enough to show, then don't show it at all. It will only make people feel sick." This is so biased. I think it's very mean to start saying that unless you conform to somebody else's idea of what's attractive, then you shouldn't be allowed to put up selfies of yourself.

你们知道吗？单子上的第六条我强烈不同意。这条是这么说的："没有好身材还天天发自拍出来秀，真让人受不了。如果没有好的东西可秀，就不要出来丢人现眼，否则只会让人觉得恶心。"这也太有偏见了。难道只有你符合别人的审美，才能发自拍照吗？我认为这种想法是非常狭隘的。

I admire your confidence in saying that you should be proud of that part, and yes, I think we shouldn't be judgmental. That should be my slogan on the show: don't be judgmental. And, when it comes to body form, yes, you shouldn't judge people or judge a book by its cover.

我欣赏你的自信，说应该为自己感到骄傲。的确，我们不应该对他人评头论足，这应该成为我在节目中的口号：不要评头论足。特别是说到人的体形、外表时，不应该妄下评论。英语里也有句老话，叫"不要单凭封面就判定一本书的好坏"。

And also, I think the one that I honestly cannot agree with as a behavior from the ladies is, "praising your ex-boyfriends". I think what essentially it's aiming at is those girls that only can see their self-worth by what kind of guys they end up with or date. And if you're with a rich guy, does that make you better? I think that kind of value system is just not good for you, and I think you should be finding your self-worth and your own values independently. And I think it's what you create for yourself that is most important, and it shouldn't be because of some guys that you date.

这个单子上的其中一条说女生"赞美前男友"的行为很掉价，这我实在不能认同。我觉得这一条实际上是针对那些以和哪种男生交往来衡量自我价值的女生。如果你现在和一个富家子弟在一起，难道你就更好了？我觉得这种价值观不好，女生应该独立寻找自我价值。你为自己创造了什么才是最重要的，而不是看你跟什么样的男生交往。

And another one that I can agree with is treating other guys as backups even if you don't like them at all. Guys sometimes can be guilty of that as well.

另一条说的是女生明明不喜欢某些追求自己的男生，还把人家当备胎。这一点我也赞同，确实是很掉价的行为。有时候男生们也会这么做，彼此彼此。

点评

Beat someone up 殴打某人；speak ill of somebody，说某人坏话。无论你有什么理由，这样对待另一半都越过了底线 bottom line。

Stingy 用来形容人小气、抠门、吝啬，中文有句俗语叫"铁公鸡"，就是 stingy person 的写照，一毛不拔。

Sponge off someone 表示"依赖于某人，寄生于某人"。Sponge 的本义是海绵，像海绵那样吸啊吸的，是不是很形象？无关性别，自己不努力，指望对方养活自己，都是极 low 的。

此外，我们不应该以貌取人，正如我们不能单凭封面就判定一本书的好坏（judge a book by its cover），因为那样也是很不公平、很掉价的行为。

　　Backup 备份，备胎。可以把它拆成动词词组 back up，意为"支持、援助"。不喜欢别人还把他们拿来当备胎，真的很自私。碰到这种人，judgmental 一下也无妨：太 low 了！

◆ 词汇小百科 ◆

　　judgmental　品头论足的
　　biased　有偏见的
　　ex-boyfriend　前男友
　　conform to　符合、遵照

（于　洋）

"鸭梨山大"怎么表达?

(素材来自《圆桌议事》2015年7月26日节目)

导　语：使用生动形象且灵活的语言可以让其他人更容易理解你当前的情绪和所处的状态，从而达到释放情绪的效果。别忘了，即使"鸭梨山大"，也要试着松一口气哦。

Yes, that's how you say that you're concerned or bothered about something. Those are two other words that can just be substituted for "worried" in that kind of sentence: bothered or concerned. And of course, when you are worried about something, it's a kind of fear. Isn't it, really? And that is reflected in another one of these phrases: "I'm afraid that I'm going to fail the exam or something". Or you can say, "I'm scared to death that I might fail the exam."

如果你感到担心或烦恼，可以说 worried about something。除了 worried，也可以用 concerned 和 bothered 这两个词。当然，当你担心某件事情时，这其实是种害怕的情绪，不是吗？所以你也可以说"我害怕这次考试会不及格"或者"一想到我考试有可能不及格，我就害怕死了"。

Another one is, they have some quite negative connotations. All of these do I think really, don't they? And another one is, again, negative: "I can't help thinking" and then you can say "that something bad is about to happen."

其实这些表达都有十分消极的含义，所以大多使用否定句式，还有一种表达——这种表达会以"我忍不住想"开头，后面接着说"有什么不好的事情马上就要发生了"。

If you can't stop thinking about something, that means that you think about it not only during the day but at night. And, that brings us to our next phrase: "it's been keeping me awake" or "I've been up all night with worry."

如果你一直想着某件事，说明你白天和晚上都在惦记。那么你也可以说"因为这件事，我一直睡不着觉"或者"我整晚都在担心着这件事"。

How do you link this "keeping me awake" phrase with the thing that you're worried about? You can say "I've been so worried about my work assessment tomorrow that it's been keeping me awake all night."

怎么把"我一直睡不着"和担心某事结合起来呢，你可以说"我非常担心明天的工作评估，以至于整晚都睡不着"。

Shall we do the opposite now, the relief when you've discovered that the thing that you were worried about isn't going to happen?

好的，我们现在来看看相反的情形。当你发现你一直担心的事情并不会发生，可以松一口气了，该怎么表达？

One of the most popular ones is, I don't think really anyone ever says it actually, but you see it written a lot in comics: "phew". It's more of what's called an onomatopoeic word. This is a word that sounds like the thing it's describing. Because when you say "phew", you exhale a big breath. And that is one of the things that people do when they are relieved about something.

有一个很流行的词，phew。其实人们并不怎么说这个词，但它经常以文字的形式出现在漫画里。它听起来就像是你呼出长长一口气时发的声音。而人们对某件事放心之后也确实经常长舒一口气。

There's another one. When people are relieved, they say "That's a huge weight off my mind." It's as though there is a big weight, something really heavy on your head pressing down on your thoughts and making you worried. But then when the bad thing doesn't happen, you say "that's a weight off my mind". In American English, they tend to say, "that's a load off my mind". And you'll hear these phrases a lot in songs as well. So that's what they mean when they say that.

当人们表达松一口气时也可以用另外一种说法"心里的石头终于落地了"。这就好比一个分量很重的担子一直在你脑海里压迫着你，让你感觉很担忧，但是当不好的事情没发生时，你就会舒一口气，来一句"心里的石头终于落地了"。

英式英语多用 a weight off my mind，美式英语多用 a load off my mind。这些说法在歌词里也很常见，就是松一口气的意思。

点 评

担心和害怕按不同的程度分，轻一点的可以说 I'm afraid that something will happen；严重的可以说 I'm scared to death about something；用否定句式来表达担忧也可以，I can't help thinking... 我忍不住会这样想，某事要发生。

当一件事情让你担心得觉都睡不着的时候，你可以说 It's been keeping me awake.

如果真的到了那种程度，肯定有损健康。所以还是相信那句老话吧：Relax, take it easy! 放轻松，看淡些，结果反而往往是好的，最终可以让你松一口气 feel relieved。

下次你也试试？

词汇小百科

worried 担心的

concerned 关心的、担忧的

bothered 烦恼的

negative connotations 消极含义

phew 唷,表示松一口气

exhale 呼出

nomatopoeic 拟声的

（于 洋）

洗澡细节暴露真实的你

（素材来自《圆桌议事》2015年10月13日节目）

> **导　语**：洗个热水澡可能是我们一天中最放松和私密的时刻。你最真实的自己也有可能在这个时候表现出来哦。和圆桌主持人们一起来看看吧！

What I definitely would do when I go into a shower is singing in the shower. It is the best thing, I mean, you go into the shower, and you are in a closed environment. It's just you, the shower and the shampoo bottle, and that becomes my microphone. That also becomes my Oscar Academy Award in my hand, and I've practiced it many times. "Thank you so much. I thank the team. I thank the crew. I thank all of those who have helped me, and most of all, I need to thank my parents. If they didn't help me and raise me up, how could I have gotten this award of best actress？"

我会在洗澡的时候高歌一曲。非常开心愉悦！你走进淋浴间这样一个封闭的场所。只有你、莲蓬头和洗发水瓶。洗发水瓶就成了我的麦克风，它还成了我手中的奥斯卡金像奖奖杯。我已经练习过（得奖感言）很多次啦："非常感谢。我要感谢我的团队和工作人员。我要感谢所有帮助过我的人。最重要的是，我的父母。如果你们没把我带到这个世上，帮助我一路走来，我怎么可能得到最佳女演员的奖项？"

But the one thing that I can confess is that I was always tempted to shave in the bath, just to save time. But I never did it, because of the reactions you just gave us, horror. Then when I was watching a 《007》 movie, James Bond movie, he would shave in the bath. After that, I thought it's all right then. What's your confession?

我可以承认一件事,那就是我一直有在浴缸里刮胡子的想法。这样比较省时间。但我没有这么做,因为我不想看到你刚才给出的那种反应——恐怖。后来我看到《007》电影中詹姆斯·邦德也会在浴缸里刮胡子。于是我想,那没问题了(我也可以这么做)。你有什么要供认的吗?

Let me just try to clarify who are the people that brush their teeth in the shower. So it's a person who will take full advantage of the multi-tasking brain. And those who like to sing, you are a confident individual who doesn't overly worry about what other people think. This will help you to go far in life. Okay, some nice words I picked up for myself and those who are in my breed.

我来说说什么样的人会在洗澡的时候刷牙。他们显然是可以同时承担多种任务并好好利用这种能力的人。而那些会在洗澡时唱歌的,是自信满满、不过度担心他人看法的人。这会让你的人生走得更远。好吧,这是我为自己和那些跟我一样的人挑选的赞美之辞。

There is a whole bunch of other types of things people do in the shower. And I have to proudly announce that it's not just singing in the shower that I do, there is also taking a long, luxurious bath. That is something I enjoy immensely too. You are showing the world there is no need to be stressed out. Then if you are in times of stress or drama, you know you can prefer letting things go and enjoy life's simple pleasures instead.

洗澡时还有其他类型的事可以做。我已经自豪地宣称我洗澡的时候会唱歌,还有就是泡澡。这个澡时间要长,泡的物质要丰富。这也是我特别享受的。泡澡就等于在向世界宣告：放轻松，没有必要太紧绷。如果感到生活中充满了压力和戏剧冲突，你会选择放手，把精力放在那些最简单的、让人愉悦的事物上。

点评

Take advantage of 有占便宜，也有利用的意思，是日常对话中常用的说法。make good use of 也是利用的意思。Let me take full advantage of / make good use of my time in school. 我得好好利用在学校的时间。

breed 有种类、血统的意思。Those in my breed 指的是我辈中人，和我一样的人。People like me. Birds of a feather flock together. 这都是类似说法。

词汇小百科

shower　淋浴
bath　泡澡
showerhead　莲蓬头
bath tub　浴缸
milk bath　牛奶浴
olive oil bath　橄榄油浴
lavender bath　薰衣草浴

（赫　扬）

关闭手机"失联18小时"会怎样？

（素材来自《圆桌议事》2015年6月3日节目）

导　语：200名大学生参加"关掉手机，挑战'失联'18小时"心理挑战。超半数人离开手机会有一定焦虑情绪，并有部分人使用了iPad等其他电子产品。对手机强烈的、持续的需求感和依赖感已经严重影响到人与人之间的交往。在本篇里，我们聊聊手机依赖症的那些事。

I think what's the really annoying part or also the addiction part is all these super functions that smart phones have that make you glue to it, that I think it evolved into an evil machine that controls you.

　　但是我认为真正恼人的部分或上瘾的部分是智能手机拥有的那些超级功能，这些功能让你无法离开手机，把手机进化成为一部邪恶的机器来控制你。

Let's have a look at some of the reactions from the participants. One unnamed student said he couldn't stand the experience. He said he felt very uneasy the whole way through, as if he's lost something very important. And he even yelled at his roommate who was trying to calm him down.

　　让我们来看看一些参与者的反应。一个匿名的学生说他忍受不了这种体验，他一直感觉心神不宁，好像丢了什么重要的东西。他甚至向试图让他冷静下来的室友大吼。

That is exactly why one of my friends, I think I told you guys on the show before, that we had a no-smartphone dinner party. So when we entered the restaurants, one of my friends confiscated everybody's phone, and we had to talk to each other. It was totally terrifying, but after the initial stage, you find people are actually boring and interesting at the same time, and it's nice to know people. And you know just be brave. I think that's the first step you need to take.

这就是为什么我的一个朋友,我记得在以前的节目中告诉过你们,我们参加了一个无手机晚餐聚会。当我们进入餐厅时,我的一个朋友收走了每个人的手机,于是大家不得不面对面聊天。这很可怕,但是在过了最初的阶段后,你会发现人们既无聊又有趣,了解一下挺好的。只要你勇敢点,这是你需要跨出的第一步。

There is a psychological phenomenon which is called "you think you're missing out on something that isn't actually happening". So people think when they are at home, everyone else is having such a great time, but really they're probably not having the great time that you think they are, all the time at least. And this is one of the things that people think when they're isolated, they don't have their phones, or iPad or tablet.

这是一种心理现象,叫作"你认为你错过了什么实际上并没有发生的事"。举个例子:人们总认为当自己待在家里时,其他人都在外面玩得特别开心,但事实上他们可能并没有你想象中那么开心,至少不总是那样。人们认为自己被孤立了,没有手机、iPad或平板电脑时,也总会这么想,觉得别人都玩得很开心,自己错过了好多。

为什么人们不愿意离开手机呢?因为他们可能对手机上瘾 addiction,

或是手机上一些超级功能让他们离不开手机 glue to it，glue 作名词是胶水，作动词是紧附于，粘上。没有手机你可能会感觉心神不宁 feel very uneasy，好像丢了什么重要的东西 as if he's lost something very important，as if 仿佛、好像，或者认为你错过了什么 miss out on something 错过某事，将某事遗漏掉，甚至认为你被孤立了 be isolated。但是如果你的手机被收走，你不得不和人聊天交谈时，你会发现了解人是件好事，因为人们既无聊 boring 又有趣 interesting，而且了解别人也是你需要走的第一步 the first step you need to take。

词汇小百科

mobile phone / cell phone　手机

tablet　平板电脑

mobile phone dependence syndrome　手机依赖症

smart phone addict / phubber　指在社交场合注意力不集中、喜欢看手机的人，低头族

（王　玮）

别让你的少女心恶化成"少女癌"

（素材来自《圆桌议事》2015年5月8日节目）

导　语：继"直男癌"之后现在又有"少女癌"，主要症状是成年女性具有和年龄不符的难以割舍的少女情怀。"少女癌"病发群年龄范围很广，因为不管多少岁，老中青年"少女"们内心或多或少都有些少女情结，即使到了三四十岁，内心深处还隐隐期盼会有完美的白马王子出现。

When it comes to romantic relationships, she has too high expectations, in terms of what they should be, the type of person that she wants, so on and so on. So definitely I think I've seen this. But I think it's interesting that only now someone has come up with this term. I think it's a phenomenon, it has been around for quite some time.

当提到恋爱关系时，她在对方应该是怎样的人或她想要什么类型的人等方面有太高的期待。当然我认为我见过这样的。但是有意思的是现在才有人提出这个说法。我认为这是一个现象，已经存在了一段时间了。

Actually *Zhi nan ai* has always been there as well. It refers to guys who are chauvinistic, and things like that. So *Shao nv ai*, these are just new words that people now use to define an already existing phenomenon.

事实上直男癌也一直都有。它指的是那些有大男子主义的男人。所以和

"少女癌"一样,这些都是用新词来解释一个已经存在的现象。

I mean you're my age, maybe a little bit younger, maybe a little bit older, and you're still acting like a 15-year-old, and I don't understand how that is attractive. I understand you want to be young at heart. Hey, look, I'm kind of young at heart, I think, I hope. I like to have fun, I like to make jokes, and things like that. But you know, not in such a way that I come across as immature or boyish, I guess.

我的意思是你和我年纪差不多,也许比我年轻一点,也许比我大一点,但是你仍然表现得像一个15岁的孩子,我不知道那样怎么会有吸引力。我理解你想做到心理年轻。嘿,我也心理年轻啊。至少我希望是。我喜欢过得开心,开玩笑什么的,但不是以让人觉得不成熟或孩子气的方式。

Yeah, I do have a feeling that whenever we accuse someone of having some sort of quote-unquote cancer, there is a condition in which that cancer becomes possible. There is a soil. And in this case if there are some girl cancer patients, the guys are there to satisfy their girl fantasy.

是的,我也有一种感觉,当我们说某人有某种所谓的"癌"时,会有这种癌形成的条件,有形成它的土壤。假如有"少女癌"患者的话,那就会有满足她们少女幻想的男人。

点 评

少女癌患者有什么症状呢?她们在 romantic relationships 恋爱关系中 have high expectations 有很高的期待,act like a 15-year-old 表现得像15岁,很 immature or boyish 不成熟或孩子气;而直男癌则是比较 chauvinistic 大男子主义的,chauvinism 沙文主义,大男子主义。这种现象一直都有,但只是现在才 come up with this term 提出这个说法,come up with something 提出,想出。

如果我们说某人有 quote-unquote cancer 所谓的"癌",那么必定有形成它的土壤,所以有少女癌患者,是因为有男人会 satisfy their girl fantasy 满足她们的少女幻想,fantasy 幻想。

◆词汇小百科◆

spoil　宠坏

act like a spoiled child　像被宠坏的小孩子一样撒娇耍赖

act pouty to get what you want　用撒娇来得到你想要的东西

怎么用英文撒娇呢?

You never ... for me.　你从来都不帮我……

If you love me, you would...　如果你爱我,你就会……

Come on! Don't be so mean.　拜托,不要这么凶嘛。

I'd love you forever if you ...　如果你……我就永远爱你。

(王　玮)

你是"出门困难症"患者吗？

（素材来自《圆桌议事》2015年6月25日节目）

导　语：你是不是经常有这样的体验：计划好出门与朋友聚会，出门前却感觉有做不完的琐事？抑或是一想到出门，就坐立不安？如果你的答案是肯定的，那么你很有可能是"出门困难症"的患者。在本篇中让我们来看看"出门困难症"的那些事。

There are people who don't go out, like the otaku thing, that's the classic one, *Zhai nan Zhai nü*. That comes from Japanese, referring to people who don't really go out, like playing a lot of video games, the anime that sort of thing. Though they would be active to some extent with friends but mostly online indirect sort of way. They don't feel the need to go out, not just the otaku thing, I think the so-called computer nerds, computer geeks.

　　有人不愿意出门，比如御宅族、宅男宅女。这个词来自于日语，指的是一类不愿意出门的人，他们玩很多电子游戏，看动漫什么的。虽然他们可能在某种程度上对朋友很活跃，但是大部分是指在网上间接的那种活跃。他们不觉得有出门的需要。不只是御宅族，还有那些电脑迷们。

That is procrastination and poor execution ability that can also be called poor time management. Procrastination is (when) you have in mind that you want to do something, but you keep putting it off, and you do other things that are more pleasurable, that are really trivial things, that are not important and you shouldn't be doing it. But still you end up doing that. What's most important just gets postponed and postponed, and in the end you don't have time to do it anymore.

还有拖延症和糟糕的执行力，也可以说是不会管理时间。拖延症是你脑子里知道想做什么事，但是你持续地拖延这件事，去做其他令你感觉更愉快的事，可能是些琐碎的小事，一点也不重要，你也不应该做的事。但是你最后还是做了。最重要的事反而一直被推迟，最后你都没有时间做它了。

But for me, how late I want to be, whether or not I don't want to be late, purely depends on the nature of the person I'm meeting, and how acceptable he or she is to people being late. If he is OK with an hour, then I'm gonna go like half an hour late. And if he or she takes being late very badly, then I'm going to be only 5 minutes late.

但是对我来说，我迟不迟到或迟到多久，纯粹取决于我要见的人的性格，以及他或她对别人迟到的接受程度。如果他能接受迟到一小时的话，那我就迟到半小时。如果他或她很抗拒迟到的话，那我就只迟到5分钟。

If it's a party, it's different. If you get there on time, it's often kind of awkward, 'cause most people won't get there on time, you are the first person there. But you could, let's say if it's a friend, you could get there early and say: "Hey, can I help set up anything?" That's a nice kind of thing.

如果是个派对，那就不一样了。如果你准时到，通常会很尴尬。因为大部分人都不准时到，所以你会是到那儿的第一个人。但是你也可以这样做：如果我们说是一个朋友（开派对），你可以早到并问他："嗨，有什么需要我帮忙准备的吗？"这就是件很好的事。

I have one foot in and one foot out of that door. Basically sometimes you really need to push yourself to get out there, you know, get out your apartment. When so many of us complain "I don't have a boyfriend." "I don't have a girlfriend." Blablablabla… because you don't go out. We think you have everything at home.

Yeah, you can go shopping, you can get people manicure for you at home. But you need to go out to meet people. That is such an essential part of being alive.

我是一只脚在门里一只脚在门外的那种。有时你的确需要推自己一把，把自己推出公寓外。我们中很多人抱怨没有男/女朋友。等等！因为你不出门。你认为你在家就有一切。是的，你可以购物，可以让人到你家给你做美甲。但是你需要出门见人，这是生活中必要的一部分。

点评

为什么有人会有出门困难症呢？They don't feel the need to go out 他们不觉得有出门的需要。也有人有拖延症（procrastination）或执行力太糟（poor execution ability），不擅长时间管理（poor time management），这些都是出门困难症的原因。这些人可能会不断地推迟某件事（put something off），Never put off till tomorrow what you can do today 今日事今日毕（或今天能做完的事不要拖到明天）。但有时候迟到也有必要，如果参加聚会的其他人都不按时到，只有你按时到达，那就尴尬了。

词汇小百科

-phobia　某种恐惧症或厌恶某事
bacteriophobia　细菌恐惧症
claustrophobia　幽闭恐惧症
decidophobia　决策困难症
mondayphobia　周一恐惧症
socialphobia　社交恐惧症
vaccinophobia　种痘恐惧症

（王　玮）

你比镜子里的自己更丑？

（素材来自《圆桌议事》2014年11月14日节目）

导　语： 不知道你是否有这样的经历：早上出门前照着镜子梳洗打扮，对自己的形象很满意。晚上回家后，随意看了一眼镜子里的自己，也觉得玉树临风。可是打开朋友圈，看到小伙伴发的你们的合影，惊呆了。你居然那么其貌不扬，接受无能啊！最近，一些科学家对这个现象给出了解释，那就是——你比镜子里的自己要丑大概三分之一！

People are actually 30% less attractive than their mirror reflections according to a psychological survey. This is why many people don't like themselves in photos.

据一份心理学调查报告显示，人们的真实长相要比镜子中的倒影难看30%。这就是很多人不喜欢相片中的自己的原因。这条新闻在网上呈病毒式传播。

And there was some research done in the University of Wisconsin–Milwaukee in the US. They show some students their normal photos and the mirrored versions. Two thirds of the students think the mirrored versions are prettier, meaning they like their reflections more. And I think it has to do with the fact that you're getting a reflection instead of a direct head-on view of yourself. But when you're looking at a photo, then you'll see yourself as how other people see you.

美国威斯康星——密尔沃基大学做了一些相关研究。他们向学生们展示了他们的照片和照片的镜像版本。结果2/3的学生认为镜像版本更漂亮，也就是说他们更喜欢自己的"倒影"。我觉得镜子里的自己更美其实也和这个有关，你从镜子里看到的是自己的"倒影"，而照片里看到的则是"正影"，跟别人看到的你一样。

I think a part of that is just going to be what you're used to. If you are used to looking at yourself through a picture, you would end up probably thinking it looks better than a mirror. I think it has a lot to do with habit. We're used to using the mirror which where the left is left and the right is right no matter what.

我觉得一部分原因在于你习惯什么。如果你习惯看照片，我想你也会觉得自己从照片里看起来比镜子里更美。所以我认为是习惯的问题。我们习惯使用镜子，左边是左边，右边是右边。忽然倒过来，当然会有点奇怪。

I just want to say something really quickly about selfies… selfies are a disease! You take a selfie and it doesn't look good enough so you take another one and that doesn't look good enough so you Photoshop it. So you spend 30 minutes on one picture and then you post that picture to the Internet and people say "you look so good" and blah blah blah… but that's not you! Selfies in general and social media in that sense, are eating away society and promoting narcissism.

我只想很快地补充一句：自拍是病，得治！你自拍了一张，看了看觉得不够美，然后再拍一张，结果还是不够美，于是你决定把它PS一下。最后你花了30分钟时间才弄好一张照片，然后把它发到网上，你的朋友们就开始说"你好美啊……"但那根本不是真实的你啊！我觉得总体来说，自拍和社交网络就是在毁掉正常社交、推崇个人自恋。

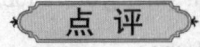

这么惊人的"科学发现"免不了在网上爆红，而爆红的英文表述就是

go viral。viral 本身是"病毒性的"意思，而 go viral 顾名思义就是像病毒一般迅速传播。如果用 go viral 形容一个网络事件，比如一张图片、一段视频或者一个故事，大多情况下会带有贬义，暗示这个走红多多少少有点哗众取宠的意味。

而最后提到的"自拍"也就是Selfie，是一个不折不扣的新生词汇。self 是自己的意思，而 selfie 就是自己拿相机或手机拍的本人照片。随着手机拍照功能的普及，自拍也在社交媒体上越来越普遍。2013年8月，selfie 正式被牛津辞典收录，受欢迎的程度随之达到了新高。

词汇小百科

narcissism　自恋

vanity　虚荣心、自负

assertive　坚定的、武断的

paranoid　偏执的

inferiority　自卑

low self-esteem　自卑

self-glorification　自命不凡

self-respect　自尊自爱

（牛翃琳）

从书架看穿你的性格

（素材来自《圆桌议事》2016年5月18日节目）

导　语：你会如何收纳书籍？按颜色、大小、题材还是年代？不同性格的人会呈现不同的摆书风格。还有人把某些书的书脊朝内放，不让其他人看出来这是什么书。看来，摆书也有很大的秘密。

I immediately connected with subject matter, because I feel like I would put books about science over here, books about space and books about art here. That would make it easier for me to get to the kind of book I wanted real quick. But I saw some other ones too like color coordinated. I am kind of a "Fengshui" kind of guy.

　　我能马上想到的是根据主题来整理书，我会把科学类的放这边，把宇宙和艺术类的放那边，这样找书的时候会容易些，也快些。我也会考虑其他方面的因素，比如颜色要协调，我还是很信风水的。

You are？I don't know you at all. I feel betrayed.

　　真的啊？我太不了解你了。我有一种被背叛的感觉。

I thought I would go by author. Because if I like a writer, I will buy almost every book that's published by that person. I want it to be grouped together, regardless of size or how it looks like. I want it to be together. Otherwise it kinda bugs me. I think subject matter kind of makes sense. But color coordination, no way does that become one thing I would consider.

我会按照作者姓名排序。因为如果我喜欢一个作者，可能会买齐他/她的全部作品，希望这些作品都在一个组里，无论尺寸和样式。我就是希望它们被放在一起，否则会很烦。按题材分类也讲得通。但是按颜色摆数对我来说是怎么也不会去考虑的一种方式。

But there was one of these categories which I was pretty surprised with. But I also feel like I could understand. And that was spines to the back. So imagine the part of the book where you normally have facing you out from the bookshelf actually goes in, so you just see the pages. I immediately thought this…this description says you are a perfectionist.

还有一种方式挺让我惊讶的，但我也能明白，就是把书脊朝里放。你通常看到书页的话，说明书脊朝里了。据说这是完美主义者摆书的方式。

I read romance novels. I'm a girl, I'm allowed. Sometimes it is a little bit embarrassing if a visitor comes to my home and sees, aren't you an educated, worldly person, and you should be reading *The Memoirs of The Second World War*, and you read this?!

我看浪漫小说。我是女生，当然可以看这样的书。只是有时候，有客人到我家，会有点尴尬。他们会觉得，我是个受过教育的、涉世的人，应该看《二战回忆录》，没想到我竟然看浪漫小说？！

点评

将书分类的几种方式：by subject matter 按主题、题材，by size 按尺寸，by color 按颜色，by author 按作者，in chronological order 按年代、编年体。

有时候你觉得很了解一个人，但他摆书的方式或者其他的行为模式让你很吃惊，你可以说 I don't know you at all. I feel betrayed.

Romance novels 是浪漫小说，还有一个贴近的词组叫 chick flick，是指符合女性口味的小妞电影、爱情文艺片、浪漫轻喜剧、言情片。flick 有"轻弹、轻打、轻抚"的意思，也有"电影"的意思。

词汇小百科

spine　书脊、脊柱、脊椎
group　组；分组、分类
embarrassing　尴尬的
worldly　世俗的、涉世的、入世的

（陈　沫）

完美主义？强迫症？

（素材来自《圆桌议事》2016年6月25日节目）

> **导　语**：你有没有一套严格的行事法则，每天必须遵守的那种？比如衣服必须整整齐齐躺在衣柜里？生病了也要做家务，容不得一点凌乱？如果是这样的话，你可能是个完美主义者，也可能有强迫症！

This type of perfectionism is characterized by excessive preoccupation with past mistakes, fears about making new mistakes, doubts about whether you are doing something correctly. So in general, while healthy perfectionism tends to be associated with good psychological well-being and high achievement both at school and at work, the unhealthy perfectionism has been associated with distress, low self-esteem and symptoms of mental illness, such as OCD.

　　这种"完美主义"过度拘泥于过去的错误，害怕去犯新的错误，总是怀疑自己是不是做对了事情。通常来讲，健康的"完美主义"伴随着良好的心理状态和在学业、工作中的"高成就感"；不健康的"完美主义"伴随着苦闷、"低自尊感"和精神疾病的症状，比如强迫症。

I am, what we call in the English language, a, hypochondriac to a lower level. For me, I know I literally have a problem where when I am walking away from the ATM, I have to check it five times to make sure A, I pull out the money and B, I got my card. And like I will leave, and like walk a couple steps, and then come back, and I have done this three times. I do know to a certainty that 'Oh yeah, I probably did it.' But there is a nagging suspicion in the back of my head. And I just can't ignore.

英语里有个词叫 hypochondriac，就是强迫症、疑病症患者。我有时候就会有这样的问题。去ATM取钱的时候，要确认五次：第一，我把钱拿出来了；第二，我把卡拿回来了，通常我离开ATM几步，会回去再查三遍。在某种程度上我知道"我已经确认过了"，但脑海里还是有挥之不去的怀疑，我无法忽视。

I think the real thing you can do to help yourself is embracing it and make it work towards your advantage. Find the way not to fight it, but to work with it and steer it in a direction that really helps your life or find ways to deal with it. But the fact is sometimes it's just how life is. But I think with a little bit of embracing yourself and not seeing it as necessarily a huge problem, but something that can help you, will help you overall in your life and especially being happy.

我觉得自己真正能做的事情就是拥抱它并且把它变成优势。我们不是去找打败它的办法，而是去找与它共处的方式，让它转变方向，真正地帮助你的生活，或者去面对它，接受生活本来的样子。我想，我们应该去拥抱自己，不一定非把这看成一个特别严重的问题，而把它看成一个可以帮助你的事情，一个能在生活里帮到你、让你快乐的事情。

As much as a free-spirited person, I think a degree of pursuing perfection is very important for any society to move forward. And those things I think sometimes are so necessary and so essential to your success. That being said, let's comfort the little OCD and the real perfectionists out there that "nobody perfect is cool and nobody cool is perfect". So maybe perfection isn't the ultimate goal. It's about making yourself better.

作为一个无拘无束的人，我认为某种程度上追求完美对任何社会进步来说都是很重要的。有时候这很有必要，对个人成功来说也十分关键。让我们安抚一下小小的强迫症和真正的完美主义者。完美的人没有趣味，有趣味的人不完美。或许完美不是我们的终极目标，让自己变得更好才是目标。

点评

根据ocduk.org的介绍，英国大概有74万名强迫症患者，症状是experience frequent intrusive and unwelcome obsessional thoughts, often followed by repetitive compulsions, impulses or urges. 经历频繁的入侵式、不受欢迎的过度思虑，时常伴有重复性的强制感、冲动感或者刺激感。典型的行为包括反复洗手或者检查各种开关。

我们很难把握完美主义perfectionism和强迫症OCD（obsessive compulsive disorder）之间的界限。一方面，人有追求极致、追求卓越的本能；另一方面，在这个过程中，很容易思虑过度、忧心忡忡。

无论如何，我们要面对它、拥抱它 face it and embrace it，把它变成对自己有帮助的一种力量，而不是拖累自己的枷锁 turn it into an advantage that could help you, not a burden that may slow you down.

词汇小百科

excessive 过度的、过分的
preoccupation 全神贯注、入神；偏见、成见
distress 苦闷、悲痛、危难、不幸
self-esteem 自尊
nagging 唠叨的、挑剔的、不安的、折磨的
suspicion 怀疑

（陈 沫）

网络社交达人反而内心孤独？

（素材来自《圆桌议事》2015年10月3日节目）

导　语：研究显示，现实生活中孤独的人特别愿意在网络世界开展社交活动。同时，也有人问：社交网络为什么让我们越来越孤独？

Lonely people or known as loners... These two things are entirely different. A loner can be someone that just prefers to do things on their own. Traveling alone for example. I've never understood how people can do that. But some people are quite happy to travel to another country by themselves for example on a holiday. Can you imagine doing that? That would be the behavior of a loner.

　　孤独的人和喜孤独者，是两种截然不同的概念。一个喜孤独者可能只是愿意自己一个人独处。比如独自去旅行。我从来不能理解怎么有人能做到这点。但确实有人很乐意一个人在假日去其他国家旅行。你能想象吗？那就是一个喜孤独者的行为。

But that doesn't mean they are lonely though. They choose to do it. They are not lonely. That's just how they'd like to go on their holiday in this example. You could find people that come from a big family and have a lot of colleagues. And they interact well. So they could say they are not a loner，because they like a big family or a big team. But you could say they are alone. You can be alone in a crowd.

但那并不意味着他们很孤独。他们选择这样做。他们并不孤单。那只是他们喜欢的度假方式。你也可以看到有的人来自大家庭，也拥有很多同事。他们相处都很愉快。也许，他们不是喜孤独者，因为他们可能喜欢大家庭和大团队。但你可以说他们其实是孤独的。你完全有可能在一大群人中感到孤独。

There's no such thing as a lonely person. This suggests there's something in their nature that can never be changed. If you start ticking boxes, classifying yourself as lonely, then you are labeling yourself as a kind of loser.

寂寞的人并不存在。（社交媒体上的"寂寞"选项）意味着人类本性中有此特质而不可改变。如果你在这个选项画钩，那就是把自己归于"寂寞"类别，那就相当于给自己贴上了失败者的标签。

I think I'm seeing a cultural difference here. Because in Chinese, when we talk about "*gu du de ren*", a lonely person, it does not have the kind of stigma or "looking down upon that person" kind of feeling towards that at all.

我看到了一丝文化差异。因为在中文里，我们提到一个"孤独的人"，并不具有耻辱的含义，也没有鄙视的感觉。

There are social butterflies among us who brag about the number of friends they have on Facebook. For that kind of people, they might feel this urge to add as many people as they can.

我们当中有社交花蝴蝶，他们会吹嘘在脸书上的朋友数量。这类人可能有一种冲动，喜欢尽可能多加朋友。

And sometimes I do think of having a cull. Like when hunting is permitted to shoot usually male deer in Scotland, to keep the numbers down…Yeah such a cruel thing.You want to cull your friends!

有的时候我真想进行一次（社交网络朋友圈）清洗。就像在苏格兰，狩猎是允许射杀公鹿的，这样就能控制鹿的数量。你的朋友也是一样，需要控制数量！

Quality rather than quantity. That is the golden rule when it comes to your friendship selection.

重质不重量。这是选择朋友的黄金法则。

点评

Social butterfly 社交花蝴蝶。顾名思义，就是非常擅长和热衷于社会交际的人。如英国男主持人所说，在西方文化里寂寞的人不被大多数人认同。擅长社交的social butterfly则被认为是健康和受欢迎的人。网络的存在给现实生活中孤单的人另一个与人交流的平台，但同时我们也可能被时时刻刻要在网上晒出自己最理想形象的心态绑架。

The golden rule 是黄金法则的意思。一旦开头字母大写，The Golden Rule 指的是己所不欲，勿施于人的道理。golden ratio 是黄金比例或黄金分割的意思。它指将整体一分为二，较大部分与整体部分的比值等于较小部分与较大部分的比值，其比值约为 0.618。这个比例被公认为是最能引起美感的比例，因此被称为黄金分割。

词汇小百科

FOMO　即 Fear of Missing Out，害怕错过
infomania　"资讯癖"或"资讯强迫症"
mania　狂躁、极度热衷

（赫　扬）

吃很重要
Food

回家吃饭，约吗？

（素材来自《圆桌议事》2015年7月20日节目）

导　语：据调查显示，北京、上海、广州、深圳不到一半的人能在七点以前回家吃晚饭，其中北京仅有38%。中国人是不是越来越不恋家了？而你晚上回家吃饭了吗？

Maybe it's the long commuting hours, the distance and the faster pace of life in first-tier cities that is stopping people from eating at home.

我觉得可能通勤时间、上班地点和家之间的距离以及一线城市的快节奏生活导致大家没法回家吃晚饭。

Only 41% of post 90s generation choose to have dinner at home. This is where China got tremendous advantage over, I think, most European countries, because in European countries, we only got two levels of eating out. It's either the McDonalds or that kind of fast food places. You don't want to go there on a romantic date as the food is not particularly healthy. Or there is the much higher level, and it is too expensive. For example, in my experience anyway back in London, I couldn't afford to go out as often as I do in Beijing to eat. I could maybe only go out once a month. I think that's on average for British people because it's quite expensive.

只有41%的90后选择在家吃晚饭。我觉得在这一点上，中国相比欧洲国家有着巨大的优势。因为在欧洲国家，我们只有两个层次的餐厅。一个是像麦当劳之类的快餐店，但你在约会时肯定不想去这种地方，因为他们的食物并不是那么健康。另一个就是高级餐厅，它们的消费都太高了。以我自身体会而言，如果我回到伦敦，我就不能像在北京那样频繁地出去吃饭。我可能一个月只能出去吃一次。我觉得这是英国人的平均水准，因为在外面吃确实很贵。

We don't have that medium level of restaurants, like the hot pot restaurant, the *ma la tang* place. We don't have that. These places are always full up in Beijing and other cities in China. So why go home, why cook? There is so much affordable food that everyone can afford at one level or another. So I think this might have something to do with it.

伦敦那边没有中档的饭店，不像这里有火锅店、麻辣烫店等。这些在北京或者中国的其他城市都很常见。所以干嘛要回家做饭呢？街上有一大堆人人都买得起的食物，而且各种不同层次的店铺都能找到，选择多多。我觉得这也是中国人不常回家吃晚饭的原因之一。

I think that's a very good point and that might be a big reason why we see this result because I think, for Chinese people, eating out isn't really as big a deal and it just seems to be the most convenient way, although by the end of the month when you calculate your expenses, then it still seems like eating out is definitely a bit more expensive. But still, you wouldn't need to deal with the cooking, getting the groceries and washing dishes. That seems to be an advantage that a lot of urbanizers are willing to pay for.

我觉得你说得很对，这是人们不回家吃晚饭的一个重要原因，因为我觉得对于中国人来说，出去吃晚饭并不是什么大事。相反，这是吃晚饭最便捷的方式，即使你在月末计算自己的开销时会发现出去吃饭确实花费更多的钱。但毕竟你不用煮饭，不用买菜，不用洗碗。这是巨大的有利因素，很多城市居民愿意为此花钱。

So I think from a healthy perspective, cooking at home is a very good option. Actually, I don't think it has a lot to do with whether you are single or whether you have a family. Because usually people think that when they are married, they tend to cook at home. But it is rather an individual-based decision. Some people who are married for years still go out for dinner every night, and some people who are single cook at home every day.

因此我觉得出于健康的考虑，在家里做饭是一个很好的选择。而且我不觉得这个选择与你是否单身有很大的关系。我会这么说，是因为人们通常认为在他们结婚之后会更多选择在家煮饭。可事实上，这还是要看每个人的具体选择。有些人结婚多年还是每晚都出去吃饭，而有些人虽然单身但天天在家自己做饭。

点 评

中国在餐饮行业上比欧洲国家要有优势。China gets tremendous advantage over European countries when it comes to the catering industry. Get tremendous advantage over... 可以理解为"比起……有巨大优势"。

中国人外出吃饭的现象更加普遍。It is more common for Chinese to eat out. Eat out 可以理解为外出吃饭。

是否单身与是否在家煮饭吃并没有太大的联系。Eating out or not doesn't have much to do with your marriage status.

有关联可以说 have something to do with，升级版的"有很大的关联"可以说 have a lot / much to do with。

词汇小百科

fast food　快餐
catering industry　餐饮行业
hot pot　火锅
additive　添加剂
grocery　食品杂货店
food safety　食品安全

（于　洋）

去度假，带什么吃的

（素材来自《圆桌议事》2016年5月7日节目）

导　语：去国外度假，怕吃得不习惯，要不要带点吃的？不同国家的人喜欢带不同的美食，就算是带个念想；也有人什么都不带，就要享受当地的食物。

A global survey found its coffee and ketchup that holidaymakers consider their packing essentials, rather than flip flops and suntan lotion. It's also showing that nearly 40 percent of Chinese mainland travelers pack instant noodles with them.

一项全球调查显示，度假者的必带行李里包括咖啡和番茄酱，而不是人字拖和防晒霜，40%的中国大陆游客会带方便面。

Maybe if we have some French listeners you guys can clear this one up for me. Bringing cheese. 53 percent of French people said they would bring either cheese or dairy products. Guys, don't dairy products go bad?

如果咱们有法国听众的话，可以解释一下这条：53%的法国受访者说他们会带奶酪或者奶制品。这是怎么想的？奶制品坏了怎么办？

I fill in the category of us Americans. And the study shows that Americans, we, tend to bring toilet paper and I'm all about that. For us, it is very hygiene-oriented, which I totally agree with.

我是典型的美国人。这个调查说美国人会带卫生纸，我就是这类游客。

我们讲卫生，我完全同意。

Maybe they want a little bit of something that reminds them of home. But still, doesn't that just defeat the purpose of travelling? You are going off to a foreign country and I would still want to try the local stuff.

带些东西可能是为了有家的感觉，但这样不是有违旅游的初衷吗？到了另一个国家，我还是要尝尝当地的食物。

Yeah, you should try the local stuff but if it's really bad, I won't blame you for going to the McDonald's, probably that's down the street, because it's seems to be everywhere. But 37 percent of Russians they bring playing cards, really smart. Playing cards is good.

没错，你可以试试当地的食物，但是不好吃的话，谁也不会怪你去街上的麦当劳吃东西，快餐到处都有。我想说的是我喜欢这个：37%的俄罗斯受访者说他们会带牌，真聪明啊，打牌不错。

点 评

旅行时各国人民都喜欢带什么吃的？方便面 instant noodles，巧克力 chocolate，奶酪 cheese，泡菜 kimchee。

要注意的是，很多国家的海关都有禁止携带的食物清单。比如，中国游客要去英国的话，要知道英国对非欧盟地区的游客有这样的规定：You can't bring meat, meat products, milk, dairy products or potatoes into the UK.您不可携带肉类、肉制品、牛奶、奶制品和马铃薯。

如果要带水果和蔬菜呢？英国对非欧盟旅客的规定是 You can bring up to 2kg of fruit and vegetables（except potatoes）into the UK as long as they are: in personal baggage / for you and your family or friends（ie you can't sell them）/ free from signs of pests and diseases. 您可以携带不超过2千克的水果和蔬菜（马铃

薯除外）进入英国，只要这些水果蔬菜：在您的个人行李里 / 为您和亲友所用（而非为销售所用）/ 不带害虫和疫病。

另外要带什么？护照 passport，卫生纸 toilet paper，牌 cards，信用卡 credit card，现金 cash，贵重物品 valuables。

词汇小百科

ketchup　番茄酱

flip flop　人字拖

suntan lotion　防晒霜

refrigerate　冷藏、冷冻

hygienic　卫生的、保健的、清洁的

（陈　沫）

吃货普大喜奔：十大垃圾食品名单是假的！

（素材来自《圆桌议事》2015年5月14日节目）

导　语：2003年以来，一份名为"世卫组织公布的十大垃圾食品"的名单在国内广为流传。后来世界卫生组织明确辟谣，表示从未发布过垃圾食品的名单。尽管如此，了解一下如何做到健康饮食、远离垃圾食品，还是很有必要的。

Tuna is one of the healthiest fish that you can eat. It is high in protein, low in fat and how you are going to get it usually is going to be in cans. Yes, of course, there're unhealthy versions, so for example, canned tunas packed in soybean oil, that is gonna be very fatty because of the oil. But if you get tuna packed in water, it's actually going to be very healthy.

　　金枪鱼是你能吃到的最健康的鱼类。它含高蛋白质，低脂肪，而且你一般拿到手的都是罐装金枪鱼。当然也有不健康的版本。比如罐装金枪鱼包裹在豆油里就会很油腻。但是如果你把金枪鱼泡在水里的话，它就很健康了。

Fresh food is better in general than pickled food, but we've eaten pickled food for thousands of years. How could it be that bad? I mean if there is a lot of salt, yes, of course, you should be careful because you're going to get dehydrated. And eating things basically processed and high in fats, salts and sugar are bad for you. But just because it's pickled doesn't mean that is automatically bad for you.

一般来说新鲜的食物比腌制的食物健康。但是我们吃腌制的食物已经几千年了，怎么可能会那么糟糕？我的意思是说如果盐分太高，当然，你要小心它会令你脱水。而且吃一些经过处理并且高脂肪、高盐、高糖的食物对你有害。但是只是因为食物经过腌制并不意味着它对你有害。

Again there are going to be exceptions-canned tuna is a great example-I love it, eat it all the time. But in general, if it's highly processed, the longer the food and ingredients have spent on the factory line, the more likely it is to be unhealthy.

还是有一些例外的——罐装金枪鱼就是个好例子。我喜欢吃并且经常吃。但是总体来说，如果食物是经过高度加工的，食物及其成分在工厂的流水线上经过越长的时间，食物就越可能不健康。

The general definition for junk food is the food that is of little nutritional value and often high in fat, sugar, salt and calories. And when I think about it, a lot of Chinese food, Chinese cooking falls into this category, too. It's really quite a broad kind of definition, I suppose.

垃圾食品的一般定义是没什么营养价值而且高脂肪、高糖、高盐、高卡路里的食物。每当我想到这点，就觉得很多中国的食物和烹饪方法也都属于这个类别。我觉得这个定义太广了。

If you look at what a balance diet is, it is about 40 percent carbon hydrates, 40 percent protein and 20 percent fat. The way I try to design my own diet is about 50 percent protein, because protein is going to be your long-term source of energy. And it is actually used by the body and many other processes whereas carbohydrates and fats too easily, in a sedentary society, are turned into fat on the body, which is unhealthy.

如果你看一下什么是均衡饮食的话，均衡饮食是差不多40%碳水化合物，40%蛋白质和20%脂肪。我努力把自己的饮食设计成50%蛋白质，因为蛋白质会成为你长期的能量来源。而且身体和很多其他消耗过程会用掉蛋白质，但是在一个人们总是坐着的社会里，碳水化合物和脂肪会很容易成为囤积在身体里的脂肪，这很不健康。

点评

什么样的食物是垃圾食品（junk food）呢？垃圾食品可能会 there is a lot of salt 盐分太高，you're going to get dehydrated 会令你脱水，get dehydrated 使人脱水，dehydrate 脱水。还有可能是 highly processed 经过高度加工的。The general definition for junk food is the food that is of little nutritional value 垃圾食品的一般定义是没什么营养价值的食物，of little nutritional value 没什么营养价值，nutritional 有营养的，nutrition 营养。什么样的食物又是健康的呢？It is high in protein, low in fat. 它高蛋白，低脂肪，high / low in something 某物成分高 / 低。

词汇小百科

protein　蛋白质
fat　脂肪
carbon hydrates　碳水化合物
pickled food　腌制食物
pickled vegetable　泡菜
calorie　卡路里

（王玮）

吃方便面哪国强？

（素材来自《圆桌议事》2014年12月22日节目）

导　语：据中国之声《新闻晚高峰》报道，世界方便面协会针对全球15个国家进行了关于方便面摄入量的调查。结果显示，2013年，中国以年消费462.2亿份方便面的总量排名第一（若按2012年人口统计数据计算，大约相当于人均每年34包）。中国人为什么会吃那么多方便面呢？泡面对于海外学子而言，真的代表了"家的味道"吗？我们来听听圆桌主持人怎么说。

I have never reached that magic number and in the old days when I was living overseas, I wanted a packet of home once in a while and it was instant noodles that I would go for, so... I used to just get it from the Chinese supermarket in Beijing and I would bring it with me overseas to make sure that it was the exact flavor of home that I would get. But actually, it's a bit sad to say it's a reference of home, because my mom's home cooking is so much better than instant noodles, but when you are overseas, that's all you can get.

我自己是从来没吃到过这个数字的。过去在国外生活的时候，每隔一段时间，我就会想念家的味道，于是就来一包方便面。我以前都是在北京的超市里买好，然后把它带到国外去。这样就能保证我能享受到准确的、我所熟悉的家的味道。不过话说回来，说方便面能代表家的味道实际上有点可悲，因为我妈做的菜比方便面要好太多了。但是当你身在异国他乡时，你也没有什么其他选择了。

Yeah, it's like McDonald's for me sometimes. I mean McDonald's tastes like home, but we all know it's pretty crappy. It's not really representative of American cuisine or the quality of my mother's cooking either, but memory is memory. Food and taste are very strong links, perhaps the strongest link, or the power to invoke certain feelings and memories.

我明白你的意思,方便面之于你,有点像麦当劳之于我,因为我也会觉得麦当劳像是家的味道,虽然我们都知道它是垃圾食品。麦当劳并不能代表美国的饮食,也不能代表我妈妈的厨艺,但是它能让你想起熟悉的味道。食物和味觉是很强大的纽带,甚至可能是最强大的纽带,可以引发我们特定的情感和记忆。

Actually I think 34 per year isn't too bad, but when you count China's base population as it is into the equation, that's really horrifying when you see that humongous figure.

实际上,我认为每年 34 包也没有太糟糕啦。但是当你把中国的人口基数考虑在内的时候,你就会看到一个大得惊人的总数了。

What I'm trying to say is that it's not as bad or harmful as people think. It's not nutritious certainly, it has some additives and it's being fried, so a lot of oil and carbon hydrates like you said. But when you say that it is poisonous or you will die if you eat too much of it, I wouldn't go that far.

我想说的是,它不像人们想象的那么糟糕或有害。方便面当然没什么营养,也使用了一些食品添加剂,又因为它是油炸的,所以有不少油和碳水化合物。但是如果说方便面含有大量有毒物质,或者说方便面吃多了会死,未免太夸张了。

So it's sort of like a buyer beware situation. But earlier there has been this discussion about the cup, the plastic inside, the polystyrene cup that carries these instant noodles, which you need to put boiled water into it, and that could be a source of unhealthy elements being released into the noodles. However, that was false information. Yes, that's true.

方便面比较像是一个"购者自慎"的情况。之前有过对装方便面的那个纸杯的讨论，有人说杯子里面的高分子聚苯乙烯对人体有害，因为你需要用开水泡面，而高温会导致部分的有害物质渗入面条。不过，这是错误的信息。

点 评

主持人说自己从没达到过一年吃34包泡面的"神奇数字"。这里的 magic number 其实是一个很好用的英文表达。它原本是一个物理学概念"幻数"，指原子核中的质子数和中子数均为某个特定数值时，原子核的稳定性就比平均值大。后来 magic number 又引申出化学、计算机、经济甚至体育领域等的特殊含义，或者处于临界点的数字。现在，我们可以把它用在任意上下文里，表达之前提到过的或是听者可以明白的任何有特殊意义的数字。这样的表达更地道一些，同时也更有色彩。

大概在小学时代，我们就会使用 big 或者 large 来表达"大"这个意思了，是时候该进阶一下词汇库了。比如主持人所使用的 humongous 就是"巨大无比、非常大"的意思。表达很大还可以使用 enormous，庞大的、凶恶的；grandiose，宏大的、堂皇的；immeasurable，不可测量的；stupendous，惊人的、巨大的；voluminous，大量的、长篇的等。

最后要说到的一个词组是 buyer beware，购者自慎，或者更通俗的说法是"一经出售概不负责"。这个词语其实比较像法律术语，另一个更专业的、来自于拉丁语的同义词则是 Caveat Emptor；这里用 buyer beware 就是要表达：其实方便面没有营养，也并不那么健康，这事大家都知道，所以选择购买并食用方便面也就是买家自己的选择了，那似乎也没什么理由事后再来怪生产者，说泡面不健康。这就是一个需要购买者自己负责的例子。

词汇小百科

soft drinks　汽水

soda　苏打水、碳酸饮料

canned food　罐头

pickle　泡菜、腌制食品

fruit preserves　果脯、话梅蜜饯类食品

barbecue food　烧烤

fried food　油炸食品

potato chips　薯片

pickled food　腌制食品

（牛翃琳）

中国人为什么爱吃辣？

（素材来自《圆桌议事》2014年10月22日节目）

> **导　语**：无论你承不承认，中国人的口味正变得越来越重，吃辣的嗜好不断扩张版图，并在2000年前后，成为中国人的第一口味。虽然沙县小吃已经在很大程度上取代了四川小吃的地位，但这种本来不崇尚辣味的福建风味，也不得不在餐桌上摆上辣椒酱。辣味扩张究竟为哪般？主持人们又是怎么看待这股重口味风潮的呢？

Recently, an article called Why Chinese People Love Spicy Dishes More and More becomes popular on the Internet. According to the article, before 2000, spicy food was only a regional cuisine loved by some people. However, it has gradually become a national craze.

最近一篇名为《中国人为什么越来越爱吃辣》的文章在网上十分火爆。该文章指出，在 2000 年前，只有部分地区的人偏好辣味食谱。而现在，吃辣俨然已经成为全国的风潮。

People who like spicy food like spicy food. It almost doesn't matter if it is a certain type of flavor or if it's not. They do it fundamentally because of the way it makes them feel. Eating spicy food, especially after a certain level or over a certain period of time, you start to feel amazing. I remember one of the first times I had spicy hot pot. After sitting down and eating for like 30 minutes of this, first it was like unbearable, and gradually you get used to it, especially if you have a beer. And I remember specifically, feeling euphoric after eating this spicy hot pot. Because you have to remember the way your brain works. When you're eating spicy food, the molecule basically creates a pain reaction in your neural system. So if that molecule comes in connect with any mucous membrane in your body, it's going to hurt. But how does your body respond to pain? It responds to pain by releasing chemicals that are basically natural pain killers. That natural pain killers also make you feel really, really good.

喜欢吃辣的人就是喜欢。至于是不是某一种特定的辣味,根本不重要。他们吃辣其实是喜欢"辣"本身能带来的那种刺激感觉。吃辣,在超过某种程度或是到达一定时间以后,你就会感觉特别棒。我记得我第一次吃四川火锅。坐下来吃了大概30分钟,最开始是辣得受不了,然后喝着啤酒开始慢慢习惯那个辣味,再然后,我开始感觉到一种吃完麻辣火锅以后的强烈愉悦。这个其实和大脑的运作方式有关。当你吃辣的时候,产生辣味的分子能在你的神经系统中产生疼痛反应。所以如果这个分子与你身体的任何黏膜接触,你都会感到疼痛。但你的身体怎么应对这种疼痛呢?它会在体内释放天然的、止疼的化学物质,而这些纯天然止痛药就会让你感觉特别好。

I think just in general, people are over-stimulated and they're over-stressed. So they need to balance it out somehow. They need other types of stimulation that can somehow break through those noises of over-stimulation.

我觉得现代社会里,大部分人其实都是被过度刺激,也承受着过度压力的。所以他们需要找一些途径来平衡这种感觉。他们需要其他类型的刺激,来冲破这种由过度刺激带来的困扰。

Yeah, but that's only the demand side. And also there's a supply side, the restaurants. Because cooking spicy food is actually a lot easier than some of the more delicate dishes that require higher quality of the material that's been cooked and also this is just easy to do! Throwing the hot chilly peppers.

我们之前只是讨论了需求方对于辛辣刺激的需要。其实供应方——餐馆，也是"辣"流行起来的原因之一。烹饪麻辣料理事实上比做其他那些更精致的菜肴要简单多了，毕竟实际操作非常简单！只要扔一把辣椒进去炒炒，就什么菜都挺好吃的了。

点评

在表达大家越来越爱吃辣这件事的时候，主持人使用了词组 inclined to，也就是倾向于的意思，incline 本身是指倾斜、斜面的意思。

类似的表达还有 be willing to 愿意做某事，tend to 易于做某事，以及 bent on 决心要做某事等。

提到辣味会给人带来的欣悦感，主持人说了 euphoric 这个高级词汇。除了开心，euphoric 其实更多用来描述临床表现出的精神愉悦和兴奋，它的派生词 euphoriant 就是兴奋剂、安乐药的意思。

当然，如果想说高兴又不想用 happy，也可以试试这些表述：joyous 喜庆快乐的，delighted 欣喜的、愉悦的，rapturous 兴高采烈的、狂喜的，和 ecstatic 心醉神迷的、欣喜若狂的。

词汇小百科

hotpot　火锅

Hot & Sour Soup　酸辣汤

West Lake Beef Soup　西湖牛肉羹

Fish Filets in Hot Chili Oil 或 Spicy Boiled Fish　水煮鱼

Spicy Chicken　辣子鸡

Sliced Beef and Ox Tongue in Chili Sauce 或 Pork Lungs in Chili Sauce　夫妻肺片

Spicy Crayfish　麻辣小龙虾

Sliced Noodles　刀削面

（牛翊琳）

吃小龙虾的正确姿势

（素材来自《圆桌议事》2016年6月14日节目）

导　语：夏日，夜晚，户外，小目标是吃点夜宵。这时候，来点小龙虾、喝点啤酒，倍儿爽。这篇会告诉你，如何用英语描述中国美食的火爆和迷人。

They glisten, boiled bright red, heaps and heaps of whole crawfish spread across a dinner table. Chinese people simply love eating crawfish, or *Xiao long xia*. Nothing compares with washing down the delicacy with a glass of ice cold beer.

闪闪发光，明亮的红色——餐桌上摆满了一堆堆的小龙虾。中国人喜欢吃这个。没有什么比边吃小龙虾边喝冰啤酒更惬意的事儿了。

Like I said I live right next to Guijie so I can totally sympathize and say yes, that smell does drive you crazy and hungry and I always see tons of people eating this and really loving it. It's like a social context.

我住在簋街附近，完全能体会那种感觉：光闻到味道就让人疯狂，让人觉得饿。我总是看见很多人吃这个，他们对小龙虾是真爱。这其实是社交场合。

Why is it so popular? Why are people just digging in and getting their hands all oily and dirty?

为什么这么火爆？为什么人们喜欢埋头大吃小龙虾，手上油滋滋脏兮兮的？

Seafood is often expensive, delicious seafood. You think, the crawfish's close cousin, a lobster is 70 USD just for the tail in a lot of restaurants in US. But here you are seeing seafood that isn't expensive, and you can have plenty of, that's like an informal thing. I think for so many reasons it's delicious, it's cheap, it's something you can get your hands dirty with your friends and you don't have to have the dinner manners of the queen when you are eating, but you can just let loose with your friends and have some beer and have some crawfish.

海鲜通常昂贵，尤其是美味的海鲜。在美国，小龙虾的亲戚，一个大龙虾尾就要70美元。在这，海鲜不贵，你可以买很多，很难得。我想小龙虾火爆还是有很多原因的，好吃、便宜，可以和朋友一起上手吃。吃这个的时候你不需要拥有女王范儿的礼仪，可以与朋友放松来，喝点啤酒，吃点小龙虾。

If you're taking your date out for the very first time, I think probably eating in a more dignified way would be more suitable. Because I mean come on... it's the first time. Let's not show our true colors just yet. Let's try to be civil and maybe this is the best idea for a third date or fourth one when you've kind of known each other a little bit, and wanna see your true personality and all that. Let's get our hands dirty and oily and see what we really are.

如果你和别人第一次约会，还是选择去餐厅以比较斯文的方式用餐更合适一些。毕竟是第一次约会呀，不要立刻把真面目暴露出来。到了第三次或者第四次约会的时候再去吃小龙虾，这时双方已经有了一定了解，更想看到真实的性格。把手弄得油油的、脏脏的，看清真实的我们，就是很自然的事了。

点评

当我们描述美食的时候，只说味道不够，还要呈现出让人垂涎欲滴的画面。比如They glisten, boiled bright red, heaps and heaps of whole crawfish spread across a dinner table. 闪闪发光，明亮的红色——餐桌上摆满了一堆堆的小龙虾。Glisten是闪闪发光的意思，bright red指明亮的红色，heap 是指"堆"，heaps and heaps of 就是一堆堆的、很多的。这样描述，画面既视感就有了。

一样东西可以好吃到什么程度？美味的delicious，yummy，tasty，让你疯狂饥饿drive you crazy and hungry，很多人爱吃 tons of people eat this and really love it。

"吃相好"可以有几种说法：拥有女王范儿的用餐礼仪have the dinner manners of the queen，有尊严的、高贵的、庄重的dignified，文明的、有礼貌的civil。

词汇小百科

crawfish 小龙虾
lobster 龙虾
shrimp 虾
crab 蟹
let loose 释放、放出、放任、不拘束
let loose your imagination 天马行空的想象

（陈　沫）

吃小龙虾的正确姿势

吃货们！中餐再次申遗你知道吗？

（素材来自《圆桌议事》2015年6月23日节目）

导　语：话说在日本和食、韩国泡菜相继成功申请联合国教科文组织世界非物质文化遗产后，有着博大精深的美食文化的中国决定再次为中餐申遗啦！中华美食申遗是否有必要呢？

When we are saying Chinese food, the concept includes the food itself, the cooking methods, the cultural elements surrounding it. That is supposed to represent us Chinese people.

当我们说中餐时，这个概念包括了食物本身、烹饪方法，以及围绕着食物的文化元素。这应该代表我们中国人。

Having said that, there might be some other reasons for doing this, which is to do with the intellectual property rights. Champagne is a good example. Champagne is a region of France. Only fizzy white wine from that area can be called champagne. There are a lot of Spanish producers producing more or less the same stuff. They have to call it the Méthode Champenoise, champagne method. They can't call it champagne. So there is a certain amount of protecting a nation's own products, which is actually a very tangible thing, to kind of register it.

话虽这么说，但还可能有其他的申遗原因，比如知识产权。香槟就是一个好例子。香槟是法国的一个地区，只有这里出产的气泡白葡萄酒叫香槟。有很多西班牙厂商制造了差不多的东西，但是他们只能叫它Méthode Champenoise，而不能叫它香槟。所以还是一定程度上保护了一个国家的自有产品。对于他们来说，想申遗成功是一件非常实际的事情，类似于注册它，给它贴上标签。

For me, I still think this is a bit of ridiculous. I don't really see the point of this, because I think for Chinese cuisine, it's already popular as it is. It is already spreading without the need of protection. You can see it everywhere all over the world.

我依然觉得这有点可笑。我并没有看到申遗的重要性。就中餐而言，我认为它本身已经很流行了，不需要保护就大范围传播开来。你能在世界的每个角落看到它。

There is one thing that makes me think it is necessary. It's exactly because of the misunderstanding of what Chinese food is, and what Chinese dishes are like, by the western population. Because yes, on one hand, there're lots of Chinese restaurants abroad, but on the other hand, what are they serving? It's not called Chinese food. Just because you serve some General Zuo's chicken or some lemon chicken, you cannot call it Chinese food, because it's not good at all.

有一件事让我认为申遗很有必要。因为关于中餐是什么，中餐长什么样，西方人有误解。一方面因为国外有很多中餐馆，但是另一方面他们提供什么菜？那不能叫中餐。不能只因为你提供左宗棠鸡或柠檬鸡，你就管它叫中餐，因为那一点都不好吃。

点 评

中餐申遗应该是怎样的？The concept includes the food itself, the cooking methods, the cultural elements surrounding it. 这个概念包括了食物本身，烹饪方法，以及围绕着食物的文化元素。That is supposed to represent us Chinese people这应该代表我们中国人，represent代表。为什么我们希望中餐申遗成功呢？I think that adds prestige我认为那能增添声誉，prestige声誉、威望。There is a certain amount of protecting a nation's own products一定程度上保护了一个国家的自有产品。

词汇小百科

Kung Pao Chicken　宫保鸡丁
Fish-flavored Shredded Pork with Garlic Sauce　鱼香肉丝
Mapo Tofu　麻婆豆腐
Braised Dongpo pork　东坡肉
Stewed Pork Ball in Brown Sauce　红烧狮子头
Tofu with Preserved Eggs　皮蛋豆腐
Sauteed Shredded Pork in Sweet Bean Sauce　京酱肉丝
Sweet and Sour Spare Ribs　糖醋排骨
Noodles with Soybean Paste　炸酱面
Steamed Pork with Rice　米粉肉
Sweet and Sour Mandarin Fish　松鼠鳜鱼

（王　玮）

如何用英文聊酸甜苦辣

（素材来自《圆桌议事》2015年6月27日节目）

导　语：中国的饮食文化源远流长，但你会用英文表达食物好不好吃、自己爱吃什么口味的食物吗？只会说delicious可一点都不高大上哦！在本篇中，我们会教大家怎样用纯正的英文和老外聊一聊酸甜苦辣。

Talking about all the different ways to describe how good your food tastes because in Chinese you often say, it's literally "good eat" or "good taste" or whatever. For a lot of people, they'll check the dictionary and say, "Oh, delicious." That's a very common phrase and it's not incorrect but the most common one, you just say, "Oh wow, that was good" or "Man, that food tastes so good." It is actually a little more common than saying delicious.

让我们聊聊如何用不同的方式来描述食物味道吧。在中文里你可能经常说什么东西"好吃""味道好"等。很多人查过字典后会说Oh, it's delicious 哦，这真好吃。这是个很常见的说法，也没有错。但是最常用的说法就是简单地说 Oh wow, that was good. "噢哇，这真不错"或者 Man, that food tastes so good. 伙计，这吃起来真棒。这些比 delicious 更加常用。

And then we also get "appetizing" there. For this, you don't actually use that much after you've tasted the food. It's more like you walk into a room, even with dinner or whatever you see on the table especially, you get the sights, and you get the smells there, and you're like, "Man, that food looks so appetizing. I just want to get a piece of that. Can I start eating now?"

还有一个词是appetizing开胃的、促进食欲的。这个词在你品尝过某种食品以后就很少有用武之地了。通常当你走进一间房间，看到桌子上的晚餐或食物，闻到香气，你就可以说："哥们儿，这些看起来让人很有食欲，我想来点儿那个，现在可以开始吃了吗？"

Another one that I personally like quite a bit is "scrumptious", "simply scrumptious." You might have seen this in one of those Willy Wonka movies over there, but it's a little bit funny 'cause it's kind of formal but if you use it in kind of a humorous or light-hearted situation, such as "Ah! Simply scrumptious! I must have some more of that." or you're kind of being mock-formal and that kind of thing. But it's definitely a compliment to whoever's made that food for you.

还有一个我个人很喜欢的词是scrumptious可口的。也许你在《查理和巧克力工厂》（威利·旺卡是其中的一个角色）电影中见到过这个词。这个词用起来感觉很有趣，因为它比较正式。但是你可以在一些幽默轻松的场合下用它，比如Ah! Simply scrumptious! I must have some more of that（啊，真可口！我必须要吃点那个！）或者只是假装正式的语气。但这个词肯定是对给你准备食物的人的赞赏。

点评

说到怎么说什么东西好吃，大家脑海里第一个蹦出的英文词估计是delicious，然而这个词可并不像你想象中的那么受老外待见。那我们应该怎样说好不好吃呢？我们可以直接用一个简单的good来表示好吃，如something tastes good。或者用appetizing这个词，这个词是从appetite胃口演变过来的，表示这个食物让你觉得很有食欲、有胃口，但需要注意的是appetizing与good不一样，一般在你开始吃这个食物之前用，而不是用来表达吃完后的评价。

还有一个比较书面化的词scrumptious，表示食物很可口，因为比较正式，所以口语中用的不是很多，但是你可以在半开玩笑的语气下，用这个词来称赞烹饪者的手艺。

词汇小百科

sour grapes　　酸葡萄

short and sweet　　简明扼要

sweet talk　　甜言蜜语

to the bitter end　　坚持到最后，一直到最后

spice things up　　把事情变得更有意思一些

spice of life　　生活的调味剂

（王　玮）

英文菜谱入门教学

(素材来自《圆桌议事》2014年9月27日节目)

导　语：俗话说，民以食为天。无论是快乐悲伤、聚会独处，一餐恰到好处的美食，都能让人立刻心旷神怡、身心愉悦。作为一个合格的吃货，除了深谙我中华美食之精髓外，一定也对西方的料理颇感兴趣。怎奈这世上的烹饪方式多种多样，煎炒烹炸、焖熘熬炖，看不懂英文菜谱岂不是"如入宝山而空回"？别急，这篇里我们就暂收口水，一起来学学相关的英文表达。

The first one we are looking at is blanching. All you do is put vegetable or fruit, but usually vegetable, into boiling water, and after a very, very short period of time, take it out and put it into iced water or cold running water to immediately halt the cooking process.

第一个词是"焯"。你要做的就是把蔬菜或水果，通常是蔬菜，放进沸水中，过很短的时间就捞出来。然后再把它放到冰水或自来水里，这样可以立刻停止整个烹饪过程。

And then the next is braising. It's a combination cooking method using both moist and dry heat. So usually the food is first seared (we will talk about that in a minute) in a high temperature, and then finish in a covered pot with a variable amount of liquid.

下一个是"炖"。这个braising的"炖"和我们中餐里的"炖"最大的差别就是braising其实是个组合烹饪法。先高温煎炸（这个我们一会儿具体讲），然后再加水，盖在锅里炖。

Yeah and there is simmering. Simmering is used a lot in western cooking. Basically you bring whatever liquid you have in your pot up to boiling and you turn the heat down to keep it just below boiling. So it's not on the lowest setting. But it's just keeping the liquid at a temperature that is not actually boiling.

西方烹饪里还有一个很常用的做法叫"煨"。煨就是先把锅里的汤煮沸，然后把火调小煮，让它保持在马上可以沸腾的温度。这里并不是要最小火，只是要保证火要小到让它将开锅又没有开锅的时候。

And then there is grilling. So here is the thing actually – grill usually refers to barbecuing. You grill something, you barbecue something on a grill, you are grilling. Grill can also be used inside. If you have a griddle, for example, or even if you have just a regular pan, but you are grilling a hamburger inside.

Grilling是烧烤的一种，grill这个词也可以指烤架。它既可以是户外烧烤，也可以是在室内用烤架、烤炉，甚至是平底锅来烤。比如在室内烤汉堡包，也是用grill这个词。

Then there is rotisserie, where meat is skewered on a big metal stick, goes from one end, all the way to the other, and then it is stuck on the machine where it just keeps rotating so that no one piece of the meat is over the fire or heat source for too long.

Rotisserie指的是用金属烤叉穿过要烧烤的食物，一般是肉类，然后在电烤炉里面一边转一边烤，这样就可以均匀加热，不会有哪一块肉烤糊。

And then last but not least is marination, one of my favorite processes when I am cooking meat. And basically you're just soaking foods in a seasoned liquid before cooking. And the best type is usually acidic marinade with vinegar, lemon juice, or wine, or the enzymatic, which I think is quite interesting, pineapple, papaya or kiwifruit. You let it sit for maybe even a couple of days before you actually cook it up. Yeah I mean sometimes marinade can be very short. But the whole purpose is just to get the flavors from the liquid into the meat. It's actually different from a sauce, because the sauce is only on the outside.

我们要讲到的最后一个方法，也是西餐里很重要的一个烹饪方法就是"腌"。腌的要诀自然就是在烹饪准备环节中就把食物浸泡在调好的酱汁里。一般常用的酱汁搭配是酸醋腌制汁加食醋，或者柠檬汁，或葡萄酒，或者酶，然后加菠萝、木瓜或猕猴桃之类的水果。腌制的过程有时可以持续好几天。当然，腌制也可以不用那么久，重点就是要让汁的味道入肉。这跟使用酱汁是不一样的，酱汁只是外部调味。

点 评

烹饪可谓是古今中外常聊常新、居家旅行必备神技。显然，这篇里提到的西餐烹饪方法其实已经不能算"零基础"入门了。像需要用凉水 cold running water 过一下的焯 blanching，或者需要认真掌握火候才能做到的煨 simmering，都不是简单的一个动作可以概括的。又比如文中提到的炸 searing，其实也和中餐里的煎炸略有区别，有一点点像炸，但不是用油浸没的深度炸 deep-fry，而是刚好要炸到表面上微微发焦，肉不需要这样煎熟，而是半熟就可以继续之后的制作过程了。看到这里，你是不是对于西餐烹饪有了更深的了解呢？

词汇小百科

boil 用开水煮、煮沸
roast 烘烤

bake　烘焙
knead　揉面
mash　捣碎
mince / chop　绞碎
dice　切小块
shred　切丝
grate　磨碎
drain gentle heat　捞小火、微火、文火
stuff　填、酿积

（牛翃琳）

吃货+技术宅=美食公式！

（素材来自《圆桌议事》2015年6月24日节目）

> **导　语**：在中国菜谱里，"少许""适量""一点"是出现频率最高的量词，但"少许"到底是多少，这就是你自己感觉差不多，只可意会不可言传的了。而一些国外学者经过研究，给出了不同的食物的最美味的制作公式。在本篇里，让我们一起学做技术宅，用公式来制作美食吧！

I think it can produce a standardized flavor, but whether that is perfect to your palate is a completely different thing. So I think standardization is really what they're trying to do, and not really trying to find the optimal flavor.

我认为它（公式）能做出标准的味道，但是这个味道是否对你的口味就是另一回事了。所以我认为他们（科学家）正在努力做的事是标准化，而不是找到最佳的味道。

But even if you don't follow perfectly, just the idea of doing this in a more rigorous sort of way instead of like "oh, I'll just grab a certain amount of salt and just kind of throw that out there," then that's probably not going to be the optimal taste and this way it makes cooking easier in a lot of ways and it can actually be healthier. It's about improving peoples' livelihoods.

即使你不完全按照（公式）来，只是更严谨地制作，而不是随便"抓点盐扔进去"，那么也许味道不是最佳的，但是这样会让做菜更简单更健康。

这能改善大家的生活。

According to this recipe, the perfect strawberry-to-cream ratio is 7:3, and I totally disagree with it because I don't really like whipped cream that much. I would prefer 8:2, so that's also a 4:1.

根据菜谱，草莓和奶油的黄金比例应该是7:3。对此我完全不同意。因为我不太喜欢生奶油，所以我更倾向于8:2或者4:1。

Xiaohua sounded like a true conservative there saying that you think that there should be a standardized rule where I think that certain variations are necessary to suit the local palate.

晓华在做菜这方面很保守，认为应该有标准化的规则，但我认为适当的改变对于适应当地人的口味来说是必要的。

点评

如何才能制作出美食呢？是按公式，还是创造出自己独特的味道呢？The formula can produce a standardized flavor. 公式能做出标准化的味道，standardized标准化的，这个词来源于standard标准，后缀-ize表示使成为，使……化，如Car parts are usually standardized汽车部件一般都是统一规格的。但是Whether that is perfect to your palate is a completely different thing这个味道是否对你的口味就是另一回事了，palate味觉、嗜好，to somebody's palate对某人的口味。Perfect ratio完美的比例或黄金比例，如the perfect A to B ratio is，A和B之间的黄金配比是……如what's the perfect coffee to milk ratio? 咖啡和牛奶之间黄金配比是多少？制作好吃的美食还需要certain variations适当的改变，variation改变，对应动词vary表示变化。好好按配比公式做美食可以improve peoples' livelihoods改善大家的生活，livelihood生活、生计，做菜不是小事情，是改善生活品质的大事。

词汇小百科

boiling 煮
stewing 煲/炖
braising 烧/焖/烩
frying 煎
stir-frying 炒
quick-frying 爆
deep-frying 炸
frying and simmering 扒
simmering 煨
smoking 熏
roasting / barbecuing 烤
baking 烘
steaming 蒸

（王 玮）

土豆拯救世界

（素材来自《圆桌议事》2016年1月15日节目）

导　语：中国一所大学筹备成立马铃薯学院，以加强在马铃薯领域内的能力建设、人才培养和科研创新。该学校为什么要开设这样一个学院？这样的学院有存在的必要吗？

This news for me is a message that potatoes have a bright future. Later on maybe they will become a staple food, so that every day on our dinner table we will have potato, instead of rice or bread or bread made of potatoes. That can happen one day.

　　这则新闻报道对我来说昭示了土豆拥有着灿烂的未来。以后它们也许会成为主食，那么我们的餐桌上每晚都会出现土豆，而不是米饭或面包。面包是不是土豆做成的？也许某天会一语中的。

We all know that for the favorite staple food—rice and sometimes wheat, we need to use a lot of water, we need to give them a lot of pesticides and a lot of care, so that we can have a good yield. But it seems to me that potato is a rather easy-to-care plant. Like The Martian, we all watched the movie; he could grow potatoes on Mars. Why can't we make it more popular in China?

　　我们都知道我们最喜爱的主食——米饭，有时还有小麦，需要大量的水（用于种植），我们还需要使用大量的杀虫剂并投入大量精力培育，才能有个好收成。但在我看来，土豆的种植过程相对简单。就像我们都看过的电影

《火星救援》里的情节，他（男主人公）可以在火星上种土豆。为什么我们不能在中国大量种植土豆呢？

I think this university has come up with a new breed of potatoes in the past. So basically, they have leading a position. Yes, I guess they have a leading position if they can breed a kind of disease resistant potato. Maybe they have some potential in further developing some other species.

我注意到这所大学曾经研发出一种新品种的土豆。如果他们能够繁育出一种对病菌有抵抗能力的土豆的话，必定会占据行业的领先位置。也许他们有潜力再开发出一些其他的种类呢。

I am not laughing at potatoes, I love potatoes! I love fried shredded potatoes in vinegar sauce. I love them. And I think for the Irish People, when they had that big famine in their history, potatoes saved millions of lives. So we have a lot to say to thank potatoes. In some Asian countries, I think some European countries too, a lot of people love potatoes. We have sausage on mash which is made of mashed potatoes and sausage. And for Indian people, potato is a necessary ingredient for a lot of vegetarian food because a lot of Indian people do not eat meat. So it is a very important staple food for quite a number of countries. Also some African countries take potatoes as a staple food. So we are not laughing at them, it's just the idea of a college with this name that tickles a bit.

我并不是在嘲笑土豆，我爱土豆！我爱吃醋熘土豆丝。我真的很爱吃的。我想对于爱尔兰人民来说，（土豆的地位更高）。他们当年经历大饥荒的时候，土豆拯救了数以百万计的生命呢！所以我们真的要感谢土豆。在一些亚洲国家，还有欧洲国家，非常多的人爱吃土豆。有一道菜叫香肠土豆泥，就是把土豆剁成泥加上香肠制作而成的。对于印度人来说，土豆是不可或缺的素食主义食材，要知道很多印度人是不吃肉的。所以土豆是很多国家非常重要的主食呢。有若干非洲国家也把土豆当作主食之一。所以我们可不是在笑话他们，只不过一想到一间大学要以此命名，有点被逗乐的感觉。

Joking aside, I think the reason why I was laughing was partially because of ignorance. When you don't understand the science behind potatoes, or rice, or wheat, or whatever object, then it's very easy to make fun of it.

玩笑之余，我想我笑成这样的部分原因是无知。当你并不知道土豆、大米、小麦或其他物质背后的科学知识时，是很容易拿这些东西开玩笑的。

点评

Breed 当名词使用是"种类，血统"的意思。当动词使用时有"繁殖，训练，引起"等意思。Tong is one of the new breed of Chinese girls who are independent, confident, and not afraid of breaking the rules. 童是新一代的中国女孩，她们独立、自信，而且不怕打破常规；Born and bred in Beijing, she will not forget her roots regardless of where she lives now. 生于长于北京，无论现在她身在何地都不会忘记她的根在哪里；Violence breeds violence. 暴力催生更多暴力。

Someone has the potential in / for / to do 某人在……方面有潜力。She has the potential to become the team leader. 她有成为队长的潜力。

让我们从小小的土豆说起。土豆、地瓜、玉米，这是美洲馈赠给全世界的礼物。在2015年上映的著名科幻电影 The Martian《火星救援》里，帮助马特·达蒙撑到最后的是土豆。土豆这种农作物的最大品质，就是对抗恶劣的环境。

不过未来中国人会不会习惯于把土豆当主食，中国土豆种植面积会不会翻番，这都难以预料。国家政策的倡导必将在一定程度上影响土豆在我国的种植情况。

词汇小百科

have a bright future　拥有光明的未来
staple food　主食
rice　大米
wheat　小麦
barley　大麦
yam　甘薯
mashed potato　土豆泥
roasted potatoes　烤土豆
potato salad　土豆沙拉

（赫　扬）

独自就餐不再是异类

（素材来自《圆桌议事》2015年2月4日节目）

导　语：快节奏的生活方式似乎让很多人习惯了一个人吃饭，既可以简单直接地解决温饱问题，也可以对食物有更细致严格的要求。几年前，日剧《孤独美食家》被小清新们引进国内：一位叫五郎的大叔在屏幕里吃饭、念叨，从头到尾都是一个人，几年如一日。就是他，告诉年轻人：在纷乱的世界里，哪怕一个人也要好好享受美食。任何原因都不能干扰吃，吃是一种哲学和信仰。

Yeah, I think it's something that's becoming a bit more popular and I think it is breaking through some of the existing social stigma of one person dining outside. It used to be frowned upon, more or less, but not that much anymore.

对啊，我觉得自己一个人出去吃饭这件事，好像开始流行起来了，不再被看成是某种污点。过去，独自就餐多多少少都会引人侧目，甚至被评头论足，但现在这种情况已经越来越少了。

When I was single and in the university, you know, after I graduated and I was working a job, I'd eat by myself all the time. Yes, I did enjoy it, but I think that in most of those cases, it was just something to do quickly and get it over with. And really now, I mean I view it very much in having a relationship with someone, whether it's a friend, whether it's your spouse, your kids, or whatever. It's sharing the food, sharing a feeling, as you said, a nourishing thing. That's really important.

之前我单身，在大学读书的时候，以及后来毕业开始工作的时候，我都经常自己一个人吃饭。的确，当时我挺享受独自用餐的。不过，大部分时候，一个人吃饭只是为了方便快捷、甚至敷衍了事。现在想想，我觉得吃饭是需要有饭伴的，不管是朋友、爱人、孩子或是其他的什么人。就像你说的，吃饭是一起分享食物、分享情感的过程，有益身心健康。这很重要。

OK, well, here I'd like to quote a little bit from this really popular Japanese TV drama called *Gu Du De Mei Shi Jia*, The Lonely Gourmand. So, it basically tells you that when you are having the food alone, it's free from the constraint of time and societal views. And you fill the appetite with happiness and in that brief moment as you are enjoying the food, one's heart and mind is set free. And that intimate moment is what I cherish so much.

我想分享一些我从日剧《孤独的美食家》里看到的观点。基本上它想说的是：当你独自用餐时，你不再受时间和社会规则礼仪的约束，在那个短短的一顿饭的时间里，你满心愉悦，胃口大开，而你的心神也是完全自由的。我自己也很珍惜那种纯粹的亲密时刻。

点 评

单身的美食家，独自一人在高档餐厅用餐时，曾经会觉得好像遭到了其他食客的鄙视。frown是皱眉的意思，可以形容不高兴、沉思、忧愁等状态。而frown on / upon something 就常常用来表示"不赞成、不许可、不同意"某件事情。

没有"吃货"精神的人，多半觉得吃饭只是为了填饱肚子，那如何表达"赶快把事情做完，结束这个不愉快的任务"呢？可以用get it over with。比如This project has been dragging on forever. Let's just get it over with already. 这个项目已经拖了很久，我们赶紧把它对付完吧。

词汇小百科

tasty　可口的、味道好的
appetizing　开胃的、促进食欲的
delectable　美味的、令人愉悦的
flavorful　可口的、充满……味道的
luscious　香甜的、甘美的
palatable　可口的、怡人的

（牛翎琳）

中外交流
Communication

外国人眼中的中国文化符号

（素材来自《圆桌议事》2015年6月15日节目）

导　语： 作为世界上最为古老的国家之一，中国一直都是神秘的代表。那么在外国人眼中，中国究竟是一个什么样的国度呢？北京师范大学发布了《外国人对中国文化认知调查报告》。在本篇中让我们来看看什么是老外最熟知和最不熟知的中国文化符号。

I'm not surprised with panda being the most widely recognized Chinese symbol. They're so cute, aren't they? They're podgy, and I just want to poke them. And also I think the Chinese government has been actively engaged in the panda diplomacy for a few decades. Now I think it's sort of been chosen as the national symbol, even for Chinese people.

大熊猫成为最为大家熟识的中国象征，我并不惊讶。它们好可爱，不是吗？矮矮胖胖的，我只想戳戳它们。而且中国政府近几十年来一直致力于熊猫外交。现在它俨然成了全中国的象征，即使是对中国人来说也是一样。

This term has really migrated its way into the English lexicon now, so I think that's part of the Chinese culture. You know, the Yin and Yang, that's the philosophy concept that's really taken off in the English speaking world as well.

"阴阳"现在已经进入英文词汇中了，我认为那是中国文化的一部分。你知道阴和阳是哲学概念，目前在英语的世界里也已经广为人知。

A lot of Americans would be educated in this way about China. If you think about it, if you try to analyze the channels through which foreigners know about China, it's all pop culture icons, pop culture symbols, right? So movies, songs, TV series, these are the places to go. Nobody would get their education through like having a master's degree or PhD on China, while some people do, but it's not how most people are educated.

很多美国人是以这种方式了解中国的。不妨想一下，尝试分析外国人了解中国的渠道，都是流行文化符号、流行文化象征，不是吗？所以电影、歌曲、电视剧，这些是了解的方式。没人会通过获得硕士或博士学位来了解中国——可能有些人会这样，但这不是大多数人的了解途径。

And also I think mass media play such a big role in stereotyping our understanding of a nation, like you know, Hollywood movies, American TV shows, those are the primary sources for us to learn about America.

我认为大众传媒在我们对一个国家教条化理解方面也起了很大的作用。像你知道的，好莱坞电影和美国电视节目是我们了解美国第一来源。

点评

外国人对中国形象的了解究竟是怎样的呢？人人都爱大熊猫 panda，因为 Chinese government has been actively engaged in the panda diplomacy for a few decades 中国政府近几十年来一直致力于大熊猫外交，be engaged in something/doing something 从事于某事或做某事，panda diplomacy 大熊猫外交，就像 Ping-Pong diplomacy 乒乓外交一样。有些中国的文化符号如阴阳 has migrated its way into the English lexicon 现在已经进入英文词汇中了，migrated into something 迁移到什么当中，migrate 迁移、移居。没人会通过获得一个学位来了解一个国家，他们的方式通常是通过 pop culture icons 流行文化符号或

pop culture symbols流行文化象征来了解一个国家，icon符号、偶像，symbol象征，如电影movies，歌曲songs或电视剧TV series，就像我们通过好莱坞电影Hollywood movies和美国电视节目American TV shows来了解美国一样。

词汇小百科

stereotype　刻板印象
cultural shock　文化冲击
cultural conflict　文化冲突
cultural difference　文化差别
cultural identity　文化认同感

（王　玮）

外国人眼中的中国文化符号

外国人看不懂的中式生活习惯

（素材来自《圆桌议事》2016年7月11日节目）

导　语：有些中式生活习惯是外国人完全看不懂的，比如把锅碗瓢盆放进闲置烤箱，拿饼干盒来储藏针线包，还有把手指伸进电饭锅来量一下需要多少水。外国人是怎么看这些习惯呢？

This one, your fingers are not always, actually, they are frequently not very clean. So, if you want to eyeball it like I do myself frequently or mostly, that's fine. But, you could also get a measuring cup like a lot of these rice cookers now; they have those little measuring cups with them. So, you can just use it, figure out how much water you want to put in exactly, how much rice, and there you go. There's no need to go by my finger.

这一条，把手指伸进电饭锅……事实上，手指不总是那么卫生。如果你紧盯着（电饭锅里的水量），我就经常这么干，这是没关系的。其实你还可以用一个量杯，现在很多电饭煲都带量杯，可以直接用啊，测算出你到底需要放多少水、多少米。没有必要用手指。

Are you kidding me? That is an extra step and you need to store for that cup. So, yeah it could be a little troublesome. But I think it shows a very different perception towards cooking and many other things that Chinese people tend to do. It is that we are into abstracts. We are free spirited sometimes. We don't want the specific degrees, the scientific mode towards cooking. No way, we want to do it as what masters do: that is according to our mood, according to our fingers, we know how we cook.

开玩笑吧？量杯也需要存放，岂不是又多了一个步骤，有点麻烦。这说明中国人在烹饪和其他很多事情上与其他国家的不同——我们喜欢抽象的境界。我们有时候无拘无束，不想用精确的刻度和科学的烹饪方法。我们希望像大师一样，做事看情绪，量水靠手指，我们知道怎么做饭。

There are bigger problems with the table manners, like for example, you had better put your cell phone down and away before eating. That's a more important one I would say.

谈到餐桌礼仪，其实还有更大的问题。比如最好把手机放在远处。这点更加重要。

Also having a sewing kit is kind of necessary in any household but storing it in a cookie container…It used to be that those cookie containers are so fancy and it's like a nice place to store things. But, no longer really is that the case as now you can just get a fabulous sewing kit container from Taobao or wherever these days. So easy and so cheap.

居家生活里有针线包是很必要的，但是把它放在饼干盒里……那些饼干盒很好看，的确是存放物件的好地方。但是，现在不用这样了，去淘宝网或者任何地方买一个超赞的针线盒，很方便，也便宜。

点评

每个国家或地区的人们都有自己的生活习惯，自己认为很平常normal，而外人觉得有点奇怪odd，比如我们有时喜欢抽象的abstract，但外国人很多情况下喜欢具体的 specific。习惯上的差异只是表象，背后更深刻的是思维方式，比如用手指量水这个小习惯，可以或多或少看出来不同的理念different perceptions，perception 是观念、认知、印象的意思。

当你不同意一件事的时候，可以委婉地表达，指出这样做的一些不良效果。比如不同意"把手伸进电饭煲"，你可以说your fingers are not always very clean. 你的手指不总是那么卫生的。Not always……是很好的提醒。又如，不同意用饼干盒装针线包，你也可以通过提供一个替代方案来表达，可以说you can just get a fabulous sewing kit container from Taobao or wherever these days. 现如今你可以从淘宝网或者任何地方买到超赞的针线盒，意思就是不要用饼干盒装了。

词汇小百科

rice cooker　电饭煲

measuring cup　量杯

sewing kit　针线包

eyeball　作名词自然指"眼球"，作动词是"打量，盯住看"的意思

free spirited　无拘无束的、自由奔放的

（陈　沫）

外国人看不懂的中式生活习惯

美国学生眼里的中国功夫

（素材来自《圆桌议事》2015年9月17日节目）

导　语：一项调查问卷显示中国对美国学生的吸引力比美国对中国学生的吸引力还要强，然而相比起中国学生对美国的了解，美国学生对中国的了解却仅限于功夫明星，这是真的吗？

Let's talk a little bit about people's interest or knowledge about cultural icons of the other country. Not surprisingly, Chinese people can name a lot of either shows or celebrities or historical figures, while there is limited number of Chinese people that Americans know.

　　我们来说一下中美两国人们对于对方国家文化偶像的兴趣或了解程度。不出意料，中国人民可以很轻易地说出很多美国的电视节目、明星或者历史人物，但美国人民对中国名人的了解却相当有限。

That's exactly what the survey found. These big Kung Fu stars and former basketball star Yao Ming are the most famous Chinese people amongst all for Americans, and also Chinese president Xi Jinping. Americans students know him too. I guess they do pay attention to world politics more or less. Nobody could name a Chinese film or TV drama. Oh, I'm sorry. The majority of these US students couldn't do that.

　　这正是研究发现的结果。美国学生只认识中国的功夫明星和前篮球巨星姚明，还有中国的国家主席习近平。看样子他们多多少少还是关注政治的。

没人说得上来一部中国的电影或者电视剧。大部分美国人都说不上来。

I suppose that they are too young to remember *Crouching Tiger Hidden Dragon*, because that came out ten years ago or more than that. If they are college students, probably they don't remember that. But that was a hugely successful Chinese movie.

  可能是他们太年轻了，不记得《卧虎藏龙》这部电影吧。这部电影上映十多年了，如果他们现在是大学生的话，当时还是婴儿，十有八九不记得了。但这是部非常成功的中国电影。

But would you be able to name the stars? It would still be difficult. Back then I remember some of my American friends say: "Oh, there is this young woman. She's amazing. She looks like sixteen." Then I realized they were talking about Zhang Ziyi. There you see a cultural difference too. Because for us, she is a full-grown woman. She must be in her twenties and she is great at Kung Fu and all that kinds of stuff. But in the eyes of Americans, the perception is completely different. But I am not surprised with this at all, especially when we talk about TV shows, Hollywood, and the influence it has over the world, it's incomparable.

  但是即便记得《卧虎藏龙》，他们能说出那些明星演员的名字吗？恐怕还是困难。我记得当时有些美国朋友说："有个年轻女演员，她很棒，看起来也就16岁。"我后来意识到他们说的是章子怡。从这里就可以看出中美文化间的差异。在我们看来，章子怡是个成熟的女人，二十多岁，擅长功夫，等等。而在他们看来，她却是个十几岁的小孩。对此我并不感到奇怪，尤其是在谈论电视剧、好莱坞电影的时候。好莱坞对世界的影响真是无与伦比的。

American culture is overwhelming and mainstream. They've got the movies, fast food and drinks and coffee shops. There is a lot of American culture coming at the same time on different sorts of levels, isn't there?

美国文化势不可当,是主流文化。有电影,快餐,饮料,咖啡店等,渗透到我们生活的方方面面。

Exactly. It is not surprising that Chinese students would know so much about cultural elements or icons in the US.

太对了,难怪中国学生知道这么多美国的文化元素和偶像。

I lived in London before. I love the city. But I never thought London is as beautiful and as modern until I watched the new version of *Sherlock*. There is a lot to be learned there. Can we do something similar to Beijing? Because I think for this city, although it has been in the news a lot, to capsulize a city's image, what the city represents and what it is like today and present it in such a natural way like they did in *Sherlock*... is something to be learned.

我在伦敦生活过,我热爱这座城市,但我在看新版福尔摩斯电视剧《神探夏洛克》之前没觉得它这么漂亮和现代化。我们能从中学到很多。我不禁在想:能否用类似的手法来处理北京呢?虽然北京也经常上新闻,但如何概括一个城市的形象,描述城市的面貌,用自然的手法勾勒出一个城市的文化,电视剧《神探夏洛克》无疑给我们上了很好的一课。

点评

电影《卧虎藏龙》(*Crouching Tiger Hidden Dragon*)可能是为数不多的为外国人所熟悉的中国电影之一,造就了一批功夫明星 Kung Fu stars。好莱坞电影代表当今世界的一种主流文化 mainstream culture。

Icon 指标志性的偶像,如文化偶像 cultural icon,时尚偶像 fashion icon,等等。

词汇小百科

historical figures　历史人物

incomparable　无与伦比的

overwhelming　势不可当的，无法抗拒的，压倒性的

Sherlock Holmes　福尔摩斯，英国作家柯南道尔 Sir Arthur Conan Doyle 笔下的大侦探

Sherlock　《神探夏洛克》，BBC根据《福尔摩斯》翻拍的新版电视剧

（于　洋）

美国学生眼里的中国功夫

中英夹杂太low了？

（素材来自《圆桌议事》2016年2月25日节目）

导　语：有些人觉得说中文的时候夹杂几个英文单词非常洋气，显得高大上。但是也有很多人觉得这种表达方式十分矫揉造作，在中文语境中显得水土不服。这样的中英文"夹杂体"，是不是太low了？

Are you still with us? Yeah? I'm grateful that you have not switched channels just yet. This phenomenon of talking in mixed languages is called linguistically "pidgin."

你还在收听吗？是吗？我很感激你还没有转台。这个使用多种语言进行混杂式对话的现象在语言学上被称为"混杂语言"。

I think it's due to the limitation of certain people's language skills that you can't find a translation. But I think for certain words like "orientation" and "presentation", these words that are used in western offices very frequently, and now you see them (being) used in China as well. But don't you find that it's usually those who work in foreign companies that are in that language environment that use this kind of mixed language a bit more than other people?

我觉得那是因为某些人的语言能力有限，才无法找到合适的翻译字句吧。不过确实有些字眼例如"任职培训"和"陈述报告"在西方工作场合较为常用。现在（此类活动）在中国（工作场合）有时也适用。但你不觉得一般是那些在外国企业中工作、拥有国际化语言环境的雇员比其他人更常用这种混合型语言吗？

There are three major points I want to make about this story.

对于这则新闻，我有三点要说。

There are two setbacks to this that I don't like. First of all, it's to do with the purity of the language. The problem is if you are using English words, that's fine, but if you are using them incorrectly, is that cool?

这样我认为会有两个问题。第一，语言的纯洁性会受到影响。如果你使用英文词汇，没有问题；但如果你的使用有误，那就是问题了。

In China these days, we like to say zhe ren hao low. I love it when we are saying that because in Chinese we are saying this person is bad, inferior, we don't like this person, bad taste amongst other things. And you say "so low!" Do you think it's used in a correct circumstance?

在现今中国，我们喜欢说"zhe ren hao low"。我喜欢这样的中文用法。我们用它来表达这个人不怎么样，较差，我不喜欢这个人的坏品位及其他问题。对这个人的评价是真low！你觉得low这样的使用方式在英文里是正确的吗？

But because the English terms that are being put into Chinese are interchangeable, it means there is no real system of right or wrong here. It's more to do with a fashion trend, for me I find that personally a bit convoluted and confusing.

但因为英语里的术语在这儿被直接挪到中文语境里，可进行互换的替补作用。这意味着这种（中英文交杂的）用法并没有一个真正的对与错的体系可遵循。这可能更是一种（语言）潮流。我个人觉得有些复杂和难懂。

But for Chinese, it's quite okay for us to use pidgin. Even the "long time no see" originally was not standard English, now it has morphed into standard English language. When people are talking around you, like this person is so "man", this is so "low", It's simple, it's succinct, and it really reflects the person's emotions. So there's nothing wrong about pidgin.

但对于中国人来说，我们使用混杂语言并没有什么问题。连现在的常用说法"好久没见"一开始也不是标准英语的用法，现在它演变成了标准英语。当人们日常会话时，有时候会说这个人好man，这太low了。这样的说法很简单明了，而且充分地反映出个人的情感。所以使用中英文混杂的语言方式没有什么问题。

点评

到底应不应该使用中英文交杂的方式说话呢？首先要看清楚对象，再说话。在双方都不反感中英夹杂的语境下，这种讲话方式才不会让人感到突兀，或者让听者觉得你"装"。比如讲话双方都为留学生，都为外企员工，或都为同行业的专业人士。

但是，假如对方不怎么在日常生活中用到英文，或者基本没有英语技能，用夹杂英文的中文对话会让对方觉得很费劲和难以理解。在这种情况下，为了沟通的顺畅，应该努力地切换为全中文模式。

最理想的情况是，根据具体的交谈语境，要么纯讲中文，要么纯讲英文。如果一个人的英文或中文足够好，他不会总出现本来在说一种语言，因为遇到某个概念用这种语言表达不出来，而要寻求第二种语言帮助的情况。

词汇小百科

setback　挫折、阻碍
convoluted　盘绕的，复杂的

（赫　扬）

去洗手间的表达方式

（素材来自《圆桌议事》2014年10月25日节目）

导　语：据说有个外国人在爬长城，因为水喝多了想上厕所，就和他的中国导游说："I want to go somewhere."（我想去方便一下。）导游未解其深意，又生性热情好客，便大方回应道："You can go anywhere!"（去哪儿都行！）显然，"方便"真的是个有点三俗，但又极其实用的话题。这一篇里，我们就一起来聊一聊上厕所，特别是上大号的表达吧！

In English, we say going pee is number 1 and going poop is number 2. But you can also say that you have to drop a deuce. And deuce, I am not quite sure where that word comes from, but it also means number 2. So drop a deuce would be the same thing as saying I need to go number 2.

在英语里，我们说上小号是1号，大号是2号。还有一个说法是你要去"扔个两点"。虽然不知道deuce两点这个词的由来，但在这个语境里，它也意味着2号。所以drop a deuce等于我需要去上大号的意思。

And then, of course, there is take a dump, right? So drop a deuce, take a dump and drop the kids off at the pool, so we can say in English there is a lot of dropping kind of imagery there.

当然，你也可以说"卸个货"take a dump，以及drop the kids off at the

pool，把孩子扔进游泳池。这些都是上大号的意思。由此可见，上大号的英文表达真的包含很多扔、降落的意象。

Here is a really funny one. Again very, very cultural. I have to take the Browns to the Super Bowl. The Super Bowl is the championship of American football of the NFL. Now the Cleverland Browns are a notoriously bad team, so it's funny obviously because they are called the Browms and poop is brown, but also because the Browns never go to the Super Bowl.

下面这个说法也很有趣，并且很有美式文化背景——"带布朗队去超级碗比赛"。Super Bowl，超级碗，是美式足球NFL也就是全美橄榄球联盟的冠军赛。因为克利夫兰布朗队的水平是出了名的差（许多体育迷戏称"一坨屎！"），而它的队名里又有屎的颜色——棕色brown，所以那些嘲讽克利夫兰布朗队"烂泥扶不上墙"的人就用"带布朗队去超级碗比赛"take the Browns to the Super Bowl这个短语来表示上大号的意思。

点评

上大号（poop）的表达，大部分都是俚语（slang）。虽然有点"三俗"，可能无法在不熟的人面前或某些正式场合使用，但时尚炫酷的欧美年轻人经常说这些话，所以很有必要了解一下。不过了解归了解，使用还是要谨慎为上。比如去面试的时候，千万别跟考官说I'm prairie-dogging，那画面太"美"，不敢想象。切记一条大原则：Don't use them in polite company.

词汇小百科

go to the loo 是英式英语中的厕所

go and see my aunt 是英国俚语的上厕所

go to the powder room / need to powder my nose　去化妆间、去补妆（仅限女性使用）

use the John，John　在俚语中是洗手间的意思

make a pit stop，pit stop　是赛车比赛中进站加油的意思，这个俚语也指上厕所。

当然你也可以说：Please excuse me, I'll be back in a minute. 抱歉我走开一会儿，马上回来。还有最普遍、最简单的go to the bathroom，上洗手间。

（牛翃琳）

去洗手间的表达方式

洋明星的中国名

（素材来自《圆桌议事》2015年2月10日节目）

导　语：卷福、阿汤哥、小李子、水果姐、火星哥、霉霉、大表姐……如果你不是欧美影迷或乐迷，不是这些当红明星的粉丝，或许并不知道这些有趣的昵称分别指代谁。这一次，爱给偶像"冠名"的中国粉丝甚至成功引起了美国CNN的注意。既然动静这么大，我们就一起来学一下那些洋明星的中文昵称吧，不然就落伍咯。

I think a lot of those nicknames just come from fans and I think these celebrities should seriously take it as a major compliment to them. Because they are foreign celebrities and stars, and they are having such a big fan base in China that people actually coin new words and phrases to address their names and what they stand for. Isn't that a great achievement?

大部分昵称都是粉丝们想出来的。我觉得，这些明星真的应该把拥有中文昵称当成是对他们的极大赞美。想想看，他们的中国粉丝群如此庞大，大到了可以集众人之力创造出新词来称呼他们，宣扬这些明星的立场。这难道不是巨大的成功吗？

It has to be that he was super popular in Sherlock Holmes, the UK version. In that TV series, he had lovely curly hair and maybe because he is so cute to his fans that they think "what a blessing he is" and there you go, "Curly Blessing". And also there is a Chinese wording for Sherlock Holmes *Fuermosi*, so we called him "juan fu", acronym（for Curly Sherlock Holmes）.

"卷福"这个外号，主要是因为本尼迪克特·康伯巴奇在英剧《神探夏洛克》中饰演的夏洛克·福尔摩斯实在太火了。这个角色的一头鬈发格外惹眼；而在中文里，"福"除了可以指代福尔摩斯这个名字外，还有幸福、祝福的意思，许多影迷都觉得由本尼迪克特·康伯巴奇这么优秀的演员来演福尔摩斯，太幸福了，所以几个原因结合在一起，他就成了"卷福"。

Then Ariana Grande is known as "xiao niu", I mean it all feels very random, like why would you call Mariah Carey "Cow Sister"? It sounds insulting.

美国女歌手爱莉安娜·格兰德被中国粉丝叫作"小牛"，因为她就像是年轻版的玛利亚·凯莉，也就是粉丝口中的"牛姐"。也许你会觉得有些莫名其妙，为什么要取"牛姐"这样的外号啊？听起来好像有点侮辱人呢。

In English, you call someone, especially a woman a "Cow", then you are saying she's fat. But "niu" in Chinese actually means awesome, fabulous, stunning, gorgeous etc. Because she just got quite good a singing talent, right?

在英文里，如果你用奶牛来形容女士，就相当于在说她很胖。但是"牛"在中文里其实是很厉害、很棒的意思，粉丝叫她"牛姐"是因为她唱功实在太牛了。

点 评

在讲到起外号这件事的时候，主持人表示，有外号说明他们红啊！所以这应该是对他们的夸奖。把什么东西看成是夸奖，用英文说就是 take something as a compliment. 如果确实不是夸奖，知道自己说出来的话会让对方难受，可以来一句"No offense 无意冒犯"；对方则可以回应"None taken 没事，我不介意"。不过说实话，铁杆粉丝对明星的热爱很多时候是不理智的，所以如果你想批评或嘲笑某人的偶像，光说一句no offense是没有用的，对方十有八九会offense taken（而不是none taken），轻则翻脸，重则开撕。所以，要记住那句老话，三思而后行哦！

词汇小百科

fans　（追星的）粉丝

idol　偶像

Internet celebrity　网红

anti-fans　黑粉，专门抹黑别人的那种粉丝

online trolls　"喷子"，在网上恶意诋毁他人的人

（牛翃琳）

英语花式"打人大法"

（素材来自《圆桌议事》2015年4月25日节目）

> **导　语**：打架虽然是不对的，但是你知道怎样用英语描述不同的打人方法吗？仅限于语言交流哦。

If you don't shut up, I'm going to bust you in the mouth. And then a variation on that is bust on. The bouncers busted on some drunk guy last night. And then clock. Clock is usually to punch someone in the face.

如果你不闭嘴的话，我会打破你的嘴。这个词还有一个变化的用法是bust on，比如保镖昨晚揍了一个醉鬼。还有一个词是clock，通常是揍某人的脸的意思。

So if you don't shut up, I'll give you a fist of fives. Get banked on. He really pissed those guys off and so he got banked on. Give a thumper, a thumper is a hit, a very strong hit, and so to give a thumper is to hit someone very hard.

如果你不闭嘴的话，我会给你一拳。还有get banked on，例如他真的把那些人惹火了，所以就被揍了。Give a thumper，a thumper表示一次很重的击打，所以give a thumper意思就是狠狠地打某人。

Then knock out, you see this a lot in boxing. So you hit someone so hard, usually in the face or in the head, that they lose consciousness. We were just playing around and I accidentally knocked him out.

还有knock out，你在拳击比赛中经常看到这个短语，表示你狠狠地打某人，通常是打脸或头，使他们失去了意识。比如我们只是闹着玩，然后我不小心把他打昏了。

And then knuckle sandwich, very similar to fist of fives, but it's usually to the face or to the mouth area, because you give them a sandwich and you usually eat sandwiches.

Knuckle sandwich和fist of fives很像。但是通常是打在脸上或嘴周围，因为你给了他们一个拳头做成的三明治，而三明治通常是吃的。

To nail is to hit forcefully with a blunt object. He got nailed in the face with the football. Or I nailed him with the basketball.

Nail表示被重物砸到。比如他被足球砸到了或我用篮球砸了他。

To pop, to hit someone on the back of the head with the flat of one's hand. It's kind of like a slap, but to the back of the head, usually used to get a person's attention or to assert one's authority rather than to inflict harm.

Pop意思是用手扇某人后脑勺，像slap（扇）一样，但是pop指的是打到后脑勺，通常是用来获得某人的注意，或维护某人的权威而不是为了制造伤害。

Sucker punch, it's basically to attack sneakily. So a sucker punch is when someone is totally not expecting it, the fight hasn't started yet, you're not necessarily in an argument, but you just punch them in the face, without giving any kind of warning, that's what we call a sucker punch.

Sucker punch是突袭。当某人完全没有预料到的时候，打斗还没开始的时候，或你并没有在争吵的时候，你就一个招呼都不打地揍他们的脸，这就是我们所谓的sucker punch。

点评

怎么样？英语里打人的词汇是不是一点也不比中文少呢？你可以打不同的部位，打头可以用beam，打头打得狠一些可以用brain，学生不注意听讲时可能被老师扇后脑勺（pop），揍脸可以用clock。打得程度不同用词也不一样，打得重一些用give a thumper，打破某个地方用bust somebody in some part，打到昏迷则是knock somebody out。当然打的方式不同，说法也有差别，比如你也可以给某人一个拳头做成的三明治（knuckle sandwich），用某物打某人（nail somebody with something），也可以偷袭（sucker punch）。虽然学了这么多词，不过大家要记住，打人还是不对的哦！

词汇小百科

straight left　左直拳

straight right　右直拳

deliver a straight right at somebody　给某人一记右直拳

left hook　左勾拳

right hook　右勾拳

flat hook　平勾拳

clean someone up with a left hook　用左勾拳收拾了某人

（王　玮）

到了国外，去银行，说点什么？

（素材来自《圆桌议事》2015年1月24节目）

导 语：我们每个人都离不开银行，但如果要用英语表达自己的需求，可能很多人会不知所措。在本篇中，我们就来学习一下相关短语，确保以后跟外国人交流时没有障碍。

First of all, if you go to a bank and you want to get money out of your account, you would go up to the teller (it's the person who is working behind the desk) and say, "I would like to make a withdrawal."

如果你要去银行提款，你应该对teller（银行的柜员）说：I would like to make a withdrawal（我要取款）。

Then the teller might ask you, "How would you like the money?" That basically means what types of notes and how many notes do you want for that withdrawal.

柜员会问你：How would you like the money？这可不是问你想要什么样的钱（美元、英镑还是人民币），而是说你想要什么面值的钞票（五元、十元还是二十元）。

If you want to put money in, you can say I would like to make a deposit, so you are depositing money. Maybe you have your check from work. And you can say to the teller, "I would like to deposit this check."

需要存钱的话就说make a deposit。另外check（支票）也是在英美国家经常用的，所以你有可能想要把某一张支票存入银行账户，这时候就说I would like to deposit this check（我要存这张支票）。

Let's say that you've never been to that bank before. And you want to open a bank account. Well, that's very simple. You just say "I would like to open a bank account."

如果你是第一次去那家银行，需要开户，那你就说：I would like to open a bank account（我要开户）。

And of course, life is not as simple or as easy as we would like it to be. Sometimes maybe you'll lose your ATM card or you'll lose your credit card. So you can call their service number or you can go to the bank and you can report a lost credit card or a stolen credit card.

当然，生活有的时候不会像我们希望的那么顺利。如果丢了银行卡或信用卡，你需要赶紧挂失。你可以拨打银行的服务热线，也可以直接去银行柜台办理。假设信用卡被偷了，你就说要 report a stolen credit card，如果只是丢了，你可以说 report a lost credit card。

In banks there are many different types of accounts, as I'm sure you are already aware. But we are gonna look at some of the broader categories. So in general, there are two types of accounts. One is a checking account and the other is a savings account. A checking account is an account that has a very low interest rate, and you are making payments into and making withdrawals (from it) on a regular basis. Whereas the savings account has a slightly higher interest rate, and it is expected that there will not be very much activity on that account.

银行里有很多种不同的账户，但总体来看，最常见的是两种。一种是 checking account，也就是活期存款账户。这种账户的利率非常低，你可以随存随取。另一种是 savings account，也就是定期存款账户。它的利率相对高一些，但在定期日到来之前不能随便提取，所以账面上一般不会有太频繁的业务。

点评

如果你去银行只是为了办理存钱、取钱之类的日常业务，用到的英语其实很简单。最关键的几个单词是withdraw / withdrawal（取款）、deposit（存款）、checking account（活期账户）和savings account（定期账户）。如果你去银行是为了咨询financial investment（理财投资）方面的信息，那用到的英语会相对复杂一些，初学者暂时不用考虑。此外，建议大家多多使用online banking（网上银行业务），一来免去排队等候的苦恼，二来也可以缓解不知道怎么用英语表达自己需求的焦虑。

词汇小百科

teller　银行柜员

withdrawal　取款（名词，对应的动词为withdraw）

deposit　存款（动名词同形）

open a bank account　开户

close a bank account　销户

ATM　自动取款机（automatic teller machine的首字母缩写）

checking account　活期存款账户

savings account　定期存款账户

interest rate　利率

（刘　彦）

"OK"是个有故事的词

（素材来自《圆桌议事》2014年6月7日节目）

导　语：OK可能是我们最熟悉的英文单词了，很多不会说英语的人都OK长OK短。可OK其实比我们想象得复杂，它的用法也非常灵活多变。在本篇中，我们就来学习一下这个神秘的单词。

OK is an amazingly mysterious word and it's also an amazingly flexible word. It can be used as an adjective. It can be used as an adverb, an interjection, a verb, a noun, and a discourse marker. For example, it can be used to show doubt or even be used to seek confirmation.

"OK"真的是一个用处非常多的词，它可以用作形容词、副词、感叹词、动词、名词，还可以用作征询意见的语气词。

As an adjective and as an adverb, it usually means adequate, acceptable, or perhaps even mediocre, in contrast to good. As an interjection, it denotes compliance or agreement, like just saying "yes." As a verb and a noun, it shows assent or, again, agreement.

"OK"作为形容词或副词的时候就是还好、还可以，甚至是凑合的意思，总之没有达到"好"的级别。作为感叹词是表示同意，相当于说yes。作为动词和名词的时候，它表示同意、肯定。

Looking at the history, it's a word shrouded in mystery. Among etymologists, the people who study the history of language or the development of language, there isn't actually any agreement on where the word "OK" comes from. Some people have speculated that it came into use in Boston in 1838 during an abbreviation fad and "OK" meant "all correct" and correct was spelled with a "k."

回看历史,"OK"的起源一直充满了神秘色彩,即使语言学家也无法达成统一的意见。比较常见的说法是"OK"最早诞生于1838年的波士顿,当时有缩写的风潮,而且喜欢用同音的错误拼法,所以"OK"其实是all correct的首字母缩写。

To be honest, there are so many other interesting theories. Maybe it comes from the Scottish "och aye". Maybe it comes from another North American, Native American Indian tribe, the Lakota, from "Hokaheh". It could be a loan word from a Greek phrase, Ola Kala, meaning "all good". It also could be a loan from the Burmese word "hou' ke", meaning yes. As we can see, we just have no idea where it actually comes from, except now we know how to use it.

还有不少其他的起源传说也都挺有意思。有说是起源于苏格兰的,有说是起源于另外一支北美部落的,有说起源于一个希腊外来词的,还有人把它追溯到了缅甸语。无论哪种说法,意思都差不多,无非是yes或者all good,跟最流行的all correct是一回事儿。所以,我们虽然无法确定它的起源,却都知道该如何使用这个单词。

And we use it in different languages. OK? OK!

神奇的是,在不同的语言里,"OK"都通用。有问题吗?没有!

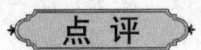

"OK"虽然看起来简单,但背后的故事却一点也不简单。如果你不是语言学者或专家,对这些故事只要有所了解就行,没有必要研究得非常透彻

thorough。有必要记住的是"OK"的用法。它是一个万能的all-purpose单词,可以当形容词、副词、感叹词、动词、名词,还可以用作征询意见的语气词。就是这么牛,OK?

词汇小百科

mysterious 神秘的

flexible 灵活的

adequate 足够的,合格的,差强人意的

mediocre 平庸的

denote 指示、代表

shroud 覆盖,包裹

etymologist 词源学家

speculate 推测、猜测

abbreviation 缩写

fad 风潮

(刘 彦)

新年快乐

（素材来自《圆桌议事》2014年12月27日节目）

导 语： 俗话说，新年新气象。我们都喜欢借着新年的契机，祝福家人、朋友和自己翻开新的篇章。在本篇中，我们就来学习一下相关的英语表达。

They almost all have something to do with becoming a new person, using the New Year as a way to realize your goals that you did not actually achieve in the year before. Whether or not this year will be different is of course a different question. But let's start with, first, ring in the New Year, so basically to celebrate the beginning of the New Year at midnight on Dec 31.

这些短语都表达了新年新气象的愿望，期盼在新的一年里达成过去一年没有实现的目标。当然，能不能真的实现另当别论，但用来当祝福语肯定是很好的。首先就是ring in the New Year，迎接新年的到来。为什么要用ring呢？因为跨年十二点的时候，敲响新年钟声是最常见的庆祝方式之一。

Right. Then there is turn over a new leaf time for a fresh start. Do something different. Interestingly enough, it has nothing to do with the leaves that fall from the tree. Rather, it has to do with the leaf, in a book, a book leaf.

还有turn over a new leaf这个短语。它可不是指翻开一片新的叶子，而是翻开新的一页书，也就相当于中文里常说的"翻开新的篇章"。Leaf在这里是书页的意思。

Then back to the drawing board. So architects and designers use drawing boards to come up with designs and they are able to translate those designs into a real actual product. The whole idea there is you go back to the drawing board to re-evaluate and re-plan for the New Year.

Back to the drawing board 也很常用，是重新开始的意思。建筑师和设计师一般都用画图板（drawing board）来画图，所以重新回到画图板上也就是说要重新开始规划一件事的意思。

Then there is start from scratch. So if you haven't begun one of your New Year's goals, you must start at the beginning. This is also interesting, because you can make something from scratch, nothing to do with the New Year.

另一个高频短语是start from scratch，从头开始，从起点开始。还有一个类似的短语是make something from scratch，从第一步开始，一点一点做起来。有趣的是，其实任何时候都可以从起点开始做，并不一定要等到新年。

And there is back to square one. So if you started a goal before and it didn't work out, you can always go back to square one. We are really not sure where this came from, but square one is the very first place.

Back to square one是回到原点、从头开始的意思，有点像back to the drawing board和start from scratch的结合体。Square one在这里就是最初的地方，起点。

Last but not least, if at first you don't succeed, try again. I think this one is fairly obvious, but somehow a clichéd phrase that we use in English on a regular basis, as if it's something new. But it is just what it sounds like. If you are not successful, try again.

最后，当然少不了那句if at first you don't succeed, try again（如果刚开始不成功的话，要继续尝试）。这听上去好像是中国家长鼓励孩子好好学习的一句话，有点陈词滥调的感觉，但在全球各地都很受用。

点评

我们都会说happy new year，但其实除了这句话，还有很多更有意义的话可以拿来当新年祝词。比如if at first you don't succeed，try again. 这话虽然听起来很鸡汤，但确实很有道理。美国已故歌手Aaliyah当年的一首冠军单曲Try Again也是反复吟唱这句话。其实学习说穿了也是归结到这句话上。既然大家都喜欢在新年之际下决心，不如就对自己说：学英语一定要坚持。If at first you don't succeed，try again!

词汇小百科

ring in the new year   迎接新年的到来
turn over a new leaf   翻开新的篇章
back to the drawing board   重新开始
start from scratch   从头开始
back to square one   回到原点，从头开始
if at first you don't succeed，try again   如果刚开始不成功的话，要继续尝试
clichéd   陈词滥调的

（刘　彦）